ETHICAL & SOCIALLY RESPONSIBLE INVESTMENT FUNDS

An Investor's Guide to

ETHICAL & SOCIALLY RESPONSIBLE INVESTMENT FUNDS

Consultant editor
JOHN HANCOCK

KOGAN PAGE

London & Sterling, VA

Publisher's note

Every possible effort has been made to ensure that the information contained in this book is accurate at the time of going to press, and the publishers and authors cannot accept responsibility for any errors or omissions, however caused. No responsibility for loss or damage occasioned to any person acting, or refraining from action, as a result of the material in this publication can be accepted by the editor, the publisher or any of the authors.

First published in Great Britain and the United States in 2005 by Kogan Page Limited

120 Pentonville Road
London N1 9JN
United Kingdom
www.kogan-page.co.uk

22883 Quicksilver Drive
Sterling VA 20166-2012
USA

ISBN 0 7494 4146 1

British Library Cataloguing-in-Publication Data

A CIP record for this book is available from the British Library.

Library of Congress Cataloging-in-Publication Data

Hancock, John, 1949–
   An investor's guide to ethical and socially responsible investment funds/John Hancock.
      p. cm.
   Includes bibliographical references and index.

   ISBN 0–7494–4146–1
   1. Investments—Moral and ethical aspects. I. Title.
HG4515. 13 H36 2005
332.63'27—dc22

                                2005000816

Typeset by Datamatics Technologies Ltd, Mumbai, India
Printed and bound in Great Britain by Scotprint

Contents

Julia Dreblow

Marginal or mainstream? Why the mainstream investment
community considers SRI issues to be marginal 5; An
introduction to how SRI does things differently from the
mainstream 6; Key aims of ethical and socially responsible
investment 7; The importance of share ownership 8; A changing
business climate 9; The difference between ethical and socially
responsible investment 11; What responsible investment
considers 12; Measuring an investment provider's commitment
to SRI 12; Indicators of fund manager or investment provider
commitment to SRI 13; A natural development 16

Julia Dreblow

How ethical funds came into existence 17; Fund choices available
today 18; Ethical approaches – defined and explained 18; How

Foreword

It appears significant and highly appropriate that John Hancock should be challenged to produce this excellent guide at a time when the twentieth anniversary of the launch of the first ethical trust has just been celebrated.

The changes in attitude of the investing public over the period has not only been apparent from the strength of financial interest in ethical unit trusts (now valued at over £4 billion of funds under management) but also in the 'institutional' concerns freely expressed.

For example, the Church Ethical Investors Group, representing churches managing assets of over £7 billion, recently announced a framework to enable members to develop a common understanding of the ethical issues affecting companies in which they invest.

Charities are rethinking their position, secure in the knowledge that recent prognostications and statistical data support the belief that companies which have good corporate governance have an improved share price over those that do not follow such practices (ICAEW). Indeed, recent research from Deutsche Bank claims an irrefutable link between good governance and business success.

The early fear that exclusion of so many companies of 'negative status' from portfolios would necessarily result in portfolio underperformance has in itself been negated. Indeed, the additional company study and increased company dialogue demanded has led to a greater company awareness and understanding among 'ethical' investment managers essential to decision making.

Similarly, the advisor who interests him- or herself in matters of social responsibility is more able to advise clients appropriately on their individual concerns and requirements thus bringing benefit to both parties.

In this book, the editor and contributors offer a wealth of information and statistics, which should help advisors to pursue these objectives.

'There are no moral absolutes, morality is relative to the situation.' So said the sage.

In his precise way, John Hancock and his contributors lead us to an understanding of the situations which become everyday developments to the financial advisor as he leads his clients into areas appropriate to their individual needs.

Charles Jacob MBE

From our sponsor

Friends Provident launched the UK's first ethically screened fund for individual investors in 1984 and remains a leading player in socially responsible investment.

There are now over 60 screened funds available across the UK from a wide range of providers, as well as substantial assets under management with approaches based around dialogue. Yet there is still a long way to go. Market research tells us that the majority of people do care about the social, ethical and environmental behaviour of companies, yet few appear to link this to their own investment decisions.

We welcome this book as part of the solution to this dilemma, and as a useful source of information for investors to consult about SRI. We hope it will help investors to gain a better understanding of the relationship between investment, investors and company activity – and we have agreed to support this book with this in mind.

We also hope this book will help investors to gain a better understanding of how their own personal values can be translated into investment decisions that meet both their personal and their financial goals. This in turn should help individuals to contribute towards solving some of the world's most complex problems.

Julia Dreblow
SRI Manager, Friends Provident

Notes on contributors

Mark Campanale, Head, SRI Business Development, Henderson Global Investors
Mark is responsible for SRI business development at Henderson. He was a founder of the original SRI business created at Jupiter Asset Management, the SRI funds at Henderson and, in Australia, the successful AMP Sustainable Future Funds.

A member of the UKSIF/Ethical Investment Association 'Retail Revolution' committee, Mark is a board member of the Fair Shares campaign, of GeneWatch UK and of the Rainforest Foundation. He has a degree in Politics and Economic History and a Masters in Agricultural Economics, and worked on development and aid projects from 1985 to 1989.

Lee Coates, Director, Ethical Investors Group
Lee founded Ethical Investors Group, independent financial advisers dedicated exclusively to ethical investment, in 1989. Annually, Ethical Investors Group donates 50 per cent of its profits to charities and groups specified by its clients. To date, over £400,000 has been donated. In 1997 Lee started a new company, Ethical Screening, dedicated to providing bespoke ethical screening solutions to individuals, charities and faith groups.

Julia Dreblow, SRI Manager, Friends Provident Life & Pensions Ltd
Julia has worked in financial services since 1989 and specialized in socially responsible investment since the mid 1990s. She is the SRI Manager at Friends Provident,

which launched the UK's first retail ethical funds, 'Stewardship', in 1984 and also has a 'responsible engagement' strategy that covers all of their equity assets.

Julia is also a director of the UK Social Investment Forum, a not-for-profit membership organization with the remit of advancing responsible investment, where she chairs the Retail Sub-Committee.

EIRIS

EIRIS is a charity set up in 1983 with the help of a group of churches and charities that all had investments, and strong convictions about what they thought was right and wrong. They needed a research organization to help them put their principles into practice when making investment decisions. EIRIS Services Ltd, a subsidiary company of EIRIS, undertakes most of the research for clients and provides commercial services.

John Hancock

John came to journalism following 22 years in financial services at various levels up to managing director, both in the UK and overseas. In the 15 years since, he has contributed to over 60 titles, written five books and edited the *Invest in Success* series since 1999 and *Selling Financial Services*, also since 1999. Working from Cornwall, John covers topics in the business, investment, financial services, technology, education and travel markets. He is the editor of *Investing in Corporate Social Responsibility* and author of *Ethical Money* (both published by Kogan Page).

Standard & Poor's

A division of The McGraw-Hill Companies (NYSE:MHP), Standard & Poor's is the world's foremost provider of independent credit ratings, indices, risk evaluation, investment research, data and valuations. With 6,000 employees located in 21 countries, Standard & Poor's is an essential part of the world's financial infrastructure and has played a leading role for more than 140 years in providing investors with the independent benchmarks they need to feel more confident about their investment and financial decisions. For more information visit www.funds-sp.com.

UKSIF

The UK Social Investment Forum (UKSIF) is the UK's membership network for socially responsible investment. UKSIF's primary purpose is to promote and encourage the development and positive impact of SRI amongst UK-based investors. The Forum was launched in 1991 to bring together the different strands of SRI nationally and to act as a focus and a voice for the industry.

Introduction

This book starts from the assumption that advisers are the key group in the financial planning and investment process for most people. But many advisers also have not yet really acquired the levels of information about ethical and socially responsible investments that, as thorough and professional practitioners, they like to have to hand when discussing clients' financial plans. Neither do they necessarily have the tools to incorporate that information into advice. Of course, organizations exist that can provide the type of information advisers and investors need in this area. The excellent work of both Ethical Investment Research Services (EIRIS) in establishing and setting out a clear framework for understanding ethical and socially responsible investment issues and funds and the UK Social Investment Forum (UKSIF) in building a body of adviser-focused material to support the inclusion of ethical and socially responsible investment in the advice process has been instrumental in the massive successes so far achieved by ethical investment and its adoption by more than 60 investment providers as a part of their investment offering.

Endorsed and sponsored by both those organizations and by Standard & Poor's, whose fund tables provide the performance information critical to investment understanding, as well as by Friends Provident Life and Pensions, the company that launched the first ethical fund, this book seeks to assemble the whole gamut of information on ethical and socially responsible investment between two covers.

The main body of the book aims to help the reader better understand ethical and socially responsible investment and the funds that define themselves as fitting within this investment sector. It considers the origins of the sector and the influences and motivations that shape the sector, the defining features and performance of ethical and SRI funds, how investors can access these funds, who are the sort of investors likely to be interested and what will be the effect of greater participation in the ethical and socially responsible investment sector. This is all essential knowledge and the quality of information of which any investor would wish to be availed before embarking on an important investment decision. It is, if you like, the material needed to become an investor. The tools to turn that material into a real investment decision are in the appendices.

The appendices are, we believe, the first time that anyone has put between the covers of one book both the financial and the ethical and social responsibility measurements, both of which will be needed to be able to offer proper advice. Using the appendices provided, advisers and investors will be able to clarify an investor's own ethical and social responsibility priorities and then match those priorities to one of the funds in this growing sector using Appendices 3 and 1 from EIRIS. When a shortlist of appropriate funds has been identified, then the reference to the relevant table in Appendix 2, and its current equivalents, will allow the usual performance questions to be answered – while past performance is not an infallible indicator of future results, it is important information.

There are a number of contributors to this book and it has been their thorough and considerable efforts that have made it all work. These contributions are more essays than chapters although we have maintained a chapter and appendix format to make navigation easier. So there may be overlaps between chapters but, as each one deals with a different aspect of the subject, those overlaps will be in context in their chapter and will help the reader to see some of the concepts in this sector from different perspectives and thus, it is hoped, obtain a more three-dimensional picture. Thanks to Julia Dreblow who not only represents Friends Provident but also has contributed two chapters based on her extensive experience of this market; thanks also to Mark Campanale of Henderson Global Investors whose knowledge of the investment aspect of ethical and socially responsible investment has been honed at the front line and who has contributed two chapters; and thanks to Lee Coates of Ethical Investors Group whose chapter is founded upon the large body of knowledge and experience he has developed while advising ethical and SRI investors over many years. Thanks to EIRIS whose untiring efforts have built for the ethical investment sector a body of knowledge second to none, to bring to this sector the kind of clarity that others might envy; thanks to Standard & Poor's for the use of their globally respected and trusted performance data and for the rating profiles of those ethical and SRI funds that they have qualitatively rated (AAA, AA, A) to date; and thanks to the UK Social Investment Forum for lending their advice, support, endorsement and a chapter to the book.

Perhaps before this introduction descends into the script for an Academy Awards speech, I should simply express the hope that readers will find it an interesting read, enlightening and useful in introducing the idea of ethical and socially responsible investment. Most of all, I hope that it makes readers feel better equipped not just to understand this sector but also to do something about it; I hope that it provides a call to action with the means to support that action.

1

An introduction to the concept of ethics in investment

Julia Dreblow, SRI Manager, Friends Provident Life
and Pensions Limited

There are two key aspects to ethical investment that any potential investors should be aware of, the 'ethical' aspects and the 'investment' aspect. To understand ethical or socially responsible investment (SRI) it is important to take each in turn and to gain an understanding of how they fit together. This book aims to do just that.

The core focus of this book is ethical and socially responsible investment, which is widely taken as meaning funds and investment management strategies run by major life offices and investment companies. However, there are other aspects to ethical investment such as ethical bank accounts that are available and important, although not covered in this book.

MARGINAL OR MAINSTREAM? WHY THE MAINSTREAM INVESTMENT COMMUNITY CONSIDERS SRI ISSUES TO BE MARGINAL

Despite rapidly growing business recognition of the importance of ethical, social and environmental matters, and the ever-increasing public concern and press attention focused on these areas, the investment management community still often considers them to be marginal or niche issues. Yet 92 per cent of people questioned in a

MORI/Friends Provident survey, conducted on 10–15 June 2004, believed it important that companies take social, ethical and environmental issues seriously.

The assets that are found in investment funds – typically equities (shares), loan stock (bonds) or other asset classes – can be traded rapidly. Fund managers typically buy and sell on the latest information so longer-term trends and concerns tend to have been sidelined. In addition, there has traditionally been insufficient research with a wider social, ethical and environmental (SEE) remit. This has meant that, for individual investors, their personal values have largely been ignored to date.

There are however two historical situations when this has not been the case. The first is effectively incidental. Mainstream funds, or in other words funds that have not been screened against their SEE values, take ethical issues into account in certain situations. Often this is either when a disaster (an oil spill, uncovering child abuse, a discovery of corruption, etc, not to mention some recent high-profile financial collapses) has hit a company and has impacted its share price or perhaps when a consumer boycott starts to bite and there are fears it may start to affect product demand and therefore the share value of the company. Such situations are not uncommon but nor are they the norm. Managing investments on this basis however indicates that fund managers are potentially failing to spot risks in advance. In many cases good management can avert such situations. The second example of when SEE values are not ignored is of course ethical investment funds and other 'responsible' investment approaches. The distinction between mainstream and ethical funds, however, is blurring as increasingly diverse options become available and as external bodies such as the Association of British Insurers (ABI), the London Stock Exchange (LSE) and others encourage companies to focus more closely on these issues.

AN INTRODUCTION TO HOW SRI DOES THINGS DIFFERENTLY FROM THE MAINSTREAM

Socially responsible investment combines the dual objectives of making values-based judgements about companies – normally prior to investment – and looking for good investment returns.

Socially responsible investments are therefore intended to be appropriate for people who wish to have their values taken into account as part of the investment process. This means that for those wishing to integrate their personal values into their investment decisions they should seek advice on their options. For example, people buying a stakeholder pension or an ISA should ask their financial adviser or product provider whether or not ethical, social or environmental issues are taken into account in any of the options that are being recommended. If they are not they should ask for an investment solution that better meets their needs. These fall into two key areas – those that impact where funds can invest, ie ethical funds, and those that do not, ie engagement-only funds.

KEY AIMS OF ETHICAL AND SOCIALLY RESPONSIBLE INVESTMENT

People choose to invest in a socially responsible manner for a number of reasons. The key motivations however have tended – according to investor research – to be because 'ethical criteria meet investors concerns' and to 'make a difference'.

Stewardship unit holder research statistics of July 2001 (source: Friends Provident-commissioned NOP research) included the following:

- 60 per cent said ethics and fund performance are equally important;
- 36 per cent said ethics are more important than fund performance;
- 2 per cent said fund performance is more important than ethics.

Investment performance is of course important and for most investors it is taken as read that any fund or investment strategy that does not give reasonable returns simply does not have the right to exist. However, within these parameters research into ethical investor opinions has confirmed that ethical aspects are equally important or more important than performance for all but 2 per cent of ethical investors.

Performance aside therefore, the two key functions of ethical funds are to have fund policies and criteria that match investor needs and to aim to bring about positive change. In fact, since the creation of ethical funds these have been the dual objectives of the funds' managers. The UK's first fund, Stewardship, was set up (in 1984) with these objectives in mind. The criteria, including some that are now happily no longer required such as anti-apartheid exclusions, aimed to be in line with the values of investors who cared about a range of issues.

The aspiration to make a difference was, however, twofold. Firstly, working on the basis of supply and demand for shares, the ethical investment pioneers hoped they would build a critical mass in ethical funds so that unethical companies would be concerned about having access to fewer investors and thus change their practices to attract more investment. Secondly, they worked on the basis that reasoned dialogue, aimed at encouraging companies to come into line with ethical criteria, would encourage change.

Since these early days, these two objectives have effectively created the two strands of the SRI market, screening and engagement, both of which are further explained below.

THE IMPORTANCE OF SHARE OWNERSHIP

Translating people's personal concerns into an appropriate investment strategy is not without its difficulties. It is not at all uncommon to hear that potential ethical investors have been told by financial advisers to invest their money in a 'normal' fund and give some money to charity as an alternative solution to making an ethical investment. However, this completely misses the point of ethical and socially responsible investment.

Companies are owned by their shareholders: their primary duty, therefore, is regarded as being to those shareholders. The directors and managers of the company aim to make profits for their shareholders' benefit, and as such gear their businesses towards meeting their shareholder demands. For shareholders to fail to communicate that they have ethical or other concerns (either by making investment in companies that behave badly or by failing to communicate concerns) means that companies are given the message that such issues are unimportant. As such, they cannot be blamed if they simply comply with their legal obligations and pay little attention to the wider impacts of their corporate activities. Ethical investment and SRI therefore give members of the public a crucial voice to communicate concerns, albeit collectively, to companies.

An analogy can be drawn here with ethical product offerings. There is little point in saying, for example, on the one hand that it is appalling that coffee growers are being treated unfairly by the multinationals and then not buying fair-trade coffee. Likewise there is little point vehemently opposing war or smoking and then being a part owner of armaments or tobacco companies – a screened ethical fund might be more sensible.

However, in line with the early aims of ethical investment pioneers, there is also a middle ground. Screening is not the only solution offered by investment institutions. In addition to the option to withhold your money from the shares in companies of whose business practices you disapprove or intentionally directing money into the shares of companies of whose corporate practices you approve, the option also exists to support investment houses and funds that are committed to having a formal dialogue with companies to help them understand that there are investors who care not only about investment returns, but also about the way a company goes about its business. As a stand-alone approach, this is relatively new and intentionally pragmatic, often termed 'shareholder engagement' or 'activism'. It involves investment companies and pension funds engaging the companies in which they invest in dialogue about how those companies can go about their business more responsibly and still give good returns for shareholders. This is a very important development as it puts a very clear emphasis on the need for both better business practices and investment returns.

It is also important as it recognizes that, as much as some people may wish it, companies that are avoided by ethical funds are not likely simply to vanish just because they are deemed unethical by some investors. There is still a market for their shares. They are still able to trade. Taken to extremes, it can be argued that by ignoring such companies ethical funds are effectively leaving those investors who debatably care the least about ethical issues to be the sole proprietors of the world's (theoretically) less ethical companies – a highly undesirable situation from a responsible investment perspective and, in some people's view, doing society a disservice.

So, assuming that these less ethical companies are not going to vanish, it is incumbent on investors to encourage them to behave more responsibly. As such, investors need to behave more like owners or even long-term business partners. They need to work with companies to find solutions to some of the issues that threaten the well-being of people and the environment, both today and tomorrow, in a way that complements other business imperatives such as profit. The potential importance of share ownership cannot be overstated.

A CHANGING BUSINESS CLIMATE

The role that investors play in influencing company behaviour has not only been recognized by SRI investors; indeed it is widely recognized that the business world is changing and that investors have important responsibilities within this new climate.

Examples of the way in which this has been recognized include the latest (second) version of the Combined Code on Corporate Governance. This is a code for company boards based on successive reports that started with the Cadbury Report in 1992. This latest report initiated the 'comply or explain' principle to corporate governance best practice. The Turnbull Report of September 1999 was the first of these reports to call for better disclosure of businesses' SEE risk and opportunity. These principles have since become an addendum to the UK Stock Exchange listing requirements for all companies that wish their shares to be traded on a UK stock market, which effectively makes compliance obligatory.

A key part of these requirements was that companies should properly manage and report all their business risks to shareholders. This specifically includes social, ethical and environmental risks and has led to increasing focus on all related areas of company activity, from both a risk and an opportunity perspective.

Following on from this the ABI, a body representing most UK life offices and whose investing value accounts for about 20 per cent of all UK company equity, issued guidelines for companies owned by their members. These SEE guidelines ask for basic disclosure standards for companies to meet, asking them to demonstrate that social, ethical and environmental risks and opportunities are understood and being properly managed as well as asking them to identify how this can affect the value of the company. The ABI requests that this information should be disclosed in full within company annual reports and accounts. This provides better information for investors, and an opportunity for them to engage with companies on these issues.

In addition the FTSE4Good initiative – an initiative launched by the index provider, following discussions with UNICEF – created an index that assesses company social, ethical and environmental performance. Only companies that meet certain minimum SEE standards in their corporate behaviour are accepted on to this index – as opposed to company size, type or location being the primary criteria for entry. The aim is for entry levels to be gradually raised in the hope that member companies will in turn raise their standards to ensure they remain in the index.

Other reviews of relevance, but primarily with their emphasis on corporate governance (ie primarily the way companies are managed), include:

- Various assessments of the role of non-executive directors and audit committee roles (most recently the 2003 Higgs and Smith reviews).
- The Institutional Shareholders Committee (ISC) shareholder activism paper – ISC membership includes the ABI, the National Association of Pension Fund Managers (NAPF), the Investment Managers' Association (IMA) and the Association of Investment Trust Companies (AITC) – published in December 2002. The paper states that shareholders ought to act responsibly – voting and intervening in companies when they have legitimate concerns.
- The London Principles – an initiative launched by UK prime minister Tony Blair at the 2002 Johannesburg WSSD summit. The principles examine the role of the UK financial services sector in promoting sustainable development. It was commissioned by the Corporation of London on behalf of DEFRA, the UK government department then responsible in this area.

The only legislation that is directly related to SRI however is a July 2000 amendment to the 1995 Pensions Act, which is expected to be carried over with the forthcoming 2005 pensions rules. This legislation calls for occupational pension schemes (primarily defined benefit and stakeholder pension schemes) to disclose in their statement of investment principles, a document that must be made available to investors on request, their position on the following:

1. The extent (if at all) to which social, environmental or ethical considerations are taken into account in the selection, retention and realization of investments; and
2. The policy (if any) directing the exercise of the rights (including voting rights) attaching to investments.

This legislation has greatly increased the profile of SRI issues in the occupational pensions community with over half of schemes responding to this disclosure requirement.

However, it has not put in place any mechanism for checking that schemes, or investment houses on their behalf, actually do what they say they do. There is currently no reporting requirement for schemes, an issue that is being addressed by the not-for-profit membership-based SRI industry body UK Social Investment Forum (UKSIF) within their 'Just Pensions' programme, details of which can be found at www.uksif.org.

The other downside to this legislation is that it is only relevant to one segment of the investment world, and as such does not give retail investors in ISAs, bonds, personal pensions or defined contribution pension schemes any means of finding out whether or not their investment has any form of SRI perspective. This issue is also being taken up by UKSIF within their retail programme. The aim of this programme is to give people greater access to better information and advice on SRI, through addressing the need for regulatory change and better information for financial advisers.

THE DIFFERENCE BETWEEN ETHICAL AND SOCIALLY RESPONSIBLE INVESTMENT

The terms 'ethical' and 'socially responsible' investment are often used interchangeably. Both investment approaches take into account personal concerns and values. The term 'socially responsible investment' has grown in popularity in the UK since July 2000 when the pensions legislation came into being. Until then, the term 'ethical investment' was widely used but, as an investment form, screened ethical investment was unpopular in the pensions market as it involved making investment decisions based on non-financial considerations.

The benefit of looking for alternative methods, as well as terminology, was recognized by those pushing for change, and the terminology used in the USA (where, according to the Social Investment Forum, one investment dollar in every eight has an ethical remit) was duly adopted. This effectively left 'ethical investment' relating primarily to screened funds (which select assets on SEE grounds) while the term 'SRI' became widely regarded as a catch-all phrase that could have a number of interpretations, including, as outlined above, 'engagement'.

Today whilst the terms may be broadly interchangeable, some people tend to see SRI or 'responsible investment' as an all-inclusive term, whereas they see ethical investment as meaning avoiding or supporting companies through the purchase of their shares for ethical reasons, ie screened ethical funds.

Another approach put under the spotlight from July 2000 was shareholder voting. This is because the legislation specifically directs trustees of pension schemes to say the extent to which they use their other shareholder rights – voting at the annual general meeting (AGM) and any extraordinary general meeting (EGM) being their primary additional 'right'. Whilst separate from SRI, this is integrally linked to the responsible investment agenda, as it is an additional, important way investors can make their views known to the companies of which they are part owners.

WHAT RESPONSIBLE INVESTMENT CONSIDERS

At the most basic level there are two aspects of companies that need to be considered: what a company does, and how it does it.

Both are crucial and relevant to any screened ethical fund that has published criteria that overlap with a company's activity. However, a strictly screened fund (either negative or positive) will initially be led by the former, 'what a company does', whereas an engagement approach, because of the fact that it is unlikely to be able to alter what a company does, is likely to focus on the latter, 'how it does it'. In addition a screened ethical fund may use the way a company operates as a means of judging companies if the fund includes such issues within its selection criteria, for example good employment practices, concern for the environment or bribery and corruption.

Issues that responsible investment approaches take into account can be broadly subdivided into three main groups – social, ethical and environmental (this phrase having been lifted from the July 2000 pensions legislation). The issues that sit within each of these areas are open to a great deal of interpretation and debate, and many can be considered to exist within more than one of these headings. However, the following issues can be considered to rest within each of these categories:

- social, eg human rights, labour standards, equal opportunities, diversity, and bribery and corruption;
- ethical, eg tobacco, gambling, pornography and military;
- environmental, eg pollution of land, sea or air, nuclear, renewable energy, environmental management, transport and mining.

Responsible investment approaches may concentrate on one or more of these and this should be made clear in the funds' published information.

MEASURING AN INVESTMENT PROVIDER'S COMMITMENT TO SRI

For some investors the only relevant aspect of making a socially responsible investment (ranging from bank accounts to pure equity funds) is where their own money is invested and the use to which it is put. For others, that is only part of the equation.

For this growing number of investors the other key aspect is the commitment the investment provider (life office, bank or fund manager) demonstrates to socially responsible investment. This is important because the more committed provider is more likely to be able to influence companies for the better or offer a screened fund that is well thought out and able closely to track market developments and changes in the way companies behave.

Some investors also look further than this and consider the firm's approach to corporate responsibility to be crucial. This too is important as ethical investors typically want to be reassured that the company handling their investment operates to the same high standards that ethical and SRI funds expect from the firms in which they invest.

INDICATORS OF FUND MANAGER OR INVESTMENT PROVIDER COMMITMENT TO SRI

The key indicator of how committed fund managers or investment providers are to socially responsible investment is the level of resources committed to that area of their business. This subdivides into three main areas, ethical/SRI analysis, financial analysis and communication.

SRI analysis resource

A firm that employs a large number of in-house SRI researchers in order to have a full understanding of ethical issues and relevant company and government activity is clearly in a stronger position than a firm that employs no one – or one or two people. Employing a substantial team allows an investment provider to be fully engaged in dialogue and help shape the agenda of many issues in line with investor expectations. Such teams act as a conduit between companies and society/investors and, in particular, can therefore work with non-governmental organizations (NGOs), governments and think-tanks, as well as arranging one-to-one meetings plus group seminar sessions with companies – in order fully to comprehend what drives the companies they work with, as well as the value of their shares (also termed 'shareholder value'). A substantial headcount also allows active participation in collaborative efforts aimed at finding solutions that suit companies and wider society.

Specialist ethical fund managers

In addition, an investment provider that is serious about understanding SRI issues will also employ one or more specialist fund managers. This is in recognition of the fact that managing screened funds is different from managing other funds when a substantial proportion of larger companies are excluded. High exclusion of this kind leads fund managers to look beyond the best-researched larger companies (company research is typically carried out both in-house and from external analysts) to gain an understanding of the financial position of many less well-researched companies. This is time consuming and requires specialist knowledge – particularly if there is international exposure within screened funds.

However, for an 'engagement-only' approach specialist fund managers are not required as investment selection is not ordinarily affected by this strategy. Engagement activity is carried out by governance and/or SRI specialists, who need not necessarily have fund management expertise, although a close working relationship with the fund managers they work alongside is crucial, and fund managers, in turn, are increasingly improving and elevating their skills in these areas in the light of changes in the business environment.

Communication and marketing output

The other key area that needs specialist resources committed to it is communications, primarily between the investment provider and investors or intermediaries, but also with the media and others. Socially responsible investment is a complex investment area; different product providers offer different solutions and this can be easily misinterpreted. If scepticism about particular funds or investment providers is to be averted, their approach needs to be properly explained. This means their activity needs to be communicated clearly by people who have a thorough understanding of the issues and how the various parts of the team fit together. There should also be provisions in place for investors and intermediaries to ask questions and debate issues as necessary. Whether or not an SRI product provider or fund manager has people in place to do this is important.

The output of these teams is also important – newsletters and other marketing and sales materials are further good indicators of commitment to SRI. Other indicators include support for the European Social Investment Forum (Eurosif) transparency guidelines (both retail and institutional) and information flows to external groups who seek to educate advisers and the public (eg Synaptic Systems Ethical Screening, and Ethical Investment Research Services – EIRIS).

Subcontracting ethical research

Unlike with communication and fund management resources it is the norm for SRI product providers to subcontract some or a substantial proportion of ethical research to specialist research houses. The largest and best known of these in the UK is EIRIS; another is Ethical Screening Limited.

This is perfectly appropriate, but can risk stifling the individuality of the fund if the product provider hands over full responsibility to a third party. In addition such an approach may be held back if the research provider has less frequent dealings with companies than an in-house fund management-linked team might.

The other side of this coin is that independent research organizations will bring a breadth of experience and understanding of the market that an individual fund manager, needing to focus on the fund's specific investments, may not be able to achieve.

However, responsibility for stock selection can never be fully delegated, as somebody within an organization has to decide the form of the fund. This can also be a hindrance or a benefit, as the person may not be expert in this area, although support can be acquired by market research and discussions with experienced intermediaries (such as ethical investment specialist independent financial advisers).

Subcontracting ethical research traditionally has been focused around screened ethical funds; however, such research has increasingly been used by funds with a balanced or engagement approach. Subcontracting engagement activity is less common in the retail marketplace, although in the institutional pensions market it is not uncommon, as pension schemes frequently delegate this activity to fund managers with expertise in this area. In addition, 'collaborative engagement' (often facilitated by UKSIF) offers opportunities for newer entrants to become involved.

Measuring commitment to corporate social responsibility

The measurement of corporate social responsibility (CSR) is a relatively new area; however, the issues and ethos that sit behind it are often as old as companies themselves. CSR is really the content of a separate book (see John Hancock (ed), *Investing in Corporate Social Responsibility*, published by Kogan Page) but it is worth briefly remarking on the overlap between CSR and SRI.

Firstly, however, the difference between these two areas must be understood. Socially responsible investment is all about investment strategies and where an investor's money is put, ie in which shares, bonds or property. This includes the way investments are bought and sold, eg screening, as well as what is done with shares that are held, ie engagement. CSR on the other hand is about the behaviour of individual companies, including the company offering an SRI fund, and the way they manage their impacts on their surroundings. Investors who care about ethical, social or environmental issues are likely to take an interest in the corporate responsibility of a product provider as well as of the companies they are invested in.

CSR is generally less populated by substantial in-house teams than SRI might be, although there is an array of external consultancies and industry bodies with companies typically employing a single CSR manager.

A company's commitment to CSR can be measured in a number of different ways. For companies quoted on a stock market one useful indicator is whether or not a company meets the standards required by the FTSE4Good index. Other indicators are Investors in People membership, publicly available environmental and social reports that measure progress towards specific goals, membership of Business in the Community (and ranking in its awards system). In addition information can be gathered on the way a company responds to criticisms and addresses its shortcomings, which, within both CSR and SRI, is often to be considered as being in many ways as important as whether or not a company has made mistakes. Another measure, favoured by some but criticized by others as window dressing if not accompanied by a strategy that addresses the fundamentals of the way the business operates, is community giving. Information on this normally appears in the annual report and accounts.

A NATURAL DEVELOPMENT

The inclusion of an ethical or SEE component in investment has grown well beyond the original concept of a means to express an objection to a particular aspect of corporate life and has, with the development of engagement, matured into a mainstream investment criterion. Institutional investors have always wished to question various aspects of the way in which a company is run, usually with a view to clarifying a policy or to considering the effects of that policy on profitability. The introduction of SEE concerns to the reasons why a question might be asked does not change this except by the fact that it recognizes some new and growing commercial phenomena – the sustainability of an activity or policy (ie will its achievements last and what will be their impact on the environment?) and the responsibilities of a company, as a corporate member of society, to other members of that society, corporate or otherwise. Seen in that way, ethical or socially responsible investment is a natural evolution of investment policy to reflect a parallel evolution in global attitudes to the way companies are run.

2

The different ethical and SRI investment models

Julia Dreblow, SRI Manager, Friends Provident Life and Pensions Limited

HOW ETHICAL FUNDS CAME INTO EXISTENCE

The UK's first ethical investment fund was launched by Friends Provident. Until the early 1970s Friends Provident invested along Quaker lines, which meant avoiding companies involved in armaments manufacture, alcohol production, tobacco and pornography alongside trying to make the world a better place by seeking to invest in companies that were doing good things. The transition between moving from this to their position as a large FTSE 100 company and one of the UK's most successful life offices meant major change for the group. As such, having decided to move away from across-the-board screening in the 1970s, the company found that the concept of creating the UK's first screened ethical fund had some appeal – both as a means of keeping happy existing investors, who were concerned about the move away from screening across the board, and for attracting new monies.

Early issues for this fund were, not surprisingly, those of importance to Quaker investors, including concerns about companies supporting the apartheid regime in South Africa. Since then the growth of the environmental movement has reshaped the screened fund movement, as have concerns about animal husbandry and the ever-evolving understanding of human rights and labour standards issues, including of course issues like child labour as well as bribery and corruption, and governance.

Despite this broad base of support the success of ethical investment was not widely anticipated. Some even referred to the Stewardship Fund, launched in 1984 (the first ethical fund), as the 'Brazil' fund – from the belief that you had to be nuts to invest in it, not from any connection with concern for the rainforests! Needless to say, history has proved otherwise.

FUND CHOICES AVAILABLE TODAY

If all the life, pensions and investment fund links that are available to individual or retail investors are added together there are around 250 ethical funds (source: Synaptics, 2003) although many of these are variations of core funds of which there are around 60 (EIRIS). This, however, excludes the wide range of funds available from the handful of highly respected investment organizations that offer funds with 'engagement' approaches as part of their mainstream funds propositions and in addition to their screened funds.

In the same way that we as individuals do not have identical values or concerns, responsible investment products too vary in their approaches. This diversification is crucial as it means that more investors' needs may be met.

Of course there are many areas where screened ethical funds are in agreement – tobacco, armaments and nuclear power are almost always excluded to some degree from screened funds. Most also cover the three key areas of ethical investment, people, environment and animals, but the depth and breadth of their screening or other involvement vary. A good example of this is the Jupiter Ecology Fund. This is essentially an environmental fund. In common with engagement-only approaches, different takes on the SRI theme should be applauded, not criticized, as they reflect the rich diversity of public opinion and make it possible for investors to find solutions that suit both their investment and their ethical needs.

ETHICAL APPROACHES – DEFINED AND EXPLAINED

There are a number of socially responsible investment approaches available. Broadly, funds consider two main areas: what companies do and how they do it. Approaches range between strict negative screening and pure 'engagement' or dialogue. This range has grown up over the last 20 years and reflects different opinions regarding not only investment strategies but also how best to influence the business community to try to make the world a better place. As such there is no 'correct' ethical policy, although the investment community is not short of people offering a solution for the world's ills or how capitalism might be improved upon.

The main approaches available, which may be offered separately or in combination, include those set out below.

Negative screening

Defined as...

The exclusion of stocks that fail to meet the ethical criteria of the fund. Funds may apply any number of ethical screens.[1] These may include areas such as tobacco, armaments manufacture, environmental pollution, labour standards, support for oppressive regimes, pornography, nuclear power, animal testing, etc.

Explained as...

A fund with numerous negative criteria, applied as 'absolute exclusions'. This will lead to a large number of companies being avoided. Such funds are termed 'strictly screened' ethical funds. A fund with fewer absolute exclusions may be termed as less strictly screened or 'lighter green'.

Most ethically screened funds have a number of negative ethical criteria, some of which are applied as absolute exclusions while others may be applied less strictly. For example, tobacco 'production' may be an absolute exclusion whereas a supermarket that makes less than 5 per cent of its turnover from the sale of tobacco products may be allowable. Or a further example – animal testing may be a negative screen, which excludes most pharmaceutical firms from many ethical funds, but the sale of medicines that have been tested on animals may be acceptable.

Positive screening

Defined as...

Ethical criteria that direct the fund to invest in certain companies. Typically, this might be companies whose activities are believed to have beneficial outcomes for or impacts on people, animals or the environment.

Explained as...

As with ethical screening, the impact of this on the portfolio is a matter of both degree and the way in which it is combined with other criteria – such as negative screening. A variation of this approach is 'best of sector' where ethical policies aim to give investment exposure to a certain investment universe or sector by accessing those companies that are considered to be leaders in their field.

For example, the UK's first ethical fund, the Stewardship Fund, views positively companies providing the 'basic necessities of life'. This includes companies involved in housing, clothing, food, energy and water where companies do not operate in such a way that they are excluded in accordance with the negative criteria.

Some other industries such as health care or companies manufacturing safety products are also favoured by many ethical funds. However, they may fail to meet the standards set by others, for example because they test products on animals.

Easier companies to assess are those providing clearly positive services or products. This can include companies such as renewable energy companies. However, such industries are often difficult to invest in either because few companies are quoted on a stock market or because the company is so small that its shares are illiquid and not easily traded.

The best-of-sector approach is regarded as a compromise between ethical standards and fund managers wishing to get broad investment exposure. They are often regarded as being in conflict, as the theoretical best investment approach is to allow investment in all companies based on financial criteria – a view that completely fails to recognize the investment benefits of giving close consideration to social, ethical and environmental (SEE) issues. It is therefore a useful attempt to balance SEE and financial issues and a way of encouraging companies in difficult sectors but trying to raise standards and address some very difficult problems.

Thematic investment

Defined as...

Investments aimed at directing money into companies that specifically focus on meeting certain positive aspirations: effectively a very pure positive approach.

Explained as...

Investment solutions that fall within this area are typically aimed at investment in newer companies, often being developed by 'pure-play', in other words highly focused, smaller companies. Technologies falling into this category may include those involved in renewable energy, recycling or waste remediation, for example.

Whilst exciting, such investments tend to focus on very small companies, which is regarded as increasing risk and, as such, is viewed with caution by many. This area is generally accepted as being appropriate only for a small proportion of an investor's money or only for the wealthier investor.

Engagement

Defined as...

A strategy that can be applied to any fund (screened or otherwise) that aims to influence company behaviour by dialogue between fund managers and the companies they invest in.

Explained as...

The aim of engagement or 'shareholder dialogue' is to encourage more responsible business practices, which will benefit the company, its investors and wider society. This is based on the premise that, all other things being equal, more responsible companies – in particular those that manage their ethical, social and environmental risks and opportunities well – will outshine their peers in the longer run.

Engagement can be used either as part of an ethical fund strategy (which is where it originated) or as a stand-alone practice. Although still the exception rather than the rule, the latter is becoming increasingly popular amongst mainstream, larger investment providers. Issues covered tend to be those that affect a large number of companies such as labour standards, supply chain management, climate change, biodiversity, forestry, and bribery and corruption.

The bribery and corruption campaign was essentially a development of George Soros's 'Publish What You Pay' campaign. The campaign aims to increase government and corporate openness about payments made and received, as a means to address and reduce corruption – often a core driver of poverty. Governments have further developed the idea, with Tony Blair taking a leading role, under the heading of 'Extractives Industry Trading Initiative'. Signatories include major oil companies and the governments of many resource-rich countries. Pressure had been put on these companies by an agreement between fund investment managers.

HOW DOES ENGAGEMENT WORK?

Engagement policies are normally carried out by specialist teams working within larger investment institutions; whereas screening can more easily be subcontracted out of the institution. For some important issues, investment institutions have chosen to work together to increase the pressure for change on companies. Areas of progress include work with pharmaceutical companies with regard to the patenting of AIDS drugs (and others), known as the 'Access to Medicines' campaign. Another project, known as the 'Equator Principles', has encouraged international banks to support a banking industry initiative to give increased consideration to the social and environmental impacts of whom money is lent to. This project now has 15, mainly US-based, bank signatories.

To date, engagement has been seen mainly as a function that operates as an addition to standard investment analysis practices for non-screened (mainstream) investment funds. In such cases, a company's shares are selected for standard financial reasons and then the management of the company is encouraged to improve further by altering certain social or ethical practices. To date, however, companies have not tended to be dropped as a result of failing to respond to engagement. The reason for this is that there is concern amongst primarily institutional investment providers that such action would alter the risk profile of a fund, so investment providers have so far steered away from doing this. In addition there are fears that the exclusion of companies on ethical grounds undermines the debate to be had between investment managers and companies, which is aimed at making them more successful as well as making the world a better place.

Engagement as a stand-alone approach was essentially born of the need to find investment solutions for large occupational pension schemes following the introduction of the pensions disclosure legislation in July 2000. As such it is still relatively in its infancy. It remains to be seen how this will evolve over coming years.

FITTING THE APPROACHES TOGETHER

Although it is a complex area, it is important to recognize that there is no single correct policy or SRI approach because investors' views and values vary widely. As such, different funds do consider different ethical issues and do apply different methods. Different investment institutions and different ethical funds will appeal to different investors, some of whom will wish to avoid companies for ethical reasons. Others will want to support certain activities while others still will want to change the world. No single approach offers a panacea and none can expect to appeal to a wide audience if it is excessively extreme.

Although it is widely thought that avoidance does not alter company behaviour, in reality, if sufficient investors withhold their support from a company, avoidance will drive the company to take action, because of the risk of either being taken over or being starved of capital. With regard to a number of issues ethical funds can be seen to indicate future trends (remember the original UK ethical fund issue was 'anti-apartheid') and may also be the tip of the iceberg, indicating the direction in which investors wish funds to move, if given the option. Companies can view the messages given out by these funds as a timely warning. Withholding financial support can be an important means of investors getting their message across to a company.

Likewise, complex issues also surround engagement. It has to be recognized that, in order to maintain its pragmatic, business-friendly front, this policy also has its limitations. For example, it is widely regarded as likely to be futile to seek to encourage an armaments company to cease making weapons or a tobacco company to cease making cigarettes – however disliked by ethical investors. This does not however mean that it is worthless to engage with such companies. On the contrary it is preferable that such companies should manage marketing, employment, sourcing and environmental issues responsibly, for example; however, engagement can only focus on these, debatably more peripheral, areas for such industries.

MEETING THE NEEDS OF THE MARKET

Given the choice and all things being equal (ie that the investment will not sacrifice performance), a majority of people claim that they would rather invest in a business that operates in an ethical and responsible manner towards people and the environment. It is also clear that, just as different people have different views on life and how to go about it, so they will wish any ethically driven investment that they make to match their views and approaches as closely as possible. The proliferation not only of ethical and SRI funds but also of different investment models is a very healthy sign, indicating that this investment sector can now offer funds that can closely match the views held by most people across the spectrum of ethical and social concerns and funds that closely reflect the manner in which people would prefer to express their views.

Note

[1] In the USA it is not unusual to apply single screens, eg a tobacco exclusion only; however, this is not common in the UK retail investment market.

3

Green legislation and other outside influences

John Hancock

A CHANGING BACKGROUND

When selecting a collective investment fund that includes among its stock selection criteria an ethical or social dimension as well as an expectation that the business will grow and generate profits through true added value while pursuing long-term developments that are sustainable, an investor will be motivated by moral considerations. However, there are also some very practical reasons why it would be sensible to consider the socially responsible, ethical or environmental investment sector. Holdings in a collective investment fund ought to be for the long term, in which case investors will wish to be assured that their investment stands a better than even chance of prospering and delivering growth and income well into the future, because plans have been laid and actions undertaken to secure that objective. The management teams of businesses that run along ethical and environmentally sustainable lines are viewed favourably for their planning and long-term thinking. But, however good a management team may be, there are other factors that can bear on a business's ability to achieve long-term success – factors that are usually outside the control of any individual company. It would, of course, be easy to talk here about the current of social sentiment, the tide of public opinion and other such lofty notions but such factors are often quoted when there is no hard evidence to prove or disprove them.

While we will talk about those influences later on, the main part of this chapter will be considering developments in the legislative climate whose effect would be to make life more difficult for businesses that disregard ethics, sustainability and their broader responsibilities to society.

The other side of this coin is that the same legislation will mean businesses that have set out their ethical and environmental agenda and have put into place the means to monitor and adhere to that agenda will find themselves swimming with the tide of national and supra-national policy, inasmuch as legislation in Western economies reflects that policy. They will certainly find it easier to operate within a legal structure that formalizes particular positive attitudes and decent standards of corporate behaviour.

Given the nature of governments in the major economies of Europe and America today (their reliance on focus groups, the need to be re-elected, etc), there is also a likelihood that, if enough people express a strong view in favour of a particular attitude or policy, the government will wish at least to appear to be moving in the same direction. So, a strong movement towards ethical and environmental dimensions in investment policy would encourage a government to consider how it might be seen to be going with that tide. This certainly appears to be happening in the United Kingdom where several government ministers have made pronouncements of positive attitudes regarding ethical and environmental issues. If and when they are translated into legislation and policy, these attitudes will have a significant effect on the conduct of business in the areas affected. So it will be a good idea to examine what is happening in these areas now and what that might mean for the future.

One note of caution, though. Of necessity, this book can only reflect the situation at the time of writing. Things may be quite different by the time you read these words. However, that does not alter the principle that the legislative and opinion climate is currently moving steadily towards an agenda that will handicap those businesses that pay no attention to ethical, social and environmental matters while it will provide a hospitable climate for those businesses that do consider those issues and incorporate them into planning and operational programmes. The content of this chapter includes only an illustrative selection of initiatives and policies with ethical and environmental implications. I would strongly advise that socially responsible investors keep up to date with the latest developments in the thoughts and actions of government and supra-governmental organizations (such as United Nations agencies) for pointers to what the future holds, as any sensible investor would wish to do in order to avoid investing in businesses whose modus operandi may, in the foreseeable future, bring them into conflict with what is legally acceptable.

The whole area of policy and legislation has to be seen in the context of a growing feeling that the warnings and predictions of environmentalists as well as the expressed concerns of campaigners on ethical issues were not simply the rantings of committed activists. But that has been a problem and it must be said that the manner in which some campaigners have put their case has often overshadowed the case itself. Some ill-advised pronouncements have been made that give fodder to parts of the press that wished to portray activists as crazy. During a protest against the transport of live veal calves from the UK to Europe, one well-known celebrity was told by a lorry driver that he had to feed his family. Quite an understandable point of view, you might think. The celebrity retorted that the driver's family was of no interest and, in a few words, reinforced the notion that protesters can be out of touch with reality. This provided free copy for anybody who wished to argue against what was, generally, a sincerely held moral stance against a particularly unpleasant form of animal exploitation. Good cause, atrocious communication. Emotions around environmental and ethical issues of the day have often run high with the result that passion has eclipsed reason. However, most of the protests have been based on genuine concerns that emanate from sound research and recorded trends in the environment. And even if the cause of change is as much a cyclical development in the earth's climate as the result of greenhouse gas emissions, so what? We'll still have to deal with it, and the arguments advanced by environmentalists seem to offer a reasonable model for economic life in the new circumstances.

With mainstream scientists now confirming that the environmental disasters first predicted by groups such as Greenpeace and Friends of the Earth (and largely rejected by the scientific and political establishments at that time) really are waiting just around the corner, most reasonable people and even governments have had to take note. With the powerful 'me first' sentiments of the 1980s now being replaced by the more 'communitaire' approach of the 1990s, we are seeing the current socio-economic cycle enter its second phase and take a step nearer to maturity, that is if you believe that a society is a little like an enterprise, which traditionally moves from a buccaneering to a reflective and then to a mature style.

On the ethical front, much the same would be true. Concerns on ethical issues have tended to be regarded as hindering progress, and the theory has been that, if the people at the top of the line prosper, prosperity will cascade down the line to increase the well-being of all, even if the differentials remained the same. However, in global terms and within any population group or work group, the reality has been that the rich, the aggressive and those with particular profit-focused skills have prospered mightily while those who were less fortunate have seen their relative (and sometimes their absolute) situation deteriorate. It does seem that some adjustments will need to be made to the way we behave in order for a balance of opportunity and progress between rich and poor to be restored without the rich being discouraged from creating wealth or the poor discouraged from doing anything at all.

On these, as on many other issues, governments have started to create policies taking account of the public's growing interest in thinking ahead, thinking sustainable, thinking honest and decent, and thinking fair. There are not many overtly ethical or environmental measures but there are many policy pointers that make it clear that those values will, in future, form an important part in the thinking of governments around the world.

ALL AROUND THE WORLD

A cynic might say that the further up the governmental and supra-governmental ladder you look, the more likely people are to have their heads in the clouds, which would make most supra-governmental efforts for the environment and ethics pretty much a waste of time. There is also the less cynical approach, which understands that, in order to get a pronouncement that is acceptable to a majority of the world's nations, it will not be possible to get much more controversial than stating that water is wet and air is dry. So, events such as the earth summits at Rio in 1992 and Kyoto in 1997 will necessarily have been long on 'motherhood and apple pie' but short on what to do about the environment or action plans to achieve even their limited objectives. However, we should not dismiss them for all that. Even if they make no immediate difference to the way the world works, the publicity generated and the issues aired help to set an agenda for national and local governments to make policy appropriate to their own requirements and priorities. And if that means compromises, well, so be it. Limited progress, hedged with caveats and generous timescales, is better than no movement at all and is more likely to be achievable. It also establishes a new and higher baseline from which to set a future agenda for even more progress.

Also, such summits do often get governments to commit to standards that they might otherwise try to fudge. For instance, in Rio, the developed nations agreed to a set of, albeit voluntary, targets on emission levels. They agreed to take measures aimed at lowering emissions of carbon dioxide and other greenhouse gases to 1990 levels by 2000. A small step, but at the follow-up environmental conference held in Kyoto the developed nations signed up to a 174-nation agreement (this time legally binding) to reduce emissions of those same gases, over the period 2008–12, to 5.2 per cent below 1990 levels. Within those overall targets, the member states of the European Union agreed to undertake an 8 per cent reduction in recognition of the high proportion of worldwide greenhouse gas emissions that occur in the EU. Furthermore, within even that challenging target, the UK has agreed to target a 12.5 per cent reduction. This will be difficult news for businesses engaged in processes that generate greenhouse gases and which have not, as yet, formulated or started to implement policies to see them coping with the new limits as a normal part of a planned programme of improvement. They may have to start from scratch and divert productive resources to this essential but non-productive task.

However, it does bode well for the manufacturers of equipment to generate power from renewable resources such as wind power, wave power and even from burning wood as the latest power plants do (wood is a renewable resource if farmed just to provide fuel). It is also good news for companies whose management teams have had the foresight to plan a steady rate of improvement in the cleanliness and sustainabil- ity of their processes. This is all useful information for investors and not only those with a socially responsible agenda. No investor or investment manager would wish to be tied into a business that, at best, faces an uphill struggle and, at worst, will be vulnerable to all sorts of attacks while management efforts are focused on catching up with the real world rather than growing and developing the business. And when it has all been done, who is to say that markets lost, while management's eye is 'off the ball', will ever be regained?

One other area in which the international efforts have made a great deal of progress is in the eradication of disease. This is not a matter of legislation, but the key organizations that do the work on the ground (inoculation campaigns, for example) get a great deal of moral and financial support from governments. As the spectre of disease recedes, so the economies of the countries in question can begin to focus on projects for economic progress. This may well benefit the type of businesses that pro- mote fair trade and the types of enterprise that provide basic economic requirements such as water purification plant and agricultural equipment as well as the more sophisticated pharmaceutical, medical and surgical products that bring about the reduction and elimination of disease.

BRUSSELS RULES, OK!

There is, though, a level of supra-national government that not only has a consistent policy on ethical and environmental issues but also has increasing power to project that policy into legislation at a national government level. The European Union started out as a trading zone called the European Economic Community with an internal tariff structure to encourage trade among the member states, enabling com- panies in those states to enjoy economies of scale that can only be achieved in a very large market. That, though, was a very long time ago and now, with a single currency and with a quite distinct social democrat slant on capitalism and economics, the European Union is well on the way to becoming a single economic and political entity that, whether you agree with that or not, will stamp a distinctive style on the legislative programmes of member states. Already, in areas such as working hours, works councils, annual leave, health and safety and a host of other areas, European legislation takes precedence over local law, and European legislation has a high content of ethical considerations and environmental objectives. While the individual directives would be too numerous to specify, we are becoming familiar with the changes in our water purity regulations, the conservation of fish stocks, working time directives, the Social Chapter, human rights rulings, even the packaging of products on our supermarket shelves. One devastating intervention from Europe was the ban on worldwide exports of British beef during the BSE scare because of fears that the meat might be contaminated with a virus that may be linked to the human condition Creutzfeldt–Jakob disease (CJD) and a new variant of that condition that appeared at about the same time that the BSE crisis was in full flow. Such ethical or environmental concern should sound a warning to businesses that poor behaviour in areas where the environment or the general well-being of people could be adversely affected will not be possible, at least not within the law.

More recently, European rules on fishing quotas and methods, even net sizes, have introduced a wholly new dimension into the sea-fishing industry and one that it is finding it very hard to cope with.

This bodes well for businesses that have been cleaning their processes, trying to find better ways of disposing of waste or recycling it, removing unnecessary chemicals from the products they make and according their workforce the type of decent work conditions and consultation channels as stakeholders in the business that will add motivation and ensure that everybody, having participated in the decision process, understands the thinking behind policy and plans. Workers may also have an opportunity to suggest alternative ways forward that might well incorporate the direct experience from the sharp end that no business model can ever replicate. On the other hand, this bodes ill for businesses that have steadfastly ignored the opportunities to improve their processes and their work practices on the grounds of cost or because they do not trust their workforce. Such businesses will find it a struggle in the short term to match the latest standards, build goodwill in the business and continue to devote the resources that the business requires to operate profitably. Their exclusion from fund stock lists will not need to be on moral grounds but on the simple grounds that they have burdened themselves with an unnecessary additional and non-productive workload and have demonstrated a management style that does not suggest the business is good at looking ahead or good at managing change.

NEARER TO HOME

When the present UK government came to power, they promised action on a number of fronts including various pledges that there would be a more human, more ethical approach to some key matters of policy. Now, whenever politicians speak of ethics (or anything, come to that) they will have in mind votes and what actions will please the most people while alienating the least number. Nevertheless, there have been a number of initiatives from the Labour government in the UK that, if translated into actions, will see British policy at home and in the world at large taking into account the moral and environmental dimension to a greater extent than ever before.

However, people are very contradictory, especially when it comes to ethical and environmental issues. For instance, everybody would agree that there should be less use of cars and yet most would also find that their own use of a car is virtually indispensable. The public also have a healthy cynicism for any policy that involves a payment to a government body at national or local level. And, unless payments that are designed to discourage environmentally damaging behaviour (congestion charging, road pricing, etc) can be clearly seen to be doing a job that will make the environmental alternative better, people will choose not to re-elect that government when the opportunity arises. It may be that they are voting against the unethical policy of charging for the behaviour to be discouraged rather than investing in the infrastructure to enable the behaviour to be encouraged.

FOREIGN AFFAIRS

On assuming office in 1997, the Labour government declared that theirs would be an ethical foreign policy. The theory was that UK policy overseas should put the pursuit of human rights matters before the need to secure orders for UK companies. If the policy is to be ethical in a pure sense, it will avoid the sales of arms to regimes with poor records on human rights or coexistence with their neighbours. However, and this is the rub, if we do not sell those arms the immediate effect will be a loss of jobs in the UK at the factories that supplied those weapons and, probably, the creation of jobs in France or another arms-producing economy that will gladly take on the business. Therefore, it is a fine line that the government has to follow between a pure ethical policy and the well-being of workers (many of whom will have voted for them) at home. And how ethical is it to cut off somebody's livelihood without taking the trouble first to find him or her an alternative? Nevertheless, in anticipation of the long term, a number of defence businesses are diversifying and, while that may not make them natural candidates for socially responsible fund managers, it will mean that the areas into which they move will become more competitive and their likely dominance of new sectors into which they enter may mean that the companies most likely to succeed are those that can offer the kind of personal, bespoke service that industrial giants sometimes find difficult. However, not far from the foreign affairs brief is the overseas development brief where the UK is implementing a different approach that seeks to help developing countries with what they need rather than what we have to sell. Although the present policy is not to tie aid to trade or other contracts, there must be a beneficial effect on businesses whose stock-in-trade includes the basic needs of developing economies. Water purification plant, simple transport systems, low-cost and easy-maintenance agricultural machinery, clockwork radios, disaster relief equipment, field medical units that can cope with the over-whelming majority of life-threatening conditions and low-technology power genera-tion all spring to mind. On the other hand, it may mean less work for the large building consortia that have provided the developed world with projects such as pres-tigious airports and buildings to compete for the title of world's tallest, largest, etc.

THE ROAD TO CLEAN AIR

There is little doubt that the motor car is one of those boons of the 20th century that has made possible comfort and mobility on a scale unheard of in previous centuries to a class and number of people who might never have left their home village in past times. But it is a terrible boon nonetheless because it delivers its bounty at a very high price. From stress to pollution and the despoliation of the countryside for road build-ing, the downside of motoring has been well documented. So the current UK gov-ernment has tried to formalize some targets on stabilization and reduction of pollution levels from cars as part of a broader policy direction with regard to pollu-tion. In November 1998, the UK Climate Change Programme was launched with a consultation paper from the Department of the Environment, Transport and the Regions (DETR) and the equivalent authorities in Scotland, Wales and Northern Ireland. The foreword to that document concludes with the following words:

> This consultation paper is designed to stimulate a national debate on how we might meet our targets [for reductions in pollution levels]. We are one of the first countries to publish such detailed ideas since Kyoto. We are inviting views at this early stage to ensure that we have a good understanding of what can be achieved practically and cost effectively. We are determined to meet our targets in ways which enhance rather than damage UK competitiveness and which increase social inclusion. We also want to hear about any more imaginative and longer-term ideas. We know that we do not have all the

answers. Solutions will require partnerships between Government, industry, voluntary groups and individuals.

After this consultation is complete, we will develop and consult further on a new climate change programme for the UK. Above all, we want to create real commitment across the UK to tackling climate change. Climate change is a threat to us all and to our children. But it is also an opportunity to change society for the better. We must now deliver on our promises.

Fine words but how will they be translated into action? Voluntary arrangements may go some of the way and there will be some scope for the government reaching agreement with individual sectors without any need for recourse to legislation (the agreement to end animal testing of cosmetics would be an example to follow). However, the only way that the fine words above will become practice will be if the government legislates and we can discern the tone of future legislation on issues affecting ethics and the environment.

CAN THAT BE SUSTAINED?

The UK government has also declared its hand on the issue of sustainable business. In this policy, the link between prudent use of precious resources and the future sustainability of our lifestyle is clearly drawn in the opening words of the same consultation document from the DETR, now DEFRA (Department for Environment, Food and Rural Affairs):

> The Government is committed to sustainable development, combining economic, environmental and social objectives [for performance in]... social progress... protection of the environment... prudent use of natural resources... maintenance of high and stable levels of growth and employment.
>
> These objectives are closely linked. For example, protecting the environment is not necessary just for its own sake but because a damaged environment will sooner or later hold back economic growth.

The document goes on to look at the opportunities and challenges that the new policy on sustainable development will set for businesses. In a section entitled 'The Sustainability Challenge', the document sets out three levels of action that will be necessary in order for a sustainable development policy to work. Right at the top of that list is the statement: 'Government must set a long-term and consistent policy framework, putting in place the correct economic instruments, regulations and incentives for business and consumers.' Clearly, the UK government intended that its drive for sustainable development would not simply be fine words but would also involve government action through the legislative programme. Further on the document asks: 'Where are the responsibilities for the issues raised by sustainable development held within your business?'

MANY POINTERS TO THE FUTURE

A further pointer to the moral attitude of the present UK government can be seen in the enactment of regulations on late payments. Although phased over a number of years, these regulations, which first applied to large organizations making payment to small businesses, aim eventually to make it very difficult to make late payments and will allow creditors to charge a statutory level of interest on late payments. And even if their impact has yet to be felt with any force, history tells us that, once this type of low-level law is in place, it usually grows into every part of the processes it seeks to control.

The UK government passes and will be passing laws whose effect will be to disadvantage businesses whose drive for profits has ignored the moral or long-term sustainability dimension. Even if you remain unconvinced by the moral argument for socially responsible investment, it is becoming clear that not to act in a socially responsible manner is not going to be a viable option for UK businesses or for businesses dealing with the UK. This will also be true of the European Union, in which the UK is a major component. So, if a business wishes to have access to these large markets, it will need to be able to comply with whatever regulations concerning the ethical and ecological aspects of operation may be applicable in the EU or UK. As an investor concerned just with the long-term prospects that an investment will perform, are you likely to put money into a business that faces some years of upheaval while the management team tries to keep up with the changes brought about by a legislative programme that favours work methods and operational standards that the business has previously ignored? Can you really have faith in the capability of managers to deal with a requirement to change in which they have previously shown no particular interest, skill or foresight? Or will investors favour those businesses that have already embraced the best practice in areas of ethical and ecological dimensions and that can face any ethical and environmental development of business law without equivocation, safe in the certainty that the business already operates in a manner that embraces the principles of decency and sustainability enshrined in new legislation?

The reality is that it is not simply a good or a decent thing for investors to include a moral and sustainability dimension into their investment criteria. To be working in a way that takes account of those issues is to be working in a way that will easily settle in to the new legislative climate promised by governments around the world – whether it be the reduction of pollution from cars or the provision of public transport; in the reduction or elimination of harmful emissions of greenhouse gases in processes of the business or the creation of non-degradable waste products; through the decent treatment of workers as human and valuable stakeholders in the business in fair return for the investment of their labour and skills; through honesty in dealings with other parties (suppliers and customers) and transparency in reporting on the activities of the business. In all of these areas, businesses can show themselves to be thinking ahead and in tune with the realization that profit at the expense of honesty, of the decent and fair treatment of others or of resources being used that cannot be replaced is not so much profit as theft from other people today or from our children tomorrow.

At this stage, many of the ideas may seem to be remote or unworkable, but if experience with the European Union has taught us anything it is that, once a legislative course has been set, there is no stopping. The only limiting factor is how long it may take to implement. The current Labour government in the UK has learnt from this, and only a reckless business would now ignore the need for moral and ecological dimensions to business practice. Certainly, to invest in businesses of the type that socially responsible funds would choose is likely to look very sensible on economic and financial grounds as well as on grounds of conscience.

And there is plenty of evidence that even current legislation and regulation can allow for businesses that ignore the reality to suffer an appropriate financial penalty. Companies that fall foul of current health and safety regulations are frequently fined, with both the Health and Safety Executive and trade unions taking an active approach to ensuring that workers' welfare is not compromised for any reason. Equally, readers will be aware of the regular and well-publicized prosecutions that follow major incidents of water pollution.

As further indicators of their intent regarding the ethical dimension in business, the UK government in 1999 put into law a national minimum wage and introduced legislation to translate the Fairness at Work elements of the EU Social Chapter into UK law. Both of these measures will make it more difficult for employers to treat workers badly or to deny them their 'rights' in a number of key areas of employment practice. Although each legislative development on its own may not cause too much additional work for a business, taken together they add up to a legislative climate that positively favours companies whose operations are already ethical and inclusive for shareholders, management and workforce.

It is not only legislation that affects the climate within which businesses operate or their behaviour. Only a very reckless management team would ignore the positive and negative ebbs and flows of public opinion. Fickle it is, illogical it can be, more herd instinct than individually considered understanding it may be, but of course few members of the public would ever know, let alone concede, that was how their opinions are formed. And, of course, many really do hold the views that they espouse, resulting from consideration based on facts and, however it has been arrived at, an opinion is a very influential moderator for our view of the world, what is right and what is wrong. Increasingly today, public opinion, as reflected in (moulded by) the popular press, is moving away from the worship of the unfettered capitalism that typified the 1980s and towards what is perceived to be a more balanced view of wealth generation within a society that places equal value on all of its members, regardless of their wealth or ability. Socialism it is not and, while to go too far down this road is as dangerous as any extreme, most people feel instinctively more comfortable with a balanced society than one that takes an extreme approach. Equally, the protests of the eco-warriors and others whose efforts have brought to our attention issues that might otherwise have been buried and forgotten, while they may have attracted censure in themselves, have succeeded in raising public awareness of those activities that are spoiling the world around us and reducing its capacity to support us and our children. Businesses must react to shifts in the public's attitudes because, no matter how they have been arrived at, the opinions of the public will influence the sales and financial success of a business. That is why some of the very largest corporations on earth are focusing so much effort on their ethical and environmental policies and why they are accommodating views that they might have rejected out of hand just a few years ago.

There are no laws as yet compelling businesses like British Airways and British Telecom to take social and ecological issues into account or to instigate environmental audits of their business activities. But very large and successful businesses want to remain that way and will not undertake a policy that is likely to bring bad publicity or offend public opinion even if they could legally do so. Equally, pharmaceutical companies that make the drugs needed to treat HIV sufferers and AIDS victims have realized that they are better off reaching reasonable agreements for the use of their patents to produce local and low-cost variants of their products in countries where the wherewithal does not exist to pay the high prices that such drugs command in Western markets. The reality is that, without the drugs, some African economies stand at risk of having no significant populations of working age and, whatever your view on that, there can be no economic or social benefit to gain from allowing whole populations to become desperate people with nothing to lose from the consequences of whatever actions they might deem likely to improve their lot. Some might say that public opinion is the real law of the market rather like a law of nature. Certainly, public opinion is now swinging towards favouring the types of businesses that can show a clean ethical and environmental bill of health, and investment managers will not ignore such factors in their calculations.

Perhaps we can hope that, in the longer term, the need for a separate ethical and socially responsible investment sector will disappear as practice, policy and track record in these areas begin to rank alongside the more traditional criteria for a good investment. However, until that time, the more discerning investors who do include criteria of conscience into their investment thinking will be comfortable in the knowledge that, as ethical investors, they have already established for themselves a place in the future.

4

Why choosing an ethical or socially responsible investment fund is different from selecting any non-screened fund

John Hancock

The growth in interest in more socially responsible investment (SRI) approaches has mirrored an opposite move in the world of collecting more tangible assets such as art and cultural artefacts. Traditional collections usually reflected, first and foremost, the tastes and passions of the collector rather than any purely objective view of monetary value. Much of the value attributed to a collectable item lay in its appearance, provenance, feel or taste. Such collections were often put on display for the sheer pride in sharing access to and appreciation of objects of perceived beauty or artefacts with a recognized place in history that had been accumulated and that, when viewed together, could bring to life a particular aspect of human achievement. In fact, wealthy collectors almost regarded it as a duty accompanying their fortune (in both senses of the word) to share some of the qualities and values that fortune could acquire and thus to give back something to balance what they had taken. This was rarely motivated by any ethical concerns as we recognize them today but, nonetheless, did ensure the enrichment of society as a whole. However, in the second half of the 20th century, value began to be more specifically defined in terms of price, ie what would this object achieve at auction? Price-value-driven collectors may still have appreciated aesthetic qualities but were as much concerned with previous form and performance in the price. Indeed, some 'collectors' such as pension funds and even wealthy individuals bought solely based on the expectation of significant price rises. The passion was transferred from the object to its sale value and, because that was the guiding principle, many great works of art or other objects of significance disappeared into the safety of bank vaults. Individual collectors of this school took their pleasure from marking the rising tide of monetary value in their particular market and collections. Those were not pleasures to be shared; such collectors regarded the objects in the same way as one regards investment assets.

Investments into financial instruments such as stocks and shares and collective investment funds that themselves invest in stocks and shares have always looked to the absolute value of price as their guiding light. Whether investing short-term, long-term, for income or for growth, the bottom line has been measured in terms of money. If any intuitive value was placed on an investment, it was more likely the speculation that it might outperform conventional expectations of income or growth for the market sector in which it was categorized. In many senses that made the management of group investment funds, if not easy, more predictable. The very fact that some investing institutions have programmed computers to buy or sell stocks according to specific trends, movements or trigger points in the price of shares is indicative of the absolute and quantifiable criteria by which investment value has traditionally been measured. In this tradition, there have been a few clear definitions of what is a good investment. Will it make money this year? Will it make money next year? Will it make money into the foreseeable future? And will it beat inflation as well as other available investments in terms of the money it makes? There has not usually been any moral dimension to investment but that has changed in recent decades.

SOME DIFFERENT INGREDIENTS IN THE INVESTMENT MIX

Ethical and socially responsible investment models reflect a change in that traditional perception of value. They have introduced values of decency and of the cost to others and to the environment of any profit. More prosaically, they have introduced a long-term approach to investing, sometimes called sustainability, which is concerned not only with this year's bottom-line profit but also about how the business is prepared to face future challenges and opportunities. Socially responsible investors have pointed up the long-term financial cost of policies that pay no heed to issues beyond the figures generated for the bottom line as well as the added financial value of policies that seek to run the business efficiently and in tune with the world at large. Socially responsible investors also recognize that a profit generated from true added value, without the need to exploit anybody or take risks with the welfare of others or of the world in general, reflects the type of long-term business and management skills that will be more likely to thrive in good times as well as survive bad times.

However, in order to take that responsible approach to their investments, fund managers of ethical and SRI funds need to know more about their investments (in both quantitative and qualitative terms) than do other fund managers. For instance, whereas it might be sufficient for a company to be able to demonstrate to an ordinary equity fund manager that it employed no child labour and sold no weapons, an ethical or SRI fund manager would need to look right down the supply chain to ensure that no unpleasant labour practices were employed and right up the value chain to ensure that the business's products were not incorporated as components into other products or systems that could be categorized as weapons. It would be untrue to say that other fund managers do not apply any moral yardstick when assessing the value of stocks in which they are planning to invest. There are many occasions in which an issue that might be seen as related to ethical or SRI concerns will also be related to bottom-line performance and assessments of future growth prospects. For instance, a business that had been judged the guilty party in a pollution incident might well find its share price affected as investors assessed the likely impact in terms of resources diverted to handling the fallout from the incident and righting any failings that may have led to the incident.

Apart from the need to research and monitor individual investments more closely than might always be the case for fund managers concerned primarily with bottom-line values, ethical fund managers have to deal with investment dilemmas – because ethical, socially responsible and environmental funds include in their investment criteria judgements based on a moral assessment of what a business does, as well as statistical performance. And because each individual will see the world from a slightly different moral perspective based on his or her own experiences and priorities, there are almost as many definitions of a good investment as there are investors with ethical, socially responsible and environmental concerns! Those concerns are often very personal, reflecting an individual's honestly and passionately held belief about what are the errors or values of human endeavour. Inevitably, those concerns cherished by one investor may well clash diametrically with the equally honestly and passionately held concerns of another. Such is human nature. Some would say that the presence of such dilemmas is a weakness in the drive to pursue a socially responsible investment policy. Others believe that it is the fact that such dilemmas exist that points to the thorough and considered approach upon which this particular investment movement is built (see above) and introduces the strength of real understanding into the investment equation. Also, in the course of resolving dilemmas, fund managers and investors alike may well improve the mechanisms by which they measure and judge the social aspects of an investment.

Dilemmas occur when two sincerely held and valid views on a particular issue lead to opposing conclusions. As there are nearly as many ethical, socially responsible and environmental stances as there are concerned investors, it is inevitable that dilemmas will arise in the approach to some potential investments.

For this reason, investors will need to ensure that the fund in which they invest holds to a similar set of values as they do themselves.

DILEMMAS

Some typical dilemmas might arise in the area of animal testing. Among ethical and SRI investors, there are some who consider all animal-based research to be wrong while others take a different approach in which, while such research is not accepted for non-vital tasks such as testing cosmetics, controlled animal-based research may be acceptable in pursuit of medical advances and new treatments. Similarly, in the universe of ethical and SRI funds, there are some that support medical research and, with that, accept the need for some animal-based experiments (albeit with strict controls and accountability) while other funds would avoid investing in any business that engaged in animal-based research for any purposes. The main concerns in this area now will not be the ethics of animal experiments but the ethics of protestors against those experiments who consider it fair game to perpetrate unspeakable acts upon those who are lawfully engaged in licensed animal-based research, and the ethics of financial institutions that bow to threats from these same people and withdraw financial support for businesses involved in animal-based research.

One emotive medical issue on which different people hold diametrically opposed but principled views is that of abortion. Because many of those who first looked to the ethical content of an investment did so from a religious belief, there was an emphasis on the sanctity of human life, including the life of the unborn child. However, those who are now taking the ethical road may well believe that a woman's right to choose is the overriding consideration when an abortion is considered. Fund managers will have to think hard on that one and may have to consider offering a choice of ethical criteria in different funds.

A subtler dilemma can arise with an issue such as child labour. In a perfect world, there would be no child labour. However, this is not a perfect world and, in some parts of this imperfect world, a ban on child labour might simply mean a ban on a child's ability to contribute to the family's financial well-being. If that child's contribution is the marginal part of the family income that means the difference between getting by and going under, then a ban on his or her working would worsen rather than improve the family's conditions. Therefore, child labour may be necessarily acceptable but any business that has such labour in its supply chain should consider how best to secure working conditions – especially age at which work can be undertaken, hours and pay rates – that will not be abusing the child and should consider how best it can contribute to ensuring those children's longer-term welfare and ability to earn a living through improved education programmes and the like. While the purest of ethical investment funds will probably still avoid any association with child labour, more pragmatic funds and those whose business model is based on responsible engagement (see Chapter 1) may well take the view that they can do more for the child's welfare by ensuring good working conditions, decent pay and hours, and the provision of a long-term education programme than by simply avoiding any contact and removing the discipline of investor pressure from the system.

Another dilemma might arise in the construction industry where a builder who is heavily involved in erecting affordable housing might also be involved in road building. While the affordable housing is easy to support, road building can cause some highly emotional reactions and not all, contrary to the image portrayed in the media, against the process. An ethical or SRI fund manager may well want to know more about the road construction programmes in which a construction firm is involved. Can their building be justified in terms of bringing work and creating economic opportunity? Do the construction plans include the restoration of damaged land after the job has been completed and has the environmental impact of the finished road been kept to a minimum level, commensurate with reasonable costs? While there are often vociferous protests against the building of another road or increasing capacity on an existing one, there will also be people who would value additional jobs being available in the areas served by the road. But the evidence shows that, even where a road increases capacity to more than projected traffic levels, the very presence of the road will attract more traffic than a straight-line extension of past figures would suggest. So another question needs to be, what long-term programme will accompany the construction programme to prevent the new or extended road becoming just as congested as before but in a few years' time?

While posing and answering questions such as those above may seem to be a departure from the usual investor/investment relationship, it does bring about a depth of understanding and a level of detailed knowledge that will prove valuable in many other aspects of the investment.

A COMPLEX JUDGEMENT

Of course, while dilemmas are important, they do not replace the key differences between the ethical and social priorities and concerns of different people, which ought to be reflected in any fund into which individual investors sink their money. Some will reflect a concern about how businesses treat their personnel, or the practices they deploy to advance the business; others will question the integrity of information used in marketing, or the fairness of any trading arrangements with countries from the developing world. Managers of funds that follow an environmental agenda can at least base their judgements on more measurable criteria – 'Does this company's activity harm the environment?' – although even that seemingly straightforward question can suggest different answers according to personal priorities. Whether the fund manager adheres to an ethical, socially responsible or environmental investment policy, there is an additional complication caused by the complex cross-ownership, joint ventures and other relationships of modern business. At first sight, the choices and dilemmas faced by socially responsible investors can seem daunting.

However, since Friends Provident first launched the Stewardship Fund in 1984, ethical and environmental fund managers have worked towards refining the definitions that govern investment criteria from the avoidance-driven criteria of the protest movement to the more sophisticated supportive approach that seeks to promote good as well as avoid bad practices. As a result, in many cases the correct approach (if 'correct' is the right word) can be considered not simply in terms of being against those activities considered environmentally or ethically poor but also in terms of how an investment might give the fund managers the opportunity, on behalf of their investors, to influence future development of policy in the business. From this has developed the policy of engagement that is enabling ethical, socially responsible and environmentally concerned fund managers to invest in a wider universe of stocks and which has moved this types of investment criteria firmly into the mainstream of investment considerations.

Also, some previously avoided investments have matured or the conditions that defined their status have lost the edge that gives rise to outrage in some investors. That, though, takes managers into difficult areas and there are now a number of investment propositions with strong arguments both for and against them on ethical and environmental grounds. Avoidance criteria still dominate this sector and that, combined with the dilemmas that ethical and environmental investment can encounter, could deter some investors from making the effort to establish which fund might share their priorities. It should not do so because, for an investor who is concerned about the wider issues, it is these different priorities and dilemmas, and the reasoning that goes into resolving them, that give ethical investment its human edge. And remember, while socially responsible fund managers do include ethical and environmental criteria in their considerations, they are, like all fund managers, still obliged to work to achieve the best financial performance they can within those parameters. It would not be socially responsible or, indeed, ethical to throw investors' money into businesses with little hope of success, however well meaning they may be.

HOW FUND MANAGERS ESTABLISH AND INVESTORS UNDERSTAND A FUND'S INVESTMENT MODEL

The resolution of dilemmas is best achieved through the application of information, a task that can, admittedly, occupy a significant amount of a fund's analysis and management resources. However, as has already been said, the additional value that comes from a richer knowledge of the businesses behind the stocks that the fund holds adds value in more ways than simply improving understanding of the ethical and social context of the business as a corporate citizen. Better understanding of long-term plans and how the business plans to position itself in the context of future changes in legislation, the market and public opinion will also yield strong pointers to how good the management team is at planning at all. Ethical Investment Research Services (EIRIS) undertakes this task for funds that retain the service as an adviser and for investors who subscribe for the regularly updated research that supports its findings (see Appendix 1). Without expressing opinions of its own, EIRIS analyses and reports on companies in terms of established and agreed ethical and environmental criteria and the specific criteria that each fund has proclaimed as its own. Investors and advisers may then use this information as a first filter against the fund's own policy before applying the usual research and financial examinations. EIRIS does, though, encourage funds to have a clear investment policy on ethical and environmental issues because it is only through such a policy that fund managers can make clear their own criteria to potential investors in such terms as will enable those investors to determine whether or not the fund stands on their general side of a dilemma. Some fund managers will also refer to ethical reference committees, independent bodies that adjudicate on whether a potential investment is within or outside an acceptable level of compliance with the policy of the fund. However, for all of the general agreement between a fund and its fund holders as far as priorities are concerned, there will be specific issues that either fall outside previous understandings as to the criteria or break new ground for which no clear criteria have been established when the fund holder first invested.

In order continually to cater for the diversity in approach of different ethical investors and their advisers, as well as the dilemmas that can arise from those differences, some fund managers operate parallel investment policies. While one group of funds may adhere to strict avoidance criteria, others may be support-orientated funds looking to the future and taking a pragmatic stance, and others still may pursue a policy of engagement to influence the future direction of corporate policy in businesses where the funds invest and to support companies that are actively working to improve their ethical, social and environmental performances within the confines of the realities of their business. For instance, an oil company could not withdraw from the extraction or fossil fuels sector without irreparably harming the interests of its shareholders in a most unethical manner but such a company can undertake a programme of social involvement that will ensure that it does the best it can for the people involved in the business and the regions or countries where it operates, like the programme that BP Trinidad & Tobago (bpTT) has instigated and funded to educate and train local people to occupy the structure that the company is setting up to manage its new oilfields off those islands. This programme envisages local personnel eventually holding positions at all levels in the business right up to the top and is being backed with actions and funding (to establish the necessary institutions) as well as fine words.

THE CASE FOR DEFENCE

An investment sector that comes to mind when speaking of dilemmas would be armaments. Who, for instance, arms the peacemakers? You may dislike arms and the trade that spreads them around the world but, if you support the principle of international peacekeeping forces, the peacekeepers must be able to defend themselves against the attacks that are all too likely in any place where the peace needs to be kept. If a force is required to keep peace then the underlying situation must be one of conflict. Without arms, peacekeepers cannot effectively maintain order, as we have seen in recent conflicts in the Balkans and Afghanistan. Particularly in the Balkans, peacekeepers who were inadequately armed on occasions had to stand by while ethnic cleansing took place almost before their eyes. It may appear to be a dilemma, but socially responsible investors will look beyond the immediate reaction and consider the full case. Operating different criteria for different funds enables the managers to cater for both sides of the dilemma in this and other areas.

Arms linkages are, like transport issues, often the cause of dilemmas – and not only for investors and fund managers. Events in Sierra Leone during 1998 posed, for the British government, the dilemma of whether it had been right to arm the forces of the democratically elected but ousted government in order to assist in the overthrow of the unelected and unpleasant regime that had seized power in the country. Had a strict definition of ethical foreign policy been observed, no arms would have been supplied but the people of Sierra Leone would have had to live for an indefinite period under the oppressive yoke of a government that operated to particularly barbaric standards. On balance and regardless of the political issues, the forward-looking observer would say that the decision to assist the elected government with arms to overthrow the unelected dictators was morally correct, whatever the legal position. Often, though, the dilemmas faced by ethical investors are much less global.

WASTE NOT

Waste management is a growing business sector and investment area. But even here, caution must be a watchword. Waste management is widely perceived as being environmentally friendly but there are still problems such as leakage. Ethical, socially responsible and environmentally concerned investors look for companies moving up the hierarchy of waste management, towards materials recovery and recycling and away from pure disposal. Indeed, the new wave of legislation that encourages reuse of artefacts and components, recycling of materials, reduction in the actual amount of waste that remains and processes to recover the value and energy locked into that waste are making some businesses seem very good long-term investments. Businesses that have devised means to minimize waste from their own products or processes to reuse, recycle and reduce waste from other products or recover value and energy from waste will prosper in the growing climate of environmental legislation. But how would fund managers view a company like Nirex, which disposes (safely, we hope) of radioactive waste that cannot be recycled? No dilemma there as yet; most funds will avoid any business involved in the nuclear industry. But for how long? After all, nobody would contend that we would be better off without their activities in the safe disposal of materials that, whether we like it or not, do exist and must be safely managed for the foreseeable future. And, looking further into the future, there is a growing body of scientific opinion that believes nuclear energy is the only practical or realistic power source to eliminate our dependence on fossil-fuel-burning systems in the foreseeable future, and that, properly managed, it would be the cleanest, quietest energy source available.

MURKY POLITICAL WATERS

Of course, politics can influence views as to what is ethical or not and, for some, that simple device avoids many dilemmas. In this vein, many ethical investors were opposed to their funds' investing in privatization shares but the reality was that these were legitimate shares to hold, subject to whatever criteria the funds would normally apply. To oppose the privatization process on grounds of personal ethical stance was no reason to deny support to those businesses, their workforces and their customers once the process had been completed. Indeed, on the other side of the argument, many felt that it was important that such large businesses with such powerful market positions in areas where they had a bearing upon the lives of millions should be held to account on ethical and corporate social grounds, and the only people in a position to do more than protest at AGMs were the fund managers who hold most UK company shares. Looked at this way, it would have been remiss for ethical and SRI fund managers with their strong moral remit to avoid shares in these businesses. No fund managers would consider it ethical to start to incorporate a political colour to their declared ethics.

Political perceptions can also change with the force of events, as when considering South Africa. During the time of apartheid, socially responsible investment managers deliberately eschewed investments in the country as part of the pressure to bring about the end of apartheid. The same managers may now view involvement in the reborn state as positive support for a regime facing many problems whose solution will depend on the speed of economic and business development. However, others now steer clear on financial and value grounds. African countries have a poor track record of success with democracy, human rights and development, and South Africa has, in some eyes, yet to demonstrate convincingly that it may be different. Also, there remain income disparities between most white and most black workers doing comparable jobs. Perhaps this is a dilemma that some would prefer to address based on faith rather than fact. It is certainly one that will challenge the decision-making powers of managers whose commitment to do their best with other people's money precludes placing that money anywhere they perceive to be financially uncertain.

Most privatized businesses have established strong environmental and ethical credentials, politics aside. British Telecom, for instance, operates a service that contributes a real plus to the environment (telephone calls, videoconferences and the like reduce the need for travel). The business also sets an example in the openness with which it addresses environmental and ethical matters including annual sustainability audits detailing, among other things, the plans for and actual disposal of all spent materials – from wire to lorries. And BT has shown some good lateral thinking when dealing with problems such as the energy needed to power cooling systems in its exchanges. Rather than address the efficiency of cooling systems, BT engineers with equipment suppliers developed equipment that could run at high temperatures, thus removing the requirement and cost of energy for cooling and saving heat that could one day be sold to warm nearby buildings – an excellent example of good environmental sense also making good business sense. The only concerns that ethical fund managers may harbour about BT would be its involvement in communications systems that can have military graphic applications and its ownership of a network over which a number of businesses offer pornographic services.

Other former state-owned businesses have had fluctuating fortunes in this area. British Airways, it was said at the time of privatization, would become the pantomime horse of the airline industry. It has grown into one of the world's most successful airlines. It seemed, at the time of writing, to be weathering early-21st-century economic storms better than many others and without the subsidies enjoyed by rivals.

Railtrack, on the other hand, was one of the last significant privatizations, and to support environmentally sound transport systems but not Railtrack could easily have led to the question, at least as far as physical movement is concerned, 'If not railways, what?' The Railtrack issue provided an example of how dilemmas can foster better communications between fund managers, their investors and investments. When NPI Global Care Investments was considering whether to add Railtrack to the list of approved investments for the fund, managers wrote to investors. The position paper sent to unit holders was a good example of a realistic and apolitical attitude towards properly privatized enterprises and illustrates the lengths to which some fund managers will go to ensure that ethical and environmental credentials are exercised based on informed decisions, as the paper's treatment of privatization shows:

> [Privatization]... is a fact we cannot stop... It is from this starting point that we must consider our best option... We now believe the most appropriate course is to invest and use our position as concerned shareholders to influence future decisions and priorities. Even groups like Transport 2000, who are opposed to privatisation, nonetheless agree that... it will be important to hold Railtrack to the commitments they have made.

Given the facts, the majority of investors agreed but the exercise added strength to the decision and was in keeping with the informed and thoughtful nature of this type of investment – a good example of how the way in which a dilemma was handled actually strengthened the final investment decision.

Of course, that particular investment has since suffered dreadfully from government interference and meddling, culminating in Railtrack's effective renationalization. Here, the questionable ethics are those of the government and officials who interfered politically in a business whose key performance measures of safety (from signals passed at red to passengers killed per mile travelled), investment and public acceptance (passenger numbers) were all improving and at better levels than had been achieved under state ownership. It, perhaps, points up the new dilemma of whether any investment in a former state industry or in a partnership with the state can be safe, whether or not it passes the ethical screen. But, while it may be a matter for fund managers and individual investors to consider, that is not an issue for this book.

COMMUNICATIONS

In their relationships with companies in which they have invested, socially responsible investment managers operate in much the same way as most investors with, perhaps, the addition that some managers will tell a company if their shares are being sold because of a deterioration in their ethical or environmental score. And it works both ways. The store group Kingfisher, for instance, informed environmental fund managers when the company adopted a policy of offering only products containing wood from renewable sources. With the ethical investment market growing rapidly, why would a company wish to exclude itself from the opportunity to attract such funds?

LIFE IS RARELY SIMPLE, SO WHY SHOULD INVESTMENT BE SO?

From the point of view of the investor or his or her adviser, there are a number of reasons why choosing an ethical or socially responsible investment fund is different from selecting any non-screened fund. It will involve an investor in establishing and clarifying his or her own priorities and then will require of that investor or any adviser involved the task of considering which among the many ethical and SRI investment funds available today operates an investment model whose ethical and social priorities most closely match the investor's own. There are dilemmas, yes, but dilemmas that are addressed by ethical, socially responsible and environmentally concerned fund managers and dilemmas whose demands for research make those fund managers better informed about the individual companies in which they invest. And the presence of dilemmas is not something to be thought of as exclusive to socially responsible investment. Life very rarely offers simple choices although we sometimes exclude the difficult ones for the sake of a quick decision. The dilemmas of socially responsible investment and the manner in which they are addressed add to the analysis and understanding of the issues in question. While the choice may sometimes include more than a pinch of pragmatism, it may be better to invest in a business that, on balance, will add value to life on earth or is striving to improve its performance with regard to these values of conscience than to continue seeking the holy grail of the perfect socially responsible business. In investment as in life, if you want more out, you must put more in. For ethical investors, this means more thought about what they really wish to avoid, support or achieve with their investment.

5

Performance: can you afford to put your money where your heart is?

John Hancock

THE BIG ONE

What we are considering is an investment of hard-earned money, your or your client's hard-earned money: savings and capital set aside to provide for the future realization of a long-cherished ambition, perhaps to put children or grandchildren through university, maybe to pay for a wedding, possibly a world cruise and visit to family in Australia, eventually to provide for retirement with dignity and in comfort without the need to compromise on quality of life including, if necessary, long-term care or, possibly, simply to provide a nest egg, the 'rainy day' fund that growing numbers of people realize will be needed for a future when the state cannot or will not provide. Therefore, all that is covered in this book will be no more than fine words unless an ethical or socially responsible investment delivers consistent high performance in a very competitive market for an investor's money to be invested in collective investment funds. Given that an interest in combining decency with the need to get a good return is more than a passing whim, no matter how concerned investors may be to do the right thing they will probably not wish to do it at any cost. Nor should they. After all, if dumping bottles or paper in the appropriate collection bank incurred a financial penalty, would so many people be prepared to support those recycling programmes? If our attitude to organic as opposed to chemically grown food is any guide, given the chemical option or the organic alternative but at a higher price, all but the most committed consumers will opt for the lower price. People are happy to be socially responsible as long as the cost is not unreasonable. Equally, if ethical or socially responsible investment is to succeed, it has to attract substantial support. For the majority of savers and investors, especially those whose future well-being and quality of life depend on the returns from their investment, underperformance is not an option. Also, the most compelling logic behind including ethical and ecological concerns in any process is that it will then be going with rather than against the natural order of things and so, in the longer term, it is the most efficient way to conduct business. More fine words! But will your investment suffer? Will there be an investment penalty as reward for a commitment to do the right thing? These are the big questions that must be answered.

NO ETHICS IN LOSSES

There are no ethics in losing money – not for the investor who needs performance and growth in order to meet investment objectives and certainly not for the fund manager entrusted with the sound management of other people's money. If, in order to meet socially responsible principles, a company cannot make a profit, then it will soon be out of business, and what value then could one put on a principled approach to work? Equally, if losses arise from a well-meaning but poorly managed business that can add no long-term value to its field of activity, that is itself unethical in most people's books. There is no good reason why a decision to invest according to socially accountable criteria should also be a decision to sacrifice performance, and the socially accountable, ethical or environmental investment movement would not get very far if that was the case. Indeed, it was this very concern – that ethical constraints would compromise a fund manager's ability to discharge his or her duty to do the best possible job for investors – that, in the UK at least, for so long delayed the approval necessary for 'green' funds to be authorized. Fortunately, the evidence suggests that it is not the case that ethics and performance are contradictory objectives.

That is not to say, though, that ethical and ecological funds always perform well any more than do funds operating to the more traditional investment criteria of growth and income opportunities. All sectors of all economies are subject to cyclical movements over varying terms. Equally, for there to be top-performing stocks, there have to be badly performing stocks and average performers. Again, this would be true of any group of stocks, however categorized. No investment can be immune from such cycles or such performance variations between different companies, but a good fund manager will be able to minimize the impact of any adverse trend and capitalize on the opportunity of any positive trend. Although not always recognized as occupying a sector in their own right (they are usually categorized under one of the equity fund groupings), socially accountable investment funds and their investments do share a number of characteristics that influence performance, but then that would also be true of any group of funds. Additionally, because the concept of an ethical business or investment is relatively new, comparisons do not go back very far and, in respect of the earlier days of the concept, do not really include enough funds to make a comparison.

However, an increasing body of data is being built up from which to draw conclusions about the performance, both relative to other investments and absolute.

NOT BETTER NOR WORSE, BUT DISTINCT

In the past, socially responsible funds have invested mainly in small companies for several reasons. During the early days of ethical business concerns, the ones that were most easily able to base their business practices on socially responsible principles were those that had no baggage of older practices, and that, inevitably, meant new companies, which were generally small. Larger businesses, rather like large ships, need some time if they are to change direction without creating too disruptive an impact on the operations and effectiveness of the enterprise. When any new idea comes along, large corporations, for all their hype, are unlikely to embrace it unless they can see immediate or very early profitability. For instance, the media world has embraced new technology ideas with all the enthusiasm that you would expect of a business whose value and profits are determined by the size of audience and who very quickly saw satellite, cable, digital and other developments as means to extend that audience and create a profit centre with each programme. On the other hand, ideas that may well better the lot of the human race and the environment but will not turn an immediate or fast profit or may even conflict with, rather than add value to, current products or services will be less enthusiastically embraced, and it may sometimes require legislation to generate a wide adoption. Catalytic converters to reduce the quantity and toxicity of car emissions would be a good example of this latter type of development. Motor manufacturers at first 'pooh-poohed' the idea and then claimed that the inclusion of converters would add too much to the cost of new cars. However, when it became obvious that there would be no choice (the US state of California made catalytic converters a requirement), the converters were built, the cost was minimal and companies began to advertise the converters as a plus point in their products.

Because of the diversity of their interests, some of the world's largest 'blue-chip' companies have a vast matrix of relationships with subsidiaries, associate businesses, other members of an alliance, franchisees, licence issuers, licence holders, suppliers, customers and so on. For these reasons, it has historically been very difficult, with such complexity and in the absence of social auditing, to be sure of the ethical and ecological strengths and weaknesses of any large global business in its entirety. Socially responsible funds have often invested in small companies and been subject to the volatility of that sector in which companies, with little fat to hinder them when things go well or cushion them in harder times, often move between the extremes of performance. However, with companies such as British Telecom and BP now committed to social as well as financial audits and, in the case of BP, also committed to improving the contribution that local communities can make to their operations and, commensurately, the value they can derive from them, as well as the likes of Boots and Kingfisher able to satisfy their criteria, it is becoming easier for socially accountable fund managers to invest in businesses traditionally regarded as 'blue-chip'. Also, when in recent times pharmaceuticals, alcohol, gambling and tobacco and bank shares led the market, socially responsible funds were largely unable to participate in those sectors or benefit from their market-leading performance. Since then, some pharmaceutical and bank shares have been added to the ethical or socially responsible fund managers' investment universe, taking the sector further than ever into the mainstream investment market. If funds begin to take a proactive approach and invest in companies whose policy they would wish to influence, that will include a further number of large and successful businesses.

Some managers overcome the constraints of being bound to particular ethical or environmental criteria by offering a 'light green' investment approach, which may take a pragmatic view of companies that have a planned programme of improvement but that have paced that programme so as not to cause any unscheduled calls on profits, such as for new, environmentally clean equipment to replace older and less environmentally friendly equipment before any replacement was planned. Equally, where an accelerated programme of equipment improvement might threaten jobs in the short to medium term, as long as the improvement programme is in place and being implemented the sustainable speed will usually be best. The combination of a proactive stance and light green credentials allows the fund manager greater freedom to select successful stock without the need to fly in the face of socially responsible criteria.

There are, of course, pros and cons to be weighed in any decision. The pros of socially accountable investment have already been addressed but investors should remember that the full return on ethically and ecologically sound business practices may take a while, just as the damage inflicted when companies ignored warnings about asbestos and other dangerous materials also took a while to materialize as costly legal proceedings (financially costly as well as in public relations terms). It is possible that if, for instance, you are within a short time of retirement, not all socially responsible investments will be suitable for the funds that you propose to use in retirement. It is for reasons such as this that the expertise of a financial adviser will be valuable.

For a detailed analysis of the impacts of including ethical and responsible criteria in investment considerations and in the running of the business, read the September 1999 EIRIS report 'Does Ethical Investment Pay? EIRIS Research and Other Studies of Ethical Investment and Financial Performance' by Ros Havemann and Peter Webster, available on the EIRIS website at www.EIRIS.org.

The advice is no different to what one would suggest to any investor on choosing a particular investment sector, whether that was emerging markets, technology, socially responsible or any of the other sectors available.

Recent research has highlighted that there is no difference in risk-adjusted returns between screened and conventional funds and, again, for those who wish to explore this in greater detail, they can go to the UK Social Investment Forum (UKSIF) website at www.uksif.org and read the report 'International Evidence on Ethical Mutual Fund Performance and Investment Style' by Rob Bauer of ABP Investments and Maastricht University.

This book you are now reading cannot offer advice to readers on the correct approach to match their own or their clients' situations but, as a generality, the evidence seems to show that there has been no significant long-term performance disadvantage in investing in a socially responsible manner in the past and, fund for fund, if an investor had chosen the right one, he or she would have achieved an advantage. However, that statement would be true of any investment. Equally, as the socially responsible sector matures, there is no reason to expect that its performance will vary wildly from the market as a whole. There are, though, sound reasons to expect that, in these times when ethical and environmental issues occupy the top line on the agendas of most international bodies and the governments of the world's largest economies, socially responsible businesses will be at an advantage.

In Appendix 2 there is a table of performance figures supplied by Standard & Poor's, the respected fund information and ratings organization.

WHAT LIES AHEAD?

Socially responsible, ethical, ecological, green... whatever you choose to call them, investment funds that include in their criteria the requirement that companies in which they invest must operate decently are here to stay and they are available now at no additional cost. The companies should also return a profit sufficient to ensure they remain strong and with access to whatever capital requirements there may be in order to continue to grow and develop the business. From investing in smaller companies the funds have seen some of those companies grow and mature as businesses. At the same time, the larger companies whose stocks traditionally stabilize funds are experiencing a growing awareness of the need to operate to socially responsible standards. Yes, because it is the decent thing to do but also because it is likely to be the best way to make sustainable long-term profits in a world where public attitudes to corporate behaviour are increasingly reflected in legislation to prescribe the way businesses are run. Not only are the socially responsible funds growing rapidly and outpacing the collective investment sector generally, but also the number of charities, local authorities and pension funds embracing socially responsible investment criteria are adding weight to the sector and volume to any views expressed by the sector. This will in turn encourage even more fund managers to take that path and will mean that a significant number of institutional investors working to that agenda will be vocally present at the AGMs of those companies whose well-being depends, at least in part, on the judgement of their performance represented by the share price. As the process progresses, so increasing numbers of boards of directors and their management teams will have to take notice of the views of investors who care for all-round and sustainable added value. From being the investment arm of a protest movement, social responsibility has moved centre stage as a key investment criterion that may one day be no more worthy of comment than the criterion that fund managers should endeavour to achieve the best possible return and growth for their investors.

The best scenario for the future of socially responsible investment is that investors will feel that they will be able to get the best value from a socially responsible fund. More and more people do feel that to be the case as well as those who have always felt that the ethics and morals of the investment overrode even their need for profit. An increasing body of evidence supports the view that the long-term benefits of such an investment policy balance any short-term disadvantages and ensure that socially responsible investment is a legitimate and productive mainstream investment choice.

ETHICAL INVESTMENT AND FUND PERFORMANCE

ISIS Asset Management

Any exercise requiring the analysis of historic fund data is naturally vulnerable to accusations of bias. Indeed, it is concern over the proclivity of fund managers to 'cherry-pick' flattering performance periods that lies behind the Financial Services

Authority's (FSA) latest tightening of the rules over how such figures are presented to the investing public.

Another difficulty in approaching this topic is that of establishing just what constitutes an 'ethical fund' these days. With this in mind, it was decided to borrow the independent ranking methodology successfully employed by *Ethical Performance*, a well-established specialist industry publication.

Learning lessons from the past

An important consideration for potential ethical investors – one that attends every investment sector – is the fund management industry's adroitness in recognizing a bandwagon when it sees one. Like the technology sector in the late 1990s, or the bond sectors of the early millennium, ethical funds have seen more than their fair share of late arrivals.

It's now 20 years since Friends Provident launched Stewardship, the prototype for ethical funds in the UK. It was followed four years later by the launch of Jupiter Ecology, the first UK 'green' fund. Since then, the sector has grown almost beyond recognition.

But while basic methodologies have improved, ethical funds have probably had more than their fair share of 'part-timers' signing up over the years as a result of managers being able to buy in external research cheaply and screen existing portfolios appropriately. The rewards for this low outlay can be substantial over time as anecdotal evidence suggests that ethical investors are a lot more loyal than their peers.

This is why, whatever fears the FSA may harbour, past performance data remain invaluable when considering a prospective purchase. While it might not have much to tell us about future returns, it's still one of the best ways to form a view as to the level of resources and commitment a manager ascribes to such funds. That said, it should be stressed that any past performance table like Table 5.1 or Table 5.2 only provides an historical snapshot at a given point in time. As a consequence, we can expect the constituents of such 'best-of-breed' tables to change constantly.

But while there may have been a few damp squibs over the years, the net result is a thriving sector where every conceivable shade of green is now on offer.

Absolute differences

There are a number of reasons why looking in isolation at absolute returns can be relatively unrewarding. For one thing it's difficult to know whether we're actually comparing like with like.

Discussions as to the screening criteria variously employed belong elsewhere but the breadth of returns generated by the funds in Table 5.1 – let alone the other 30 or so such funds in the UK – suggests that a wide range of criteria continue to be employed.

Absolute figures also necessarily ignore the impact of asset allocation. For example, on an absolute basis part of the performance of the market's top fund, Stewardship Income, will be attributable to outstanding management and part will be as a result of the sustained bear market, which heavily favoured the dividend-biased funds in the UK Equity Income sector.

We can see the magnitude of such allocation issues when we consider the fund currently placed 11th in Table 5.1, NPI Global Care Income. While it labours at close to the bottom of its IMA sector over all time frames, its high dividend bias has seen it outperform all but eight of the UK All Companies funds in Table 5.1.

A similar question could be asked of the second-placed fund, Aegon Ethical Income, originating as it does from the UK Corporate Bond sector.

Naturally the equity bear market galvanized bond returns. The average one-year fund return from the UK Corporate Bond sector of 3.7 per cent may not seem a king's ransom compared to the 30 per cent or more on offer from the average UK All Companies fund, but the fact that over three years the former has returned 14 per cent – resulting in a 31.6 per cent differential between the average fund performance of each – has clearly yet to wash through current results.

Whether existing ethical investors are sitting on a top performer, then, is likely to rest partly on their risk tolerance at the time of investment. A bullish equity investor of three years ago would have initially suffered for his or her growth convictions while a more income-conscious or risk-averse investor will probably have done very well over the same period.

Absolute necessities

As we've seen, absolute figures offer little guidance as to the impact of portfolio construction or asset allocation. However, comparing absolute returns to external measures such as the rate of inflation or deposit returns provides a useful measure of the 'real' value of an investment.

For instance, with 10 months of rising markets safely 'banked' (at the time of writing), it should come as no surprise that every fund in the 'Top 15' beat inflation over the last year. Unfortunately this was no mean feat. Over the last three years, RPI has been sufficient to keep all but Stewardship Income and Aegon Ethical

Table 5.1 'Top 15' UK ethical funds – absolute returns

Fund name	Percentage change (%)			Volatility	Rank (by 3-year percentage change)
	1-year	3-year	5-year		
Stewardship Income	30.5	18.5	43.3	3.59	1
Aegon Ethical Income	6.8	17.1	n/a	1.48	2
Allchurches Amity	27.1	–8.8	4.6	4.83	3
Insight Inv Europ Ethical	27.0	–10.3	n/a	5.04	4
Standard Life UK Ethical	33.0	–11.1	–0.9	5.01	5
Scot Wids Ethical A Acc	18.5	–16.3	6.2	4.51	6
Stewardship Grwth	34.3	–16.9	4.9	4.98	7
Aegon Ethical	33.1	–18.5	0.9	5.75	8
CF Ethical Inc	12.3	–20.4	–3.0	4.02	9
CF Banner Real Life	30.5	–21.9	9.6	5.66	10
NPI Global Care Inc	20.3	–22.6	1.1	4.56	11
Scottish Amicable Ethical	32.4	–22.7	n/a	5.82	12
Jupiter Environ Opps	25.0	–22.8	n/a	5.15	-13
Norwich UK Ethical	36.1	–22.8	n/a	5.84	14
Family Charities Ethical	32.4	–24.0	16.6	-	15
FTSE All-Share	26.1	–19.6	–10.2	5.03	

Source: ISIS Asset Management. 'Top 15' fund names, and three-year volatility based on *Ethical Performance* (newsletter for socially responsible business) criteria. Fund volatility as at 1 December 2003. One, two and three-year percentage change data provided by TrustNet as at 22 January 2004.

Income out of 'positive' territory. Over five years, the only 'Top 15' fund to beat RPI proves to be Stewardship Income.

Another worthwhile measure of 'real' value is to compare fund returns to the risk-free rate that investors could have enjoyed by putting their money on deposit. If we take the Moneyfacts Building Society Index to 31 October 2003 as a proxy for deposit returns over the period, we see that over one year every fund beat the 2.1 per cent of the index, but over three years we quickly see the impact of the bear market in equities. Again only Stewardship Income and Aegon Ethical Income actually provided a better return. Without a five-year record Aegon's fund naturally drops from consideration, leaving only Stewardship Income.

Similarly, ten of the 'Top 15' funds beat the FTSE All-Share in the last year. Only the best eight performing funds share this plaudit over three years while ten of the 'Top 15' beat the FTSE over five years.

Relative values

A far more revealing approach is to compare ethical fund returns to those of their unrestrained peers. It's only through such comparisons that we can get a fuller picture of the time and resources that fund managers choose to dedicate to such products.

Over one year the best performing ethical fund in Table 5.2 proves to be Norwich UK Ethical, scoring an impressive 13th percentile ranking in the UK fund universe. It's followed in quick succession by Stewardship Growth (17th percentile), Aegon Ethical A (17th percentile), Scottish Amicable Ethical (20th percentile) and Stewardship Income (25th percentile).

Over three years, however, only Stewardship Income and Aegon Ethical Income place in the top quartile of all UK funds.

Refining the process further to compare ethical returns against those of their IMA sector peers probably provides the fullest picture of a fund's true performance merits.

It's here that an unassailable leader emerges from the pack for the first time. In relative terms, Stewardship Income managed by Ted Scott at ISIS Asset Management has generated a level of performance that's simply never been seen from an ethical fund before. The fund hasn't left the top quartile of the UK Equity Income sector for over five years while over one year it stands around the 18th percentile and over three years the 6th percentile. Importantly, it's the only fund in Table 5.2 to maintain top quartile sector placings over both one and three years.

The best of the rest are lead by Aegon Ethical Income (15th percentile in the UK Corporate Bond sector) and Norwich UK, which enjoys similar stature in the UK All Companies sector. While the former slips to the second quartile over three years, the latter actually falls to the third quartile. Notably, the other top quartile ethical

Table 5.2 'Top 15' UK ethical funds – relative returns

Fund name	Total fund universe		IMA sector	Ranking in IMA fund sector	
	1-year	3-year		1-year	3-year
Stewardship Income	434	93	UK Equity Income	15/81	4/69
Aegon Ethical Income	1514	106	UK Corporate Bond	14/93	30/73
Allchurches Amity	566	530	UK All Companies	141/315	39/260
Insight Inv European Ethical	694	575	UK All Companies	201/315	48/260
Standard Life UK Ethical	348	604	UK All Companies	80/315	53/260
Scot Wids Ethical A Acc	1129	705	UK All Companies	301/315	82/260
Stewardship Grwth	290	747	UK All Companies	67/315	91/260
Aegon Ethical A	302	788	UK All Companies	69/315	103/260
CF Ethical Inc	1291	888	UK All Companies	311/315	141/260
CF Banner Real Life	397	919	UK All Companies	88/315	155/260
Abbey National Ethical	666	920	UK All Companies	190/315	156/260
NPI Global Care Inc	1008	962	UK Equity Income	70/81	67/69
Scottish Amicable Ethical	354	980	UK All Companies	81/315	182/260
Jupiter Environmental Opps	608	937	UK All Companies	160/315	164/260
Norwich UK Ethical	221	946	UK All Companies	47/315	168/260
Total funds	1745	1447			
FTSE All-Share Tracker	579	825			

Source: ISIS Asset Management. 'Top 15' fund names based on *Ethical* Performance (newsletter for socially responsible business) criteria. Rank within investment sector/fund universe data provided by TrustNet as at 23 January 2004.

funds over one year in the UK All Companies sector such as Stewardship Growth and Aegon Ethical also drop back to the second quartile over three years.

According to Table 5.2, the worst ethical performers of the UK All Companies sector prove to be CF Ethical Growth, which, two places short of bottom, places in the 99th percentile over one year and 54th percentile over three years, and Scottish Widows Ethical, which scrapes in at the 96th percentile for one year but improves to the 32nd percentile over three years.

Probably the outright worst relative performance comes from NPI Global Care Income, which delivered 86th percentile performance over one year and a truly depressing 97th percentile over three years.

Getting what you paid for

Probably the greatest disservice done to ethical investment in its 20-year life has been the insistence of the financial press and others in repeatedly asking: 'What does ethical investment cost in terms of lost performance?' The problem with this, and it's not a minor one, is that the question itself is based upon a false premise. This is because, all else being equal, it's the individual ability of the fund manager that determines the difference between being a market beater and an also-ran – not the screening.

Previous investigations into ethical returns have tended to overlook the consistent market-beating performance of funds such as Stewardship Income. They also seem to ignore the fact that, as Table 5.2 demonstrates, the majority of ethical funds tend to occupy the top half of their sectors showing that at least 50 per cent of the non-screened fund universe struggles to keep pace with those managing more restricted portfolios!

Probably most importantly, such thinking completely fails to consider the part played by investment risk. Because the link between risk and return can never be broken, any discussion of lost performance that doesn't focus on relative levels of risk becomes moot. It simply becomes another instance of comparing apples and oranges.

In terms of the risk generated by the 'Top 15' funds, we can see that Aegon Ethical Income, thanks to its bond portfolio, is naturally the lowest-volatility fund. It's worth noting though that this is still slightly higher than the average volatility of funds in its sector.

In all, 7 of the 12 UK All Companies funds in the 'Top 15' operate at lower than the average volatility for their peer group. Similarly both Stewardship Income and NPI Global Care Income offer lower fund volatility than the sector from which they hail. This though does the former an injustice as it operates at something like 20 per cent less volatility than its ethical rival, having long been found to be the lowest-volatility retail fund in its entire sector.

This underlines another important investment consideration of which awareness is continuing to grow. This is the understanding that market risk, ie some measure of volatility broadly linked to an index or a sector, does not constitute low risk. In fact, it can mean just the opposite.

This is something that's attracted the attention of more knowledgeable IFAs and spawned another industry first for Stewardship Income, namely the marketing of the fund to income investors on its investment credentials alone.

The proof of the pudding

Clearly there are good managers and bad in every sector. Poor results might be the fault of the individual manager in question or they may reflect a reluctance on the part of a company to cede sufficient resources to such efforts.

Whatever other factors we might point to, the one immutable truth for fund investors is that it's the quality of the fund manager more than any other single factor that will dictate the quality of the return. Inevitably, while there may be no shortage of managers riding the 'ethical bandwagon', there are still more than enough pulling it to maintain the integrity of the sector and its returns.

6

How can an investor secure a stake in an ethical or socially responsible investment fund?

Lee Coates, Director, Ethical Investors Group

So far, this book has looked at the general principles of socially responsible investment (SRI): what it is, how different criteria are applied and how investment returns are affected by applying those different criteria. This chapter will now consider the practical ways in which socially responsible investors can apply their values to their financial arrangements.

The main point that we all need to understand is that any financial arrangement has potential social responsibility connotations. Even the simplest form of insurance, or the most basic bank account, can have negative social, ethical or environmental consequences. Importantly, it is possible for concerned investors to steer a path to a socially responsible financial position with little or no compromise on their returns or payments.

Working from the most basic necessary financial arrangements through to complicated and sophisticated investment portfolios, this chapter will outline how (we've already considered why) to create the most appropriate socially responsible financial plan.

BANKING/SAVINGS ACCOUNTS

The days of a cash-based society are years in the past, so at some point we will all need to hold a bank account. With changes in government policy on the payment of pensions, the majority of those who are retired now have to hold a bank account. The question is, which institutions offer a comprehensive range of services without an ethical compromise? The answer really depends on whether you wish to use a socially neutral organization or a socially positive organization. The institutions to avoid, where possible, are those that lend money to companies without applying any social, ethical or environmental criteria.

If, when making an investment decision, you wouldn't invest your money in a company manufacturing, for example, weapons, then why would you have a bank account with an institution that will lend to the same arms company? After all, it could be your money that the bank is lending to the arms company. Better, instead, to use a neutral or socially positive institution.

Ethically neutral institutions

These are mainly building societies or former building societies where there is no lending to companies. The problem of lending to arms companies, heavy polluters and those abusing human rights is generally restricted to the main banks. In this category, most lending is made to individuals in the form of mortgages, personal loans, etc.

Ethically positive institutions

These are institutions that positively vet their customers on social, ethical or environmental grounds. Here, your money will be lent to those individuals, organizations and businesses that you would feel most comfortable with. Unlike most other areas of socially responsible investment, this is one of the few areas where being socially responsible may produce a slightly lower return. This is not always the case, but in some ways the slightly lower interest paid to savers is reflected in the lower rates charged when socially responsible charities, organizations and companies wish to borrow.

For the majority of savers, the most appropriate approach is to employ a combination of ethically neutral/highest-return accounts and the socially positive/ marginally lower-return accounts. By striking an appropriate balance, the overall effect on total return will be absolutely minimal, especially in an era of low interest rates generally.

Cash ISAs

It is possible to invest in a mini cash ISA each tax year. Not only does this ensure a good gross rate of interest, often better than non-ISA accounts, but all of the interest is tax-free. Any money held on short-term deposits should be held in a cash ISA, unless the focus is on maximizing long-term capital growth. In this case, a stocks and shares ISA might be better. Choosing your cash ISA involves the same process as choosing the place for your bank account and general savings. The same ethical issues apply in all cases.

National Savings and Premium Bonds

These are very common investments for many people, especially those looking for absolute security and index-linked savings. In very simple terms, opening a National Savings account or buying Premium Bonds is a loan to the government. Putting aside party politics, there are some very interesting socially responsible investment issues relating to loans of this type.

A loan to the government can be used for a very large number of good things, including education, the NHS, social services, overseas development and many more. However, there are also some negative aspects that may be relevant to certain groups of investors. The Ministry of Defence is funded from central government, so those with strong conviction in this area (for example Quakers) may consider National Savings accounts inappropriate. Another group would be those concerned with animal testing. Via research grants and universities, the government is involved in financing animal testing. This is almost exclusively in the medical research area, but many investors consider all animal testing to be unacceptable and this group may wish to avoid National Savings investment.

So, for those who are risk averse or are looking to save for the short to medium term (less than five years), the most appropriate investment is an interest-paying savings account. For those looking to achieve a higher rate of return (especially where interest rates are low), the most common form of investment is the stock market.

LONG-TERM SAVINGS

In the best tradition of Western capitalist economics, there are a mind-boggling number of savings products available, from thousands of companies. Individuals need to sift through all of the various institutions, products and funds to find the most appropriate product for their needs. In addition, each product and fund will need to be assessed from a socially responsible perspective – doubling the work involved compared to those who do not invest in a socially responsible way.

To some people, mere mention of the stock market can begin alarm bells ringing and lead to cold sweats developing. In some ways, these feelings could be seen as quite natural, especially given what has happened to the stock market of the last few years. The problem, however, is that these feelings are usually the result of misunderstanding how the market operates rather than being based on a firm understanding of some of the basic principles that underpin the market and its operations.

If the rate of interest earned from, say, a building society savings account achieves a return, after tax, higher than the rate of inflation, then the difference is known as the real rate of return. Matching the rate of inflation does not offer any growth at all, as you are just keeping up with price increases. Anything in excess of inflation is a real return and this is where you build capital. While this looks like a good advertisement for having all of one's money in a building society account, the important thing to consider is that the quoted inflation rate is an average of most prices. None of us structure our lives in such a way that our personal cost of living matches the assumed weekly shopping basket.

For instance, education, health and entertainment costs have consistently risen at a rate in excess of the prevailing rate of inflation. If we are investing for the future, these three areas have to be taken into consideration. The further ahead one looks, the greater the return above inflation one will need in order to ensure a quality of life beyond the average weekly shopping basket.

As mentioned above, the further off one's investment horizon, the more important it is to ensure that the highest possible real return is achieved. Otherwise, one runs the risk of doing nothing more than treading water. Keeping up with the cost of a loaf of bread is no basis for a long-term investment strategy in any of the examples given below:

- saving for a child's university costs;
- saving for retirement costs such as travel, entertainment etc;
- building funds to cover health/care costs in old age.

The above are just three simple examples of areas that require a sensible attitude to investment, and one that will include, but not be entirely based on, building society savings accounts.

Let us look at two simple scenarios, where attitude to risk is tested. These can be seen as producing opposite investment strategies, although the financial planning process will ensure that the correct balance is achieved.

Scenario 1

We will start with the conventional risk associated with the stock market. If one does invest in stocks and shares, the risk is that all one's money could be lost. Technically, this is quite true. Investing in a single company or a highly speculative investment fund is very much like backing a horse, even if the odds are 1,000 to 1 (we will disregard the ethics of gambling at this stage!). If all goes well, one will make a fortune. But, of course, there is the strong possibility that one could lose everything – money, house, shirt and any other item of clothing placed on the 'sure-fire winner'.

This may be an extreme example, but it does reflect the feelings of many investors. When looking at investing in the stock market, taking financial advice is the most important first step. The purpose of this report is to guide you through the issues of risk, investment and finally the myriad of investment vehicles available. When considering a stock market investment, the advice process will consider the issue of risk. As you will see later, many investment contracts are geared to reduce investment risk by not having all their eggs in one basket. Sensible investment management is about managing risk. This is often best achieved by diversification, holding different types of investment and different stocks and shares.

Scenario 2

Let us assume that an investor decides to take no risk with the stock market and leaves all his or her money in a building society account for 20 years until retirement. This carries very nearly as much risk as Scenario 1. The difference is that this scenario does not feel risky. The risks are unknown and unseen, but the main point is that the interest on the building society money will keep going up.

This feeling of security can so often be a false one. At retirement, our hypothetical investor decides that he or she now wants to spend more time travelling. The problem is that the cost of travel has risen faster than the rate of inflation. Therefore, it is accepted that whilst some travelling can be done it will not be as much as was hoped for.

A few years later, the earlier promise to support a grandchild comes back to haunt our investor. The problem is that education, accommodation and other costs associated with university have risen faster than inflation. What to do? Deplete the accumulated capital more than expected or go back on a promise?

A few more years into retirement, the investor looks at the issue of protecting what is left of his or her estate from the effects of long-term care costs. The problem now is that health costs also have increased so much that the investor cannot afford to pay for care, nor can he or she afford to buy the insurance needed to cover the costs. Therefore, the investor is left to hope that he or she will not need care in later years, or accept that the legacy to children and grandchildren will be spent.

Twenty years before retirement, quite unwittingly, the investor took a very substantial risk. This was to avoid one type of risk, namely the stock market, and hope that nothing would increase more than the rate of interest earned on his or her building society funds. Clearly, this is a hypothetical client, but experience has shown that this is an all-too-common scenario.

Assuming that investors are looking for a balanced approach to short-, medium- and long-term needs, then the case for a stocks and shares investment has been made. The decision must now be made as to what constitutes the most appropriate way to hold stocks and shares.

LUMP-SUM INVESTMENT

Holding individual shares

This is probably the most direct and personal way of investing. From the thousands of UK companies whose shares are available for investment, individual companies can be selected as potentially good long-term investments. Each of these can then be assessed against the social, ethical and environmental criteria that the investor wishes to apply. This can be via one's own research, or by using the services of an independent ethical research company.

Unless one has a very large amount to invest (normally accepted to be above £250,000), holding shares directly is considered to be one of the higher risk options for investing in the stock market. It also requires the greatest degree of personal involvement, unless the portfolio of shares is handed over to an investment manager to look after.

For the majority of investors, the most appropriate way to invest is via a collective investment scheme. Some examples of these are given below.

Investment trusts

Investment trusts, although they are marketed as collective investments, are themselves companies whose sole assets are the shares of other companies. As such, investment trust shares are traded just like any others and they are susceptible to takeovers. Also, investment trusts are not open-ended in that they cannot simply create more shares to accommodate a new investor although new issues can be launched from time to time. The shares will have to be bought in the usual way. Investment trusts can borrow money to add value to the portfolio (gearing), which if it is done shrewdly will reap a return greater than the amount borrowed plus the cost of interest. However, borrowing to buy shares can have its downside if the shares fall in value or interest rates rise. The directors of an investment trust are accountable to their shareholders as are the directors in any company. The value of an individual investment will reflect the underlying values of investments held by the investment trust adjusted by a factor to take account of the market's estimation of the prospects for the market and the quality of the investment management team. This will be reflected either as a discount to value, where the total value of shares is less than the value of assets held by the trust, or a premium over value, where the total value of the trust's shares is greater than the value of its assets.

Unit trusts and OEICs

A unit trust/OEIC (open-ended investment company) is a fund of stock market investments divided into equal portions called units. Their prices are calculated regularly – normally on a daily basis. Unit trusts/OEICs normally pay dividends to investors twice a year. These dividends can be paid out to the investor looking for income, or reinvested back into the plan for the growth-orientated investor.

The price of units is governed by the value of the underlying securities in the fund. This price will rise and fall with movements in the price of shares in which the plan is invested. The value of a unit trust/OEIC investment and the income from it can therefore go down as well as up.

When you sell your units, you may be liable to capital gains tax in the usual way. However, you are entitled to the annual exemption from capital gains tax. Any tax liability can be kept to a minimum by selling units over different tax years or by holding the investment in joint names.

Investment bond

This is a lump-sum investment policy issued by an insurance company, where the investment is included as part of the overall life assurance funds of the company. As such, there are certain advantages on offer to some investors. Whilst the life assurance fund of the company is subject to taxation, in reality the level of tax is between 2 and 4 per cent below the basic rate amount. Therefore, although a slightly lower rate of tax is paid within the investment fund, all investors are deemed to have paid tax at the full basic rate.

Although these plans are often very widely sold, in the majority of cases they are most suitable for higher-rate taxpayers. Even for this group, the benefits are limited to issues of access and timing of investment. For the majority of investors, the investment bond is generally an unsuitable plan. This is not because it offers any different investment risk, but simply reflects the tax position.

On the investment side, it is common to find the same funds available through an investment bond as through a unit trust or OEIC from the same company. The fact that the majority of the population can invest in a unit trust or OEIC and benefit from using their capital gains tax allowance makes the investment bond generally a redundant contract. The tax deducted from an investment bond investment fund cannot be reclaimed or mitigated, so the financial planning options are quite limited.

Many investment bond contracts are sold linked to with-profit funds. In the past, these have offered access to the stock market, with many of the short-term risks removed. Their popularity has declined considerably over recent years, as many contracts, although not subject to the ups and downs of the market on a daily basis, can suffer exit/surrender charges of as much as 15–20 per cent of the value of the fund. Uncertain stock market conditions and the unfavourable tax treatment are likely to see a reduction in the number of people buying with-profit bonds (although this may not necessarily stop the rate at which many advisers are trying to sell them). At the time of writing there are no socially responsible with-profit bonds available to investors.

The above are specific investment plans in themselves, but for the majority of investors the first investment in the stock market should be via a stocks and shares ISA.

Stocks and shares ISA

From an investment perspective, the most common investment to hold within a stocks and shares ISA is a unit trust or OEIC. The ISA account itself is simply a wrapper, into which you place your unit trust or OEIC fund. The advantage offered from investing in a stocks and shares ISA is that profits are not subject to capital gains tax and the ISA can hold a wide range of different funds, thus improving the spread of investments and reducing administration requirements.

A big mistake currently being made by many people is buying a maxi ISA from their bank or building society, initially only using the cash element. If they subsequently wish to use the stocks and shares component of the ISA they will be forced to obtain this from their bank or building society and may be forced to invest unethically.

REGULAR SAVINGS

It is possible to invest in stocks and shares ISA, investment trust, unit trust or OEIC on a regular monthly basis, rather than investing a lump sum. For long-term investment, this is a very efficient way of accumulating capital. One of the most common uses of a regular investment plan is to cover university costs for children.

Whatever plan is chosen for the actual investment, each regular contribution swells the number of units attached to the plan. The objective is that the market value of each unit will increase over the longer term. As the market value of the assets fluctuates, so the unit prices will go up and down. For continuing plans, falling unit prices provide the added benefit of pound cost averaging. This is the benefit that

Year	Contribution	Price	Units
1	1,000	1	1,000
2	1,000	1.25	800
3	1,000	1.55	645
4	1,000	1.8	556
5	1,000	2	500
6	1,000	2.25	444
Total units purchased			3,945
Value after 6 years			£8,876

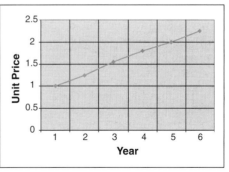

Figure 6.1 Investing £1,000 a year for six years in a rising market

Year	Contribution	Price	Units
1	1,000	1	1,000
2	1,000	0.6	1,667
3	1,000	0.4	2,500
4	1,000	0.55	1,818
5	1,000	0.85	1,176
6	1,000	1.25	800
Total units purchased			8,961
Value after 6 years			£11,201

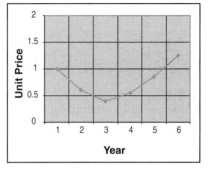

Figure 6.2 Investing £1,000 a year for six years in a falling market that later recovers

accrues to the investment of a fixed regular amount into units with fluctuating prices. When unit prices are low, the regular amount buys more units than it does when prices are high. Over the longer term, the average cost per unit to the investor is lower than the average unit price over the period, giving the investor a more favourable growth rate.

Detailed in Figures 6.1 and 6.2 is a graphical representation of two different performances in the stock market, over a six-year period. The clients invest £1,000 per annum, and then surrender their investments at the end of the six-year period. One would assume that the investor benefiting from the rapidly increasing unit price will make the most money but the figures prove differently.

Other savings plan

Many companies and advisers offer savings plans with fixed terms, many with interesting names such as 'Wealth Plus' or similar. In reality, these are endowment-based savings plans with high setting-up costs, tax paid on profits (if any) and very little flexibility. Unless an investor's circumstances are exceptional, these plans should be avoided.

Retirement planning

Since 2001, the most appropriate way of saving for retirement for those who don't have access to a company pension scheme is the stakeholder pension. A stakeholder pension is not a state pension – it's a new private pension on top of the basic state pension. Stakeholder pensions are available to people in employment, fixed-contract workers, the self-employed and people who may not be working but can afford to contribute. From 6 April 2001, those who give up work to care for relatives, start a family or take a break from work can contribute to their stakeholder pension, up to £3,600 per year gross (£2,808 net).

As with most other pension plans, you can pay in contributions regularly to build up your own stakeholder pension fund. You can also make occasional lump-sum contributions. Your stakeholder fund is used to buy a pension (usually called an annuity) from a pension provider when you retire (this does not have to be the same provider with which you hold your stakeholder pension fund). So, your pension will depend on the size of your fund and the annuity rates available at the time you take your pension. You cannot withdraw any part of your fund before you retire but you can convert part of it to a tax-free lump sum when you take your pension.

The manager of your stakeholder pension fund will invest your contributions and income tax rebates in assets, such as shares and bonds. This is why it's important to start investing early if you can – the longer your contributions are invested the greater opportunity they have to grow.

Companies offering stakeholder pensions must make sure that these pensions meet strict standards laid down by the government. The standards include:

- **Charges.** There is a limit on the management costs that stakeholder pension providers can charge – the limit is 1 per cent of the value of your fund each year. The fund manager takes these charges from your fund.
- **Flexibility.** Stakeholder pension plans are flexible and you can make contributions regularly or occasionally. It is always best to discipline yourself to make regular weekly or monthly contributions but you can change the amount you pay in if you need to. All stakeholder pension plans will accept contributions of as little as £20 gross (£15.60 net). You can stop paying in for a while if you need to, without having to pay any penalty. If you are employed and your employer provides a stakeholder pension, the employer will, if you wish, deduct your contributions direct from your pay.

Although it is still possible to invest in (and for advisers to recommend) non-stake-holder pensions, it is unlikely that these would be of any benefit to 99 per cent of pension investors. They may carry higher charges and be less flexible.

Some of the largest and most respected pension companies in the UK offer stakeholder pensions and most of these offer at least one ethical fund. So the choice, whilst not as great as in the general investment market, is still considerable for those interested in a socially responsible retirement plan.

For those who have access to a company pension, there are also ethical decisions to be made. From Monday 3 July 2000, new rules formally introduced ethical investment to pension schemes. From this date, all company pension schemes in the UK are forced to declare their ethical policy. This is an ideal opportunity for all ethical investors to have a real influence on the social and environmental policies of their pension fund.

The new rules insist that all schemes amend their statement of investment principles (SIP) to declare: 'The extent (if at all) to which social, environmental or ethical considerations are taken into account in the selection, retention and realisation of investments' and 'The policy (if any) directing the exercise of the rights (including voting rights) attaching to investments.'

There are two initial steps for each scheme member to take. These are: 1) Ring your pensions department and ask them to let you have a copy of the new statement of investment principles. Under the Pensions Act 1995, you have a right to see the SIP at any time. The wording of the SIP will give you some idea of how far, if at all, the pension scheme trustees have adopted social and environmental policies. 2) Write to the pension scheme trustees to increase the pressure in relation to social and environmental issues. On the evidence to date, it is likely that most trustees will adopt very non-committal criteria relating to positive investment or engagement to encourage better practice. This wording can be used to great effect, but can also be used to allow a business-as-normal investment philosophy, where no companies are excluded or no real engagement takes place.

Life assurance

It is generally accepted that the need for life assurance cover arises when one's personal liabilities are at their highest. Some form of life assurance policy usually covers mortgage debts, with the cover extending only as long as the term of the mortgage. Probably the other most important liability is that of children.

There are two main types of life cover available in the UK, with each subdividing into various options to meet individual needs. However, the two core types are described below:

- **Combined cover/savings plans.** These can either be fixed-term plans such as endowments, or they can run throughout life, known as whole-of-life plans. The plans offer a level of life cover in conjunction with a savings 'pot'. The cost of the savings pot and life cover is included in the same premium. The investment element is invested in the same way as an investment bond, and is therefore not very tax efficient for most investors. The cost of the life cover is often more expensive than other options.

  Many of these plans (especially whole-of-life) are sold on the basis of providing life cover with the option of 'getting something back'. The reality is, however, that the investment element is often too small to produce any sensible return and the average investor may be better off buying a simple life assurance policy (see below) and investing in a building society account for the savings account (such as a tax-free ISA).

  Because there is an investment element, it is vital that anyone buying one of these policies ensures that there is an ethical fund available.

- **Term assurance.** Under this type of plan, you select the level of cover and the term of the policy. If death occurs within the term the sum assured is paid as a one-off lump sum or a regular income, to your survivors. There is no savings element with this type of plan. In structure, it is similar to a general insurance policy where the sum assured is paid if you claim but at the end of the term the policy ceases and there is no residual value.

These plans offer the most cost-effective way of buying life assurance cover for mortgages and family protection. There are many different plan types available and these can be used to meet the different needs of individuals and their families.

As there is no investment element, the same ethical considerations do not apply in the same way as they do for endowment and whole-of-life policies. However, it is still important for those buying these plans to consider the ethics of the company issuing the policy.

7

Is there a psychological profile to the ethical investor?

Mark Campanale, Head of SRI Business Development,
Henderson Global Investors

SUMMARY

Being successful in marketing socially responsible investing requires an understanding of the issues and the SRI investment process. Most importantly of all, it requires an understanding of the client. Finding out which of a wide range of topics is the most important ethical issue for an individual client is not always straightforward. However, ethical investors as a group have a remarkably high frequency of common characteristics by way of background and occupation. This chapter delves into some of these characteristics and how they might be used as targeting tools for advisers keen to build confident client relationships.

What is the key message for investors? Is it an investment-based message? Or is it an ethical message? Broadly speaking, there have been two approaches for marketing to the investor. The first is directed at experienced investors who understand and are attracted to the investment proposition behind the funds. The key message for these customers is the market opportunity and potential investment returns. The second customer group is values-based investors who are, by and large, relatively new to equity-based investments but are attracted to the idea of investing responsibly and helping to shape the world around them.

ETHICAL INVESTORS

Whilst there is a case to argue that SRI is a proposition that is attractive to all investors, in practice IFAs with responsibility for developing new business (or profiling existing clients in a new way) cannot have the time or resources to tackle all the market, all of the time. But they can target some of the market in a focused and rewarding way. For that to work at its best, the market and its component investors need to:

- have clearly identifiable psychological profiles that are common, such that firms promoting their services can use appropriate media and marketing channels to access them in a highly targeted way;
- be identifiable by gender, education and occupation such that each of these is an indicator of suitability and appropriateness for marketing campaigns;
- remain an untapped group for financial services and be relatively under-served by IFAs or direct providers of savings products;
- have characteristics that are specific such that marketing and sales promotions should, once the brand and fund concept awareness threshold is reached, prove to offer above-industry-average responses and conversion rates to marketing campaigns.

TRADITIONAL RETURNS-BASED INVESTORS

There are compelling arguments to position SRI funds as returns driven. This is either from the perspective that detailed corporate social responsibility (CSR) analysis of prospective investments in businesses can help identify hidden risks and rewards or from the perspective that certain sectors, such as clean energy, health care and social housing, can generate above-market returns.

It was the latter that was behind the success of the sales of the NPI Global Care Funds through the 1990s in the conventional marketplace, growing from just £10 million in 1994 to over £850 million of assets by 2000. Mainstream investors bought the funds for their investment themes/stories, and as an alternative to a 'one-sector-only' approach taken by technology funds. And 'mainstream' could be defined as investors already holding a portfolio of equity-based investments. Success in reaching this audience was dependent upon:

- presenting a product as having returns-based investment appeal;
- engaging investors in an intelligent way around stories on companies that generate investment returns;

- focusing on 'solutions-based' companies as part of the promotional message in adverts.

Other investment companies successful in positioning their funds as 'solution providers', where the companies held in the portfolios had strong growth characteristics, included the Jupiter Ecology Fund and Jupiter Environmental Opportunities Fund, while funds that made a mark in the mainstream investment consciousness because of their thematic investment characteristics included the Framlington Health Fund, the Impax Environmental Markets Fund plc, the Merrill Lynch New Energy Fund and the (short-lived) ISIS EcoTech Fund. During a period when funds such as the Invesco Global Dynamic Theme Fund (an example of a multi-thematic mainstream fund) were gaining investor attention, SRI funds such as Global Care also benefited. To a degree, the investment attractiveness of these funds appealed to the traditional economic model of self-interest.

THE TRADITIONAL ECONOMIC MODEL OF SELF-INTEREST

Classical neo-economics and rational choice theory assume people's behaviour is driven purely by self-interest and personal welfare maximization. This model of the 'rational economic person' ignores moral dimensions in decision making and instead accepts that people are selfish and individualistic in their actions.[1] SRI challenges this model. The SRI investor shows that decisions are not always based solely on utility maximization; instead they can be altruistic and determined by personal non-monetary values. The SRI investor is, in short, a more complicated actor than the rational economic person of textbook theory.

Recent literature on economic psychology and behavioural finance is able to offer an insight into the motivations and behaviour of consumers in an attempt to explain the SRI investor. Economic psychologists argue that beliefs, attitudes and values are central in the analysis of economic behaviour.

THE VALUES OF THE ETHICAL INVESTOR

The term 'cultural creatives' was developed by Ray in the mid-1990s to describe a growing movement of values-based consumers who translate their strong social and environmental values into their consumer behaviour.[2]

The demographic profile of the cultural creatives is, unsurprisingly, very similar to that of SRI investors. They are typically wealthy, well educated, in socio-economic class AB and are female dominated.[3] In addition, they believe in altruism and 75 per cent do voluntary work.[4]

Cultural creatives have strong psychological and spiritual interests. They take environmental and global issues very seriously and find some elements of the modern world unacceptable. They dislike modern consumerism and business culture. These are careful and well-informed consumers; they are knowledgeable about brands and the market, seek information on companies and read consumer reports.[5] Cultural creatives are systems thinkers; when investing they want to know how company profits are generated and how they are spent.

Cultural creatives are less money sensitive than other groups and are willing to pay more for sustainable products. They are also experimental consumers; they want an enlightening experience when consuming. There is therefore great opportunity in developing an ethical investment proposition to these groups.

The values of cultural creatives as defined by Ray[6] can be illustrated as shown in Figure 7.1.

The values of cultural creatives are distinct from those of mainstream investors. Ray argues that mainstream markets do not recognize this as a coalescing and coherent world-view and therefore the products and services available to people with cultural creative values are not a true reflection of their market size. Consequently, Ray found that cultural creatives are aware of SRI but are not typically investing in it.[7]

Kaagan Research Associates, in their work for Calvert in the US in 1996, found the characteristics set out in Table 7.1 to be typical of the SRI investor. They are characteristics that overlap with the values of cultural creatives.

How pervasive is the view that ethical concerns can have an influence in investment decision making? To some extent, retail customer surveys tend to overstate interest in ethical investing. However, they do indicate a sense of the wider public wishing to understand more and discover solutions to their concerns. Table 7.2 provides an indication of the importance of ethical behaviour in the investment decision.

The 55–66 per cent 'important' or 'very important' figure in Table 7.2 has an interesting parallel with UK voting patterns, where a similar proportion of the adult population support so-called socially progressive politics (Labour, Liberal Democrat, Green) where there is a focus on the responsibility of the individual towards society.

Some of these attitudes are reflected in the Friends Provident Stewardship surveys. Table 7.3 presents responses to investor attitudes.

Once investors have accepted their interest to invest ethically, there is a steady switch into ethical investment options. This is highlighted in the Henderson Ethical Fund Survey. Table 7.4 illustrates that 68 per cent of unit holders have other ethical unit trusts aside from the Henderson Investors Ethical Fund; 32 per cent of unit holders do not have any other ethical unit trusts. The same survey showed that 51 per cent

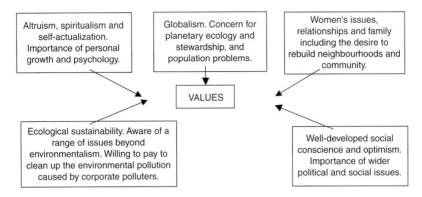

Figure 7.1 The values of cultural creatives

of unit holders have non-ethical unit trusts as well as the Henderson Investors Ethical Fund and 49 per cent of unit holders do not have non-ethical unit trusts; 48.7 per cent of females have a non-ethical unit trust and 53.4 per cent of males have a non-ethical unit trust.

The high proportion of investors stating that the Henderson Ethical Fund is their only equity-based investment alongside other ethical funds is, I believe, reflective of the large number of new investors attracted to equity markets by the ethical choice. Most investment managers do seem to expect a degree of cannibalization where they secure transfers of funds from other investment managers. But relatively few have succeeded in building a business from completely new investors (unless of course they spend greatly on building brand awareness). It is easy to forget that, outside of

Table 7.1 Typical characteristics of SRI investors

1. SRI investors feel empowered and in control of their own destiny and also on a wider global scale.
2. SRI investors have a good level of global ecological awareness.
3. Those who invest in SRI tend to consume ethically in general.
4. SRI investors are empathic and understand their actions can have wider implications.
5. SRI investors believe that corporations should be responsible to citizens, the environment, etc, and have high expectations of businesses.
6. SRI investors believe they belong to the 'global village'.
7. SRI investors reject the authority of large powerful corporations. They tend to examine the legitimacy of institutions and people who exert authority and do not respect institutions solely by virtue of their being big and powerful.
8. SRI investors often belong to small affinity groups.
9. SRI investors tend to be involved in the community.
10. SRI investors have a desire to explore 'life experiences'.

Table 7.2 Importance of ethical behaviour in retail investment decisions

Importance of ethical behaviour	Investors %	Cumulative %
Very important	23	23
Important	32	55
Neither unimportant or important	11	66
Unimportant	8	74
Irrelevant	13	87
Don't know	12	99

Source: Gallup Survey for NPI, 1995

Table 7.3 Responses to investor attitudes

	Agree %	Disagree %
'I would like to make a profit without anyone getting hurt in the process.'	92	6
'I couldn't care less where my money is invested, so long as I make a profit.'	26	72
'One of the things that puts me off unit trusts is the thought that my investment could benefit companies which do things I don't approve of.'	69	22
'I would rather invest in an ethical unit trust than any other sort of unit trust.'	60	26

Source: NOP Research Group for Friends Provident Stewardship Fund's Second Annual Survey, May 1995

Table 7.4 Investments in other ethical unit trusts

			Gender		
			Male	Female	Total
Do you have any other	Yes	Count	256	264	520
ethical unit trusts		% within gender	67.9%	68.0%	68.0%
	No	Count	121	124	245
		% within gender	32.1%	32.0%	32.0%
Total		Count	377	388	765
		% within gender	100.0%	100.0%	100.0%

the with-profits (and capital guaranteed product) marketplaces, a relatively low pro-portion of the population hold pooled equity products. So why are investors attracted to ethical funds, in a way that seems to conflict with the rational economic person? Some of the explanation can be found from the theories of Maslow.

Looking into the profile of the ethical investor (examined in more detail in the sections below) shows that those of socio-economic class AB, who have the benefits of wealth and education, are more likely to be ethical investors. The use of Maslow's theories, known as 'Maslow's Hierarchy of Needs', is an attempt to explain why this is the case.

Maslow's theory claims that people's basic needs (at the bottom of the pyramid in Figure 7.2) need to be satisfied before higher needs can be. Using this logic, once individuals' 'deficiency needs', such as psychological well-being and safety, have been satisfied they can then begin to look to their growth needs. In the final stage, 'self-actualization', they are able to fulfil their wider needs and feel empowered. Thus it is usually those in higher socio-economic classes and of greater affluence who take up environmental causes and invest in SRI.

It is these people who believe that ethical consumerism can make a difference, ie influence corporate behaviour and improve the surrounding environment and society. As disposable income increases, people have more choices, and their purchases and

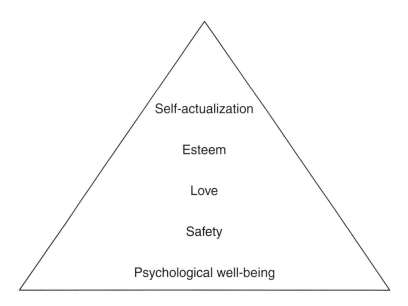

Source: Robert Gwynne (1997) *Maslow's Hierarchy of Needs*, University of Tennessee Department of Speech Communication

Figure 7.2   Maslow's Hierarchy of Needs

investments can become more influenced by their personal values. MORI found that 25 per cent of those in socio-economic class DE are ethical consumers compared to 42 per cent in class AB. This appears to support Maslow's theory.

The greater wealth held by ethical consumers may explain why Ray found the cultural creatives are less price sensitive than other groups in society.[8]

What does this mean in terms of market opportunity? Advisers focusing on this part of the investment marketplace can expect a higher proportion of customers to be high net worth individuals (HNWIs). Focused marketing campaigns, to be successful, do need to understand both these clients' values and where to locate them in the marketplace. In Europe alone, HNWIs own \$8.4 trillion.[9] This makes them powerful consumers who are able to influence markets. There are approximately 150,000 HNWIs in the UK.[10] If directed into SRI – as well they might be – the combined wealth of HNWIs in the UK could make them a significant driver for a more ethical and responsible tone in UK business.

Does the definition of consumers into psychological profiles work in practice? RISC segments consumers according to psycho-graphic/attitudinal behaviour, and the following characteristics and concerns are most prolific amongst SRI purchasers:

- personal expression;
- integrity;
- cultural mobility;
- introspection;
- flexibility;
- social participation;
- ecosystem.

In 2002, AMP UKFS undertook a study to compare the characteristics of their SRI customers with those of their typical, mainstream customers. The RISC profile comparing SRI investors and non-SRI investors indicates that the former group have comparatively high scores for personal expression, integrity, cultural mobility, introspection and flexibility. This indicates:

- people who are happiest expressing their beliefs and ideals through personal ideas and styles;
- people who are likely to be interested in social and political issues; and that
- many may assert themselves against established rules and conventions.

It is this coherence between deeply held, well-considered beliefs and actions that helps SRI investors determine and express their identity. This profile has considerable overlap with a great number of Ray's theories on 'cultural creatives'. These are empathic people, able to identify and relate well to the positions of others. They are therefore likely to respond to media that provide the potential for, or represent, social interchange or an involvement in a human context. In a similar manner to their constant questioning of social and authoritarian systems, these individuals tend not to have a strict personal framework in which they live. They prefer variety and spontaneity in daily habits and consumption patterns. This experimentation extends to sampling the ways of life from other cultures. SRI investors are relatively likely to change their familiar surroundings and experiment with other cultural backgrounds.

There are comparatively lower scores for polysensuality, enjoyment of consumption, achievement, self-conditioning and new roots. This reinforces the idea of:

- individuals who make considered purchases based perhaps on personal ethics rather than impulse purchases based on the product's novelty value;
- people who make decisions with their head rather than their emotions;
- people who prefer to weigh up the pros and cons tactically before committing themselves so the products they purchase may be as much for their functional value as their appearance or 'sensual' properties.

However, that said, there is openness to novelty in both new and existing brands provided they meet with the stringent purchase criteria. Reflecting the global perspective outlined above, these are not people who anchor themselves in familiar places or in social and personal history. They are explorers, open to influence from other cultures and from traditional as much as modern trends. SRI investors do not strive for personal development and achievement inasmuch as they prefer to invest their energies in activities that are likely to drive society as a whole forward.

To summarize, these are individuals whose lives are determined primarily by their belief systems, which drive them to explore new sensations and to question existing systems. They have a strong global perspective rather than being influenced solely by local or personal issues and it is the circumstances of the global or fellow human community that concern them most. Consumer behaviour is dominated by considered rather than novelty purchases, and product uptake is likely to be supported by advertising messages that detail both the benefits of purchase and reassurance that the product in question has qualities in harmony with personal beliefs.

WHO BUYS RETAIL SRI PRODUCTS?

General investment

Since 2000, the number of new consumers attracted to invest has continually decreased. In the year to June 2001, just fewer than 1 million people first acquired shares, compared to nearly 1.8 million in the previous year, as the adverse market conditions of 2001–03 created a fall in consumer confidence.[11] Market conditions ultimately determine consumer attitude toward investment in general, but there are also varying attitudes to specific investment issues that appear to correlate fairly well with socio-economic and demographic differences. The investing public can therefore be broken down into 'sets', albeit with overlaps, requiring tailored approaches to break down the barriers to SRI uptake.

Around 44 per cent of better-off empty nesters and 48 per cent of working managers own shares, compared to 27 per cent of the general population.[12] Therefore, key market targets for any investment products are ABC1s aged 16–54, middle-market tabloid and broadsheet newspaper readers (around 9.7 million adults in the UK).[13]

As illustrated in Figure 7.3, most smaller investors are looking for long-term capital growth as savings. Many are therefore inclined to back safer, less volatile or guaranteed investments; 78.6 per cent of ethical investors are looking for capital growth, and only 12.9 per cent for regular income.[14]

The typical ethical investor

The typical ethical investor is a middle-aged, middle-income professional, eg a retired female academic or a male headteacher. A total of 35 per cent of ethical investors possess a first degree and 45 per cent possess both a first degree and a higher degree.[15]

Professionals account for 72.7 per cent of ethical investors, and 13.3 per cent are in managerial positions (ABs).[16]

Ethical investors also tend to take an active part in established political parties, religions, charitable institutions and pressure groups; 63.3 per cent are members of a

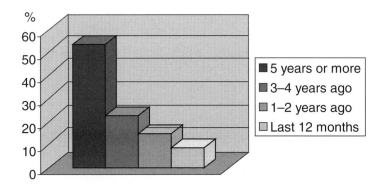

Source: Mintel, 2001 (sample 11,305)

Figure 7.3   Initial acquisition of shares

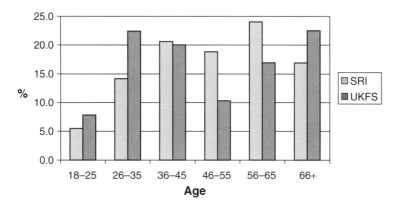

Figure 7.4 AMP UKFS SRI customers

cause-related group;[17] 85.7 per cent of Henderson's Ethical Fund holders are members of a charity or NGO.[18] Income and gender affect the degree of importance placed on individual criteria within ethical investments.[19] More information on this is set out below. SRI was found to be an extension of an overall lifestyle, as high percentages of investors are involved in other related activities.

Profile – age

A significant number of SRI customers are from the 46–65 age group. In an earlier analysis of PEP customers, sold directly off the page through marketing campaigns and mailshots, the NPI customer had a slightly different profile – perhaps reflecting the nature of PEP lump-sum investments and regular savers from individuals in regular employment.

In the case of PEP investors, the NPI survey of 280 individuals discovered the breakdown of figures shown in Table 7.5. You will see a clear bias to investors in the 35–54 age band (in bold), compared to the UK adult population as a whole. The age breakdown covers all the main age groups for regular savers PEPs, lump-sum PEPs and retirement planning.

Profile – household composition

Just over 15 per cent of SRI purchasers are single females; 10 per cent are in pseudo-families and just under 60 per cent in families or extended families. The largest group of SRI purchasers are from the 'Aspirers' segment (27.9 per cent).

Table 7.5 Age profile of PEP investors

Age	% of ethical investors by age band	% of adult population by age band (Office for National Statistics, 1991, LBS table 1991)
Up to 25	6.4	13.2
25–34	19.5	19.7
35–44	25.2	18.0
45–54	23.8	15.0
55–64	13.1	13.3
65+	12.1	20.8

These statistics reflect the female, professional and wealthy characteristics of SRI investors compared to non-SRI, mainstream retail investors.

In other surveys of the demand for ethical investing, 35 per cent of better-off empty nesters (45–64 ABs) claim to be positively inclined to invest ethically, partly because they are most likely to understand what ethical investment means.[20] The Mintel study that is the source of this information confirms and underpins the experience of NPI's customer profiles of SRI investors.

Occupational groups

Occupation is perhaps the defining factor as to whether an investor will have a preference for ethical investment. The key occupational groups are those in 'caring

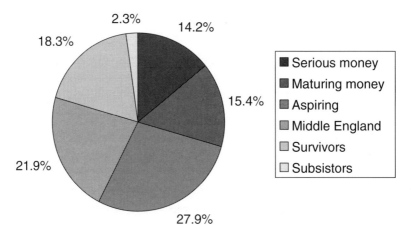

Figure 7.5 SRI purchasers by segment

Table 7.6 Profile – household composition

Household composition	SRI%	UKFS %	Index
Female home-sharers	1.9	0.5	343
Mixed home-sharers	1.8	0.8	238
Male home-sharers	0.5	0.2	229
Pseudo-family	10.1	5.5	183
Single female	15.1	11.1	136
Multi-occupancy dwelling	0.3	0.2	133
Single male	6.0	5.3	113
Abbreviated female families	1.1	1.2	90
Families	43.4	48.6	89
Extended household	4.1	4.8	85
Extended family	15.3	20.9	73
Abbreviated male families	0.5	0.9	51
TOTAL	100.0	100.0	

professions', namely occupational groups that are directly involved in looking after the needs of other people. But the list can be extended into caring professions that involve animals or protection of the environment.

There is a high concentration of individuals describing themselves as 'professionals', again reflective of the occupational profiles set out below, from the NPI Global Care PEP Survey in 1996:

alternative therapist	environmentalist	ophthalmic optician
ambulance person	farmer	optician
aromatherapist	fisherman	osteopath
childminder	florist	physiotherapist
chiropodist	forest/park ranger	record/film/TV industry
clergyman	gardener	social worker
counsellor	hatchery	teacher
craftsperson	hospital consultant	therapist
credit/debt counsellor	hospital staff	tree surgeon
dental technician	local authority employee	veterinary assistant/nurse
dentist	missionary	veterinary surgeon
doctor	nurse	voluntary
education	nursing home owner	

And of these occupational groups, the analysis in Table 7.7 of PEP holders of Global Care in 1996 emphasizes that the typical holder was a higher-income-earning professional.

Pressure group activity

Ethical consumerism, whether purchase of fair-trade coffee or selection of ethical investments, enjoys the support of a wide variety of pressure groups. In the last five years, Friends of the Earth and WWF have each appointed campaigners to focus on financial markets and to highlight to their supporters alternative, sustainable financial approaches such as ethical investments. In the case of Oxfam, this has involved campaigners working with financial institutions around 'access to medicine' – and Oxfam regularly promotes ethical funds to its membership bases. Amnesty International works with shareholder campaigners and it too promotes ethical investment products to its members.

The campaign by War on Want and Traidcraft over pension fund responsibility led to the development of the 'Just Pensions' project, with £400,000 backing from the UK government's Department for International Development (DfID). Just Pensions is administered by the main UK ethical investment trade body, the UK Social Investment Forum (UKSIF), and provides regular updates on the attitudes of investors towards socially responsible investment; for example, it published a study on the charity sector.

Morals and markets: the case of ethical investing

A University of Bath study in 1997 undertook an empirical study of a group of ethical investors, supporters of EIRIS (Ethical Investment Research Services), which

Table 7.7 PEP holders by occupation

Occupation	Percentage
Professional	56.6
Retired	17.4
Managerial	10.0
Director	6.4
Skilled manual	3.6
Not currently employed	2.1
Clerical	1.8
Sales	0.7
Secretarial	0.7
Unskilled manual	0.7

Table 7.8 University of Bath study of ethical investors

Occupation	Sex	Age	Memberships
Retired physician	f	79	Green Party
Chartered surveyor	m	41	National Trust, Friends of the Earth (FoE)
Accountant	f	61	Greenpeace
Dental radiologist	m	58	–
Homoeopath	f	49	Quaker, Green Party
Research chemist	m	67	Labour Party, FoE, Greenpeace
Retired accountant	m	67	Quaker
Teacher	m	47	Amnesty International
Businessman	m	59	Amnesty International, Greenpeace
Retired accountant	m	69	Greenpeace

Source: Craig Mackenzie, School of Social Sciences, University of Bath

profiled occupation, sex, age and memberships of organizations. This study appears to support the research from occupational classifications and age into support for ethical investment (see Table 7.8).

The activist groups are increasingly sophisticated in their tactics, eg focusing pressure on pension fund and charity fund trustees, and are very successful in drawing media attention and the interest of the charity fund membership. This inevitably further raises public awareness of ethical investment issues.

CONCLUSION

In many senses, SRI-inclined investors are the type of potential clients that advisers are seeking. They are wealthier than average with a combination of intelligence and education that ensures they are open to cogent presentations of the case for an investment. Their comparative wealth gives them the ability to consider the long term so that, once they have chosen an investment and understand why they have chosen, they will be less inclined to, and less likely to need to, bail out in difficult times. Also, because of their strong commitment to considering the impact of their own actions on others, once convinced of the efficacy of an ethical or SRI-fund-based investment they will not be easily dissuaded from that view.

Such investors do require a well-prepared and firmly founded set of reasons to invest with an absolutely transparent presentation of the pros and cons of a particular investment. They will respect a thorough and honest approach. However, an understanding of this type of investor will place any professional adviser in a very strong position to leverage growing levels of concern at corporate activities and accountability, which most individuals can best express through their decision of where to invest their money.

Notes

[1] A Lewis (2002) *Morals, Money and Ethical Investing: Ethical, green and socially responsible finance*, Pearson Education, Harlow.

[2] PH Ray and SR Anderson (2001) *The Cultural Creatives: How 50 million people are changing the world*, Random House, New York.

[3] R Hanson (2003) The Cultural Creative Market Grows: New report documents cultural creative consumer, Co-Op America Business Network News and Social Investment Forum, www.coopamerica.org/CABN/connections/issue38/ feature. html.

[4] S Valentine (2003) Values Based Investing Enriching the Soul of American Culture: Socially responsible investment, www.creatingwealthresponsibly.com/green-investing -1.htm.

[5] Ray and Anderson (2001).

[6] Ray and Anderson (2001).

[7] Ray and Anderson (2001).

[8] Ray and Anderson (2001).

[9] Cap Gemini, Ernst & Young and Merrill Lynch, 2003.

[10] Cap Gemini, Ernst & Young and Merrill Lynch, 2003.

[11] Mintel Research, December 2001.

[12] Mintel Research, 1999.

[13] Mintel Research, December 2001.

[14] Profile of the Ethical Investor, Woodward, University of Bournemouth, 2000.

[15] Profile of the Ethical Investor, Woodward, University of Bournemouth, 2000.

[16] Profile of the Ethical Investor, Woodward, University of Bournemouth, 2000.

[17] Profile of the Ethical Investor, Woodward, University of Bournemouth, 2000.

[18] Henderson Investors Ethical Fund Unit Holder Questionnaire, 1999.

[19] Profile of the Ethical Investor, Woodward, University of Bournemouth, 2000.

[20] Mintel, 2001.

8

How well do you know your client?

Helen Harrison, Retail Investment Officer, UKSIF

How well do you know your client? Does your fact-find tell you everything you need to know about a customer? Would you consider asking your clients whether their personal values would affect an investment choice? A total of 70 per cent of people consider ethical issues when buying goods and services (NOP/Friends Provident, 2000). However, it appears that financial advisers are missing out on this expanding market opportunity.

The UK Social Investment Forum is intending to help financial advisers take advantage of this opportunity through launching our 'Retail Revolution' programme. By addressing three key areas – parliamentary and regulatory work, the development of adviser toolkits and guidelines, and awareness raising – the programme will help the client and adviser better match individual investment needs.

At present ethical consumerism is one of the fastest-growing areas in the UK. According to the Ethical Purchasing Index published by the Co-operative Bank, ethical business activity contributed a weighty £13.9 billion to the UK economy in 2001. The growth rate of 9 per cent far outstripped the average economic growth of 2.1 per cent in 2001. There are many reasons for the increase. In the past the rise in ethical consumerism has been closely linked with the growth of key social and environmental movements, such as support of anti-apartheid, and with the growth in membership of organizations such as Greenpeace, Amnesty International and Friends of the Earth. In addition to this, shifts in economic trends such as the increasing financial independence of women and young people, the growth of employment in the voluntary sector, the emerging power of multinationals coupled with the reducing power of democratic governments have all impacted on an individual's purchasing decisions.

Apart from the previously identified market opportunity we must comment on why selling these types of products is of benefit to the adviser. Firstly, the feel-good factor is the most obvious benefit and can result in significant job satisfaction and client loyalty. This, as every adviser knows, can only help to achieve increased referrals of business. Secondly, ethical investors are more likely to be faithful to their investment. According to Noel Smyth, SRI product specialist at Morley Fund Management, 'Non-SRI investors have been cashing in their shares this year whilst the socially responsible investors have stayed put.' He also commented, 'People are buying more than just an investment product. They are buying a piece of philosophy. We encourage investors to take a long-term view, and SRI does too, encouraging companies to move towards more progressive policies and human rights, producing goods and services that improve way of life.'

The UKSIF 'Adviser Guidelines and Toolkit', launched in 2004, will help inform financial advisers on how to provide their clients with the most appropriate advice for this type of product.

One challenge for the investment industry is that the average person's understanding of finance is quite limited. While it seems that ethical consumers are more knowledgeable about their product choice than standard consumers, illustrated by the growth in the purchasing of fair-trade products for example, consumer interest and knowledge are not always transferred to their investments. To emphasize this, it seems odd in the current climate of investors campaigning against companies (eg against 'fat-cat' pay) that more people are not questioning how they can use their money to influence companies. The recent opposition to war in Iraq demonstrates that people are concerned with world issues and could potentially be interested in avoiding investments in arms. This again displays the market opportunity for these types of investments. There were a lot of protestors! UKSIF's awareness-raising and education programme will help consumers to make the link between their ethical concerns and investment decisions. Indeed we believe that ethical investment can be a useful tool to engage individuals on personal finance issues and help them to understand stocks and shares.

Investment in socially responsible and ethical funds need not lead to poorer performance. A CIS report in 2002 reviewed many studies of performance and concluded that, generally, screening resulted in no negative effect on performance. In fact in several cases the use of sustainability criteria for including stocks in a fund has resulted in superior performance compared to the FTSE index average. Another performance study carried out by ABN Amro Asset Management in September 2001 found that SRI has generally not led to a long-run risk-adjusted underperformance. Indeed a report published in 2002 from Co-operative Insurance Society, 'Sustainability Pays', sets out that there could be a 'business case' for SRI. Investors who consider the social, ethical and environmental (SEE) risks and opportunities that companies face could make higher returns from their investments and, furthermore, by encouraging companies to improve their corporate social responsibility (CSR) and sustainability, investors can add value to these companies and, in turn, to their investments.

Another area that UKSIF's 'Retail Revolution' will participate in is parliamentary and regulatory work. We intend to make sure appropriate legislation preserves and enhances consumer choice and promotes transparency. A recent initiative from our sister organization Eurosif, the Transparency Guidelines, was launched at the beginning of July 2003. Based in part on current best practices, the guidelines are focused on the retail SRI fund sector in order to increase accountability primarily to consumers. The guidelines are also envisioned to create more clarity for asset managers, research providers and other stakeholders. We will be supporting Eurosif through the process. Other countries are also seeing changes. In Australia advisers have recently had news of progressing regulatory changes from the Australian Securities and Investment Commission (ASIC), which released a policy statement outlining that 'good practice' advice requires advisers to enquire about their clients' views on labour standards and environmental, social or ethical considerations in their initial fact-find. Here in the UK our programme will be aiming to build on and stimulate moves in the financial services industry. An example of something that has occurred recently was the FSA's announcement that ethical considerations could be integrated into the curriculum for the revised examination framework for financial services, following on from its consultation paper 157. It is in areas like this that we will be hoping to advance change.

Along with the UK government's commitment to addressing the savings gap, UKSIF will help to promote the ethical area of the investment market. By providing advisers with information and support we aim to ensure consumers' ethical values form an integral part of their investment decisions.

COULD HIGH NET WORTH INDIVIDUALS BE KEY DRIVERS FOR SOCIALLY RESPONSIBLE INVESTMENT?

Kirstie CE Smith-Laittan

Socially responsible investment (SRI) is when environmental, social or ethical considerations are taken into account when making financial investments (a triple bottom-line approach). This research examines whether high net worth individuals (HNWIs) could be key actors in driving SRI out from the niche market position it currently occupies in the UK.

The main research objectives explore the current level of HNWI interest in SRI, the SRI approaches and products that are preferred by HNWIs and the challenges currently limiting their investment into SRI. Finally, recommendations are given for developments in the wealth management and SRI industry to make SRI more attractive and available to HNWIs. Based on these recommendations a framework has been developed to illustrate how SRI could be integrated into HNWI wealth management.

There are currently many challenges limiting HNWI investment into SRI. Most importantly, many HNWIs do not appear to be receiving adequate information and advice on SRI, which is limiting their ability to make an informed opinion on the SRI options available. In addition, fear of lower financial performance from SRI is a concern for HNWIs and wealth management professionals including trustees who may discourage HNWI investment into SRI.

When investing in SRI, HNWIs want to be catalysts of change and as a result many HNWIs are interested in moving away from negative screening to more visionary approaches to SRI. In general the younger generation of HNWIs are more interested in SRI than the older generation, suggesting that HNWI demand for SRI could increase significantly in the future. The SRI industry and wealth management industry will need to respond to this demand by developing their SRI product and service range, integrating SRI into their core values, SRI capacity building, etc. There will be significant commercial benefits for the wealth management enterprises that realize this emerging business opportunity.

Executive summary

This project examines whether high net worth individuals (HNWIs) could be key actors in driving socially responsible investment (SRI) out of the niche market position it currently occupies in the UK.

The aim of this research is to understand the current level of HNWI interest in SRI, explore whether there are SRI approaches and products that are of most interest to HNWIs and assess the challenges currently limiting HNWI investment into SRI. Finally, recommendations are given for developments in the wealth management industry (WMI) and SRI industry to make SRI more attractive and available to HNWIs.

Context

SRI is when the investor takes environmental, social or ethical considerations into account when making financial investments. There are many approaches to SRI, ranging from mainstream SRI to programme-related SRI. The choice of approach will depend on investors' investment objectives, risk tolerance and extent they wish their values to be reflected in their investments.

HNWIs are those with liquid assets of over US $1 million. The research includes wealthy family-established trusts and foundations in its definition of HNWIs, as some, such as the Nathan Cummings Foundation (USA) and Joseph Rowntree Charitable Trust (UK), are excellent examples of the influence that HNWIs can have on SRI.

Methodology

The research methodology is based on a qualitative, inductive approach. Thirty-three semi-structured interviews with key and emerging SRI players, private client fund managers and HNWIs were carried out. The interviews typically lasted one hour.

Could HNWIs be key drivers for SRI?

The HNWI market is very diverse and the level of SRI interest varies greatly. SRI is not a core investment strategy for HNWIs at present. However, the younger generation of HNWIs appear to be more interested in SRI than the older generation, suggesting that HNWI demand for SRI could increase significantly in the future.

What SRI approaches and products are of most interest to HNWIs?

It is very hard to generalize the type of SRI product and approach that HNWIs favour, as it depends on their personal experiences, business and financial knowledge, values, etc. However, it can be concluded that, as expected, the foundations /trusts and light green HNWIs tend to advocate the mainstream and engagement approach to SRI, while other HNWIs may favour alternative and higher-risk SRI strategies.

When investing in SRI, HNWIs want to be agents of change, which may explain why some HNWIs are interested in moving away from screening to more visionary approaches to SRI.

What are the challenges currently limiting HNWI investment into SRI?

It is important to understand why HNWI demand for SRI is low and why many of those who are interested are not actually investing in SRI. The main challenges identified from the interviews include low awareness of SRI, fear of lower financial returns and complexity of SRI. These challenges can cause some investment advisers to discourage investment into SRI. Therefore low HNWI demand for SRI cannot purely be attributed to a genuine disinterest; instead the challenges identified appear to contribute to the low HNWI interest and demand that exists.

Recommendations for developments in the WMI and SRI industry to make SRI more attractive and available to HNWIs

To boost HNWI investment into SRI there needs to be an increase in awareness, confidence and access to SRI across the WMI and HNWI market. The provision of SRI services and products to HNWIs will be consumer led. There are a number of developments and initiatives that could be taken to drive this consumer demand. They include: targeting SRI marketing to HNWIs and the WMI; integrating SRI and capacity building within the WMI; partnership building between SRI specialists and the WMI; and creating new SRI products and services.

Conclusion

Most HNWIs are not receiving adequate information and advice on SRI and as a result are not in the position to *become interested* in SRI. It addition, those who are interested in SRI can be discouraged by the lack of support available to them, suggesting that the current level of demand we are seeing is not a true reflection of potential HNWI interest in SRI.

To conclude: there is very positive evidence suggesting HNWIs could drive SRI. As the younger generation of HNWIs age there will be an increase in HNWI demand for SRI. A framework has been developed to illustrate how SRI could be integrated into wealth management with the aim of shifting potential HNWI demand to effective demand. There will be significant commercial benefits for the SRI and wealth management enterprises that realize this emerging business opportunity.

9

The investment implications of choosing an SRI fund

Mark Campanale, Head of SRI Business Development,
Henderson Global Investors

SUMMARY

The socially responsible investment market in the UK has grown significantly over the last 20 years and a number of the pooled funds, such as the Friends Provident Stewardship Funds (over £1 billion) and the Henderson Global Care Funds (over £700 million) have reached market-respectable sizes. Investors have sought to invest in these SRI funds not only to deliver investment performance, but also to make a positive social and environmental contribution as part of their mandate. But as this range of funds has increased, so the market has evolved a wide array of social and environmental criteria – from just 20 common criteria in the early years to now well over 500.[1] Consequently, how these criteria are combined and the extent to which they are used now mean that the funds exhibit different types of investment characteristics. These funds now behave in different ways from each other (they certainly can't be treated as a 'common group') and produce different types of financial returns. This chapter looks at the funds in more detail: how client preferences can produce different investment portfolio characteristics (asset type, portfolio risk, style bias, market capitalization bias) and, consequently, different performance outcomes.

INTRODUCTION

What is common to all of the SRI funds is a consideration of how the non-financial activity of companies contributes to their selection for an investment portfolio. 'The purpose of the research,' says Nick Robins, Head of SRI Funds and Research at Henderson, 'is to complement our financial analysis of a company to give us a complete picture of what a company does and how it operates. We want to understand what a company stands for, its vision and its corporate social responsibility track record.' 'Furthermore,' says Tim Dieppe, an investment manager of the Henderson Global Care Funds, 'we closely analyse companies for what they do, not just how they do it. So we are naturally attracted to companies in the healthcare, renewable energy or water treatment sectors.'

For many investment managers, what counts more is not what a company does, but how well it does it. So sectors such as oil, chemicals, mining or mainstream banking might feature. Some fund managers don't want to exclude sectors at all and adopt a 'best-in-class' approach. They have no problem, for example, in including large tobacco companies in the funds. Other managers follow simple negative screens and, comments an anonymous fund manager, 'so long as it doesn't breach a negative screen the company is in'. Lastly, there are other managers who do not believe that social or environmental analytics have any place in portfolio management and promote 'engagement only' as an SRI approach to invest then in the same companies that mainstream investors hold.

These contrasting approaches produce different outcomes, which the investor does well to note. Best-in-class approaches, low thresholds for negative screens and 'inclusive' as opposed to exclusive approaches can often produce portfolios that do appear, at first glance, to be fairly conventional. So it's worth revisiting the different approaches to incorporating social and environmental performance in investment portfolios and the different product frameworks.

SRI PRODUCT DELIVERY

Environmental and social analysis is a core process in designing an SRI product. There are two major methodologies used to make this analysis, negative screening and positive selection.

Negative screening

The earliest of the SRI funds adopted a negative screening approach. This approach works by excluding sectors that are believed to have a negative social or environmental impact from the potential investment universe. The most common sectors that are excluded are tobacco, armaments, the nuclear industry and companies with a poor environmental record, such as energy companies using fossil fuels. The avoidance approach also tries to take into account investor concerns about issues such as human rights, for example, which tend not to work on a sector avoidance basis, but on a company-by-company basis.

Positive selection

Whilst the latest investment management arrivals to offer SRI-based funds always try to claim that they are the first to incorporate a positive selection approach, or are the first to incorporate a social responsibility evaluation into the financial risk analysis of a company, 'positive selection' has actually been around from the earliest years. In the UK, the Merlin (now Jupiter) Ecology Fund is commonly recognized as the first to select companies on this basis. The positive approach is used in a number of different ways. For example:

- **Pioneers/innovators**. This approach seeks to identify companies that are 'pioneers' or innovators in sustainability and is an approach found in funds such as the SAM Pioneers Fund, the Jupiter Ecology Fund or Henderson Global Care Growth. This approach tends to focus on 'what companies do' (more than 'how companies do it') and so includes companies from sectors ranging across pollution control, social housing and urban regeneration, renewable energy, training and health care. Sometimes referred to as 'industries of the future' there are some funds that take strong sector themes. Examples of this are the Framlington Health Fund[2] in the UK, the SAM Water Fund and Pictet Water Fund in Switzerland. More recently, the UK saw the (short-lived) ISIS EcoTech Fund. Two examples of UK sector-focused funds are the Merrill Lynch New Energy Fund, which focuses on the low-carbon economy, and the IMPAX Environmental Markets Investment Trust.[3]

  This style of fund tends to produce spectacular returns when financial markets want to reward specific sectors – for example, the Framlington Health Fund has produced excellent returns. However, when a sector falls out of favour, these returns can be quickly reversed and diverge considerably from the rest of the market, which has exposure to a broad range of sectors. An example of this is the New Energy Fund, which quickly fell owing to the links of solar and fuel cell companies to the technology boom of 2000. Thematic funds therefore result in a higher weighting towards specific industry sectors such as health. Or they might have a higher weighting towards emerging and small businesses that are still in their (sometimes financially vulnerable) growth stage.

● **Best-in-sector approach.** In using this approach, a manager seeks to identify the best-performing companies within a given share market sector. This approach compares companies in the same industries on a range of social and environmental criteria and selects those that are 'best' overall. This style of analysis allows for the selection of larger, more traditional (and long-standing) 'blue-chip' companies in the market. Best in sector/best in class can also differ from fund to fund – for example, some funds will exclude companies involved in the gambling, armaments and brewing sectors but still seek best-in-class stocks from other sectors. In the 1990s, the NPI funds published best-in-class studies for sectors as diverse as printing and publishing to the listed football clubs. Whilst these studies stood up to academic scrutiny, ethical investors in Newcastle were rarely happy to see their club out of the fund and, say, Manchester United in. So best-of-class approaches also have their own perceptual problems.

HOW ARE THE PORTFOLIOS MANAGED?

Just as for other investment funds, the investment management process for SRI can be passive or active, style neutral or style bias. This section looks at some of the options and their investment implications.

Passive (index-based) products

The passive investor is attracted to index funds for three broad reasons. The first is the implicit assumption that, as 'markets are perfect; the numbers of buyers equal the numbers of sellers and therefore everything is in the price', there is no point trying actively to beat the market. The second is that investors want to track a broad index (the MSCI World, FTSE All-Share) and want to get as close a return as possible to this index. Often driven by risk control factors, the decision makers want to avoid the possibility that the returns of their assets deviate from the average returns of their peer group (particularly noticeable in the case of institutional pension funds). The last reason is cost – passive investing gives a market return at typically less than the management fee charged by active funds. So what SRI indices are available?

There are a surprisingly large number of SRI indices from which investors can select. Perhaps the best known was the first launched, in the US in the early 1990s by Domini Investments, called the Domini Social Index, which tracked the S&P 500. The first in the UK was the NPI Social Index, a FTSE-tracking index launched in 1998 (and withdrawn following the takeover of NPI by AMP), and the first MSCI-tracking index was the Dow Jones Sustainability Group Index, offered by Sustainable Asset

Management (SAM). Other SRI index trackers are offered by groups such as E Capital Partners in Italy, and Kempen in the Netherlands, which offers an SRI European Smaller Companies index. Today, one of the most successful (along with SAM) international SRI index products is offered by FTSE, called the FTSE4Good index.

So how do SRI indices work? Typically these products rank companies within industries in a systematic manner using company scoring methods that reflect social or environmental criteria (or both). Only those companies ranked in the top percentage for each industry are included in the SRI index. This approach is particularly useful as (contrary to the general public's understanding of indexes) many index trackers do not fully replicate the market – often excluding the smaller end of the market – so introducing a useful (though somewhat unusual) 'selection' into the index. This enables index funds to replicate the overall character of the stock market (for example, sector weightings) whilst actively choosing the best companies. Some index trackers also avoid sectors, on negative criteria grounds, though others do not. The DJSI, for example, includes a controversial tobacco company on a best-in-sector basis.

SRI indices face a number of criticisms on theoretical and practical grounds. Each of these needs to be considered by the SRI investor. The first is that, by tracking a market, investment decisions are made 'negatively'. That is, a large number of companies are only included in an index not because of any great social or environmental attribute, but because the 'risk' of not including them in the fund greatly increases the tracking error risk (the total market risk of not holding important stocks) of the portfolio. For example, in the UK, 20 stocks constitute approximately 50 per cent of the total market value of the market. Excluding just two or three of these stocks can greatly increase the total risk of the portfolio relative to the benchmark. Secondly, in replicating the main market constituents, SRI investors are basically buying some of the most controversial companies on the market and their funds inevitably look very 'mainstream'. Thirdly, it means holding sectors – such as natural resource stocks and energy stocks – whose financial value a growing number of environmental economists believe do not reflect their replacement value. Scarce minerals or old-growth forests are priced by today's short-term markets as being replaceable – when quite clearly they are not. Whole sectors, such as oil and coal, are included in SRI indices when the total environmental cost – for example, the contribution to climate change – is not reflected in their share price. It is this latter criticism that probably makes many of the larger market (FTSE All-Share, MSCI World) SRI indices flawed. What index tracking is basically saying is that there is scarcely any investment value derived from the detailed social, ethical or environmental analysis of companies and sectors. For many SRI investors, it is the flaws inherent in the financial markets that need reforming (for example, their failure properly to reflect the social or environmental damage caused by companies or whole sectors such as the oil or coal industries) and so index tracking, possibly quite gullibly, accepts these flaws.

Active portfolio management

Any investment decision that chooses to include companies or avoid companies and sectors on ethical grounds is called 'active' portfolio management. There is a double hurdle for companies to meet: they need to qualify on social, ethical or environmental criteria as well as on financial criteria. In the UK there have been three main methodologies for actively selecting an SRI portfolio. The first and perhaps most common method has been to specify a number of 'avoidance' or negative criteria. Companies are passed through these filters and all those companies that have passed through are deemed to meet the criteria and can be included in the fund. The second is positive screening whereby the best companies from within all industry sectors are selected, with minimal negative screens, and so the evaluation of corporate social responsibility plays a particularly important part in the analysis. The last actually looks at what companies do (the sectors they operate in, for example health care or renewable energy) and only chooses stocks from within a limited number of sectors. This latter approach can combine the best of the positive selection with the best of the negative selection (on the basis that a healthcare company, for example, is rarely involved in the armaments industry). Whichever SRI approach is adopted, there is common consensus that there is no such thing as an 'ethical' company. There are companies that meet ethical criteria (they don't sell tobacco, for example) and there are companies that operate to high ethical standards. Ethical funds do not choose from a list of 'ethical' companies – rather, they invest in traditional companies listed on stock markets that have some social or environmental characteristic that merits investor consideration.

Each of these different approaches for constructing an actively managed SRI portfolio has implications for the management of 'risk'. So it is worthwhile turning for a moment to a discussion of 'risk', as investors can understand this to mean different things. There is asset-based risk – for example, an investment portfolio that combines different assets, such as bonds, cash, equities (whether global or UK only, 'value biased' or 'growth biased'), property or more recently hedge funds, is considered to have 'diversified' risk. If equities perform poorly but property performs well, then a balanced portfolio of assets will still produce a return and so can be considered less risky than, say, investing wholly in equities (as regrettably many ethical investors did through the late 1990s).

But 'risk' can also be considered in terms of market risk. For example, avoiding whole sectors of the market or the largest companies introduces a high level of risk relative to the market as a whole – the total percentage difference between the portfolio and the rest of the market is commonly known as the 'tracking error'. The greater the tracking error, the larger the difference between a fund's returns and the chosen index. SRI funds have tended to be 'higher-risk' because they have a high level of uncorrelation from the rest of the stock market. However, investors can get confused by terminology. Some funds are quite well diversified by assets – for example, 'managed' funds tend to balance equities with bonds, cash and property – and can be considered 'medium-risk' by asset type. But if the equity content of the managed fund has a high tracking error relative to the main equity market, then what can be considered a medium-risk investment by asset type suddenly becomes 'high-risk' once the equity component is taken into account.

Therefore one specific difference between active SRI funds is the weighting of each market sector within the fund. Active funds can range from the sector neutral, which weights all market sectors close to the main market's index weighting and then chooses shares within each sector, to a more best-in-market approach, where the best shares meeting all criteria are selected, regardless of sector weightings. A best-in-market approach can result in significant overweighting in those sectors that provide SRI-focused solutions, such as those funds in the 'pioneers' or industries-of-the-future classification.

SRI funds in the UK have tended to combine different elements of the differing approaches, either in the method of the social and environmental screening or in the portfolio management process. Some SRI funds have been quite content to have portfolios directed towards specific sectors or to have what are in effect smaller company investment portfolios. The chosen combination will reflect the manager's preferred investment style or the fund mandate. Most ethical funds in the UK are found in the UK Growth Sector or perhaps the Global Growth sector. In terms of risk, this immediately means that UK ethical funds, with their (often) smaller company bias, have to compete against mainstream funds that typically invest 50 per cent of their portfolio in just 20 companies (the largest ones). This is why most UK funds found amongst mainstream investment providers are surprisingly similar. Some UK SRI funds have tended to look at this and then – particularly during volatile periods of stock market performance – move their portfolios into line with 'mainstream' funds, whilst other SRI funds have taken their chance, alongside other active (or increasingly 'contrarian') investors, and built portfolios that bear little comparison to 'mainstream' funds and aim to look totally different as a result.

Engagement and engagement-only investment

Engagement with companies is another important part of socially responsible investment and is usually part of an actively managed, stock-picking SRI fund. It grew out of the recognition that even the 'better' companies (in relative terms) weren't addressing all of the issues that the best and most progressive companies adopt as common practice today. Simply put, the engagement process is where the fund managers actively participate in a dialogue with companies in which they invest. Engagement also includes proxy voting on social and environmental issues as well as taking part in shareholder resolutions.

When engagement is used in partnership with an active, stock-picking SRI fund, the manager has a couple of options with which to influence company behaviour. For example, the manager can engage in dialogue with companies not held in the portfolio to encourage action that may allow their inclusion in the fund. Or the manager can sell a stock if activity within the company no longer meets the required social and environmental criteria, or buy a stock if the company is willing to change.

In recent years there has been a creeping attempt by financial institutions to portray their mainstream funds as being part of the SRI movement simply by virtue of the parent companies 'employing dialogue and engagement' across all of their investment activities. The danger with this is that it may dilute and weaken the thrust of values-based investments if companies feel that they can gain a place in a fund that is designated as SRI by its manager even if it makes no difficult demands on the behaviour of companies in which it invests.

COMPARING SRI PRODUCTS

Table 9.1 provides a comparison of some of the SRI approaches offered in the UK so as to give a sense of the impact on performance and risk of different product variations.

SRI INVESTMENT CHARACTERISTICS

This chapter has so far looked at different approaches to SRI and how different approaches lead to different levels of investment risk. It is worth now looking in more detail at additional characteristics of SRI funds such as sector bias, market capitalization bias and style bias. Each of these, in turn, assists the investor's understanding of how his or her SRI portfolio might behave at different times.

Industry and style biases

The most common share market industry sectors avoided by SRI funds are:

- tobacco;
- armaments;

Table 9.1 Comparison of SRI approaches

Environmental and social analysis	Portfolio management	Targeted environmental and social focus	Targeted outperformance
Negative screening only	Active, traditional	Low. This product has strict approach on the negatively screened sectors, but tends to invest in a traditional manner across the balance of the fund.	Low–high. The bulk of the fund is managed in a traditional manner. The negative screens tend to produce a bias towards medium and smaller-sized companies.
Best in class	Active, sector neutral	Medium. Because this product considers the entire market on social and environmental issues, it will tend to have a more significant environmental or social focus, compared to a negatively screened fund. However, because it invests across all sectors, and has a low tracking error, it will tend to include a reasonable range of contentious companies from an SRI perspective. As a result its overall social or environmental focus can be described as medium.	Low. Its low-risk, sector-neutral approach means taking limited positions and a relatively lower targeted out-performance of its benchmark.
Pioneers/innovators	Active, best-in-market	High.	

Source: SRI, the Market and its Delivery, Research paper, February 2002, AMP Capital, Australia

- gambling;
- animal testing;
- resource companies (mining, poor environmental practices, climate change).

When investors look at the financial returns of a given market, such as the FTSE All-Share Index, these returns tend to be given as an aggregate of the overall performance. Sometimes commentators will pick on one section of the performance and record this performance – typically the FT 100 Index. However, this aggregate can often hide from view substantial differences in the financial returns of some of the underlying sectors that make up that performance. For example, if on one trading day the most significant companies in the pharmaceuticals sector generated a loss while those in the mining plus the oil and gas sectors recorded a gain, then the market as a whole would tend to mark a gain – though investors in a pharmaceuticals-focused fund would lose. Whilst this is obvious, it is worth describing because it is precisely these sectoral gains and losses that have historically had such impact upon the returns of UK SRI funds, particularly during the 1995–2000 and 2000–04 periods of stock market history. Analysing these factors tends to be described by investors as 'performance attribution'.

In the context of performance attribution, information technology (given its extreme performance) is the most commonly mentioned industry in which SRI investors are overweighted. This is probably followed by industries such as communications and finance.

For advisers and personal investors wishing to invest in a socially responsible way, considering some of these factors can be a good idea because they have, and will continue to have, important impacts upon financial returns. Some questions worth asking are the following. Is the bias the result of the ethical screens (which tend to restrict investment in so-called 'dirty' industries), or is there investment logic (an investment preference) to these biases? Are these biases permanent, or can they be reversed during different parts of the economic cycle?

Biases in size are more common to SRI funds in the UK, where a good number of the largest 20 companies listed on the London Stock Exchange either are avoided because they breach negative criteria or are, quite simply, unpalatable to the SRI investor wishing to make an active, ethical choice. Inevitably, this means that SRI funds will have a natural small and medium-sized company bias. During most of the 1990s, with a few important exceptions, this group of companies as a whole did not produce sparkling investment returns. However, during 2003, as the UK stock market showed strong signs of recovery, it was led by smaller companies – much to the benefit of UK ethical funds.

Table 9.2 Comparing typical SRI style and size bias

Manager with all of following characteristics	Growth vs value	Small vs large
Negative screening	Growth – as nil weight in value sectors such as tobacco and gambling.	Mid- to smaller company bias – as much of the old-economy, dirty industries are avoided.
Best in class in traditional sectors	Value – tends to be blue-chip, mature companies in economically and financially defensive sectors.	Larger companies.
Pioneers/innovators – industries of the future	Growth – tend to be in high-growth companies.	Smaller company – pioneers tend to be emerging industries such as renewable energy.

Comparing typical SRI style and size bias

How important is 'style' bias in evaluating SRI portfolio risk and what are the potential performance implications? Simply put, the SRI funds in the UK grew at their fastest between 1995 and 2001 – which just happened to coincide with a period of market history where 'growth' as a style was in favour. A good number of the SRI funds doing well at that time had distinct 'growth' style biases, and have now done relatively poorly compared to mainstream funds where there are more 'value' style funds to choose from. SRI funds have therefore to be considered in light of their investment style bias and should be considered collectively as just another investment style or theme, such as momentum, contrarian, value or growth.

As an example of this, the Henderson Global Care Growth Fund generated competitive returns to investors during the bull market run of 1995–2000, outperforming its mainstream rivals in the global growth sector. This is illustrated in Figure 9.1. It has, however, underperformed the market in 2000–03. What market explanations are there for this performance?

In the three years 2000–03 of what had been a bear market the fund was at a disadvantage relative to the market, as the top-sector performers were largely value based, many of which the fund either had not held in its past (oil) or that fell under its avoidance criteria (alcohol, armaments, tobacco). The impact of sector avoidance on the relative performance of SRI funds to their mainstream peers is best illustrated by the defence sector performance.

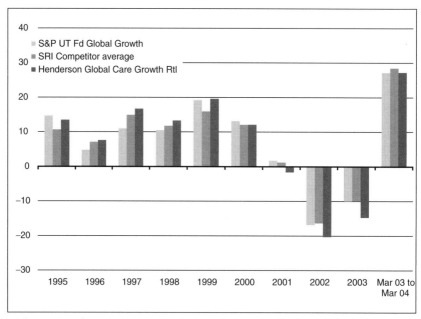

Source: Henderson

Figure 9.1 Global Care Growth rolling three-year performance annualized

In the UK, the FTSE Aerospace and Defence sector carried its strong performance in 2003 into the first six months of 2004, posting the highest return of any subsector in the FTSE All-Share over the year to 14 June 2004. Following on from 2003, when the sector saw growth of +30.16 per cent compared with +21.35 per cent from the All-Share, over the first half of 2004 the subsector generated a return of +21.21 per cent against a +0.34 per cent rise from the index. Ethical funds, by not investing in the armaments industry, missed out on the strong performance seen from these industries during this time period. But is it always the case that some of these contentious sectors will always outperform sectors favoured by ethical or SRI investors? Not so.

Table 9.3 illustrates that the biggest sector contributor to the total return of the MSCI World in 1994–99 was the technology and hardware sector – which made significant negative returns in 2000–03. Therefore during the latter period, funds with a growth bias took quite a hit owing to the cautious nature of the bear market, particularly those funds that historically held a large exposure to technology (which did include many SRI funds).

Another way to show this is to look at the contribution to the total return of the market by stocks found within these two distinct styles, growth and value. It illustrates that, as a group, value stocks made the greatest contribution to the total return of the market between 1991 and 1995; but growth stocks made the greatest contribution between 1995 and 2000. A style reversal took place after the tech bubble burst,

Table 9.3 Sector contribution to return

1994 to 1999 MSCI World			2000 to 2003 MSCI World		
MSCI industry group	Total return	Contribution to return	MSCI industry group	Total return	Contribution to return
Top 5 industries:			Top 5 industries:		
Software and services	1116.37	10.83	Healthcare equipment and services	41.10	0.16
Technology, hardware and equipment	565.56	23.15	Food, beverage and tobacco	20.56	−0.05
Telecommunication services	251.06	14.16	Banks	11.53	0.27
Pharmaceuticals and biotech- nology	243.10	19.85	Utilities	3.58	−0.35
Media	223.13	6.44	Real estate	0.70	−0.07
Bottom 5 industries:			Bottom 5 industries:		
Materials	45.06	4.63	Semiconductors and semiconductor equipment	−46.10	−1.09
Healthcare equip- ment and services	37.62	0.78	Media	−46.29	−1.97
Utilities	36.64	2.60	Software and services	−62.39	−4.30
Transportation	20.56	0.86	Telecommunication services	−63.84	−5.74
Real estate	1.98	−0.18	Technology, hardware and equipment	−71.65	−6.85

Source: Henderson
Note: The chart shows growth vs value in Pan-Europe as at 19 March 2004.

between 2000 and 2004. Figure 9.2 illustrating growth versus value shows that growth outperformed strongly from 1995 to 2000 but underperformed by 50 per cent between 2000 and 2004. Crucially, despite the market rally, the growth theme remains on the floor. Therefore on a relative basis, SRI funds with distinct growth style biases, such as Henderson Global Care Growth, have not performed well. A potential problem for SRI investors is that, as a whole, amongst the 60 or so funds available in the UK, too many of them are distinctly growth biased and relatively few have made a distinction about them being value biased.

Figure 9.2 Growth versus value 1991–2004

At the point of writing, what ought investors to consider when they are looking at their SRI funds, particularly growth funds that have underperformed the market? Henderson has taken the view that at a tactical level the fund managers ought to stick to the 'growth' theme as valuations across the market have converged and it is unlikely that the 40–50 per cent relative underperformance of growth versus value should continue. Once the divergence in valuations disappears, so should the divergence in the performance of growth-orientated SRI funds relative to their mainstream peer group.

CONCLUSIONS

In the 20 years since it started, the ethical SRI funds sector has grown in several ways: sheer volumes under investment, choice of investment styles and numbers of managers offering funds that fit into this sector. As, perhaps, you might expect, different SRI approaches generate different characteristics and different returns in different market conditions. Asset allocation remains the basis for good portfolio construction but, in the context of SRI, style bias is also a major factor. It is important to note that there are few SRI funds that offer value style approaches – which does mean careful analysis of risk, or the adoption of informed approaches that take style bias into account during periods of stock market turbulence.

However, the breadth of choice now available does mean that ethical or SRI-minded investors are more likely to find a fund that reflects their concerns and it also means that those with larger sums to invest or who are saving over a longer term will be able to create a portfolio of fund investments all of which suit their basic priority to invest ethically or responsibly but which will spread their exposure among funds whose performance will vary at different times in the economic cycle.

Notes

1   Source: EIRIS.
2   The Framlington Health Fund tends to be included in tables of ethical funds because of its historical avoidance of tobacco and armaments. Other funds in the healthcare sector, such as the Finsbury Biotech funds, the Schroeder Medical Discovery Fund and L&G Pharmaceutical Index Tracker, do not. But it would be surprising to see these funds included in lists of 'ethical' funds even though many investors might believe that they have the attributes of an SRI fund, namely support for social well-being.
3   There are other environmental sector funds in the UK that are less well known to social investors; for example, the Ecofin Environmental Funds is a €150 million-plus fund that invests in the environmental and water sectors and is managed by a specialist environmental investment boutique, Ecofin - see www.ecofin.co.uk.

10

The impact of green investment

John Hancock

BUSINESS FIRST – GET THE MESSAGE!

The theme throughout this book is that ordinary investors, whether through involvement with collective investments or directly by buying shares in businesses of which they approve or in the running of which they would like to have a say, can send a message to organizations with the power to make a difference. You should know by now the message they wish to communicate, whether they wish to send that message and how to send it. However, it is one thing to send a message; the real question is, will it be received and will the recipients do anything about it? Then the further question arises: are those recipients in a position to make any difference or are they simply small, insignificant or ideologically motivated organizations that, whatever they decide to do, can make no difference to actions and activities in the real world? These are very important questions because the answers will determine whether corporate socially responsible business practices are to be condemned to linger on the fringe of the real world, well regarded but largely ignored, or whether they might eventually become the standards and protocols for the conduct of all businesses. In order for that to be the case, the ranks of companies practising corporate social responsibility will need to cover the full spectrum from service providers to manufacturers, from small specialist new ventures to large established, respected and successful businesses, from local enterprises to multinational conglomerates. In fact, the recruitment of large and successful businesses to the ranks of those who regard decency, integrity and environmental responsibility as integral to good business practice will be essential to the long-term success of the socially responsible agenda. And the news on that front is good.

The arrival of the FTSE4Good index of companies screened for the quality and extent of their corporate social responsibility policy has introduced the idea of corporate responsibility to a much wider audience in the business world and has highlighted the efforts of many of the world's largest companies to be good corporate citizens. Corporate giants from the worlds of IT, energy, banking and pharmaceuticals have all been listed on the index. Some of them may well operate in contentious areas for many ethical and SRI investors but inclusion in the FTSE4Good recognizes that, within the constraints of their sector, they are making an effort to operate well. A good example, mentioned elsewhere in this book, is the manner in which BP is exploiting its new-found reserves off the islands of Trinidad and Tobago. Doing business ethically is not the preserve of small or emerging businesses; it has become a core value in the operation of the largest businesses.

HOW COULD YOU TELL?

But how would a business know whether it was operating to socially responsible standards? That is not a flippant question for a large global business with a number of subsidiaries, with contractual arrangements to buy from a range of suppliers and to supply components to customers worldwide, and with a workforce of thousands spread across many sites in several countries. Even for a relatively small business, it can be difficult to keep track of the activities of all suppliers (especially when components are bought through an agent or wholesaler) or to know the ultimate use for all items sold as components to other companies who, in turn, manufacture further sub-assemblies to sell on. BT fell foul of this problem when it took over a business whose interests included premium lines, one of which offered a 'colourful' chatline service. Pornography is one of the absolute avoidance areas for some ethical investors and so the situation briefly threatened BT's standing as a clean business. However, it was accepted that the company had not been aware of the nature of all interests held by the acquired business. BT instigated steps to avoid such an unplanned situation arising in the future. For most investors or fund managers with a socially responsible agenda, it is the attitude reflected in how the company deals with the problem that says as much as anything about its general approach. Marks & Spencer similarly had to take Granada Television to court over an implication that the store group had knowingly sourced products from a company that employed child labour. M&S won the case, not because there were no child workers involved in the production of its goods but because it was able to establish that the fact was not known to it. This pointed up the difficulties encountered by even the most scrupulous and thorough businesses in establishing a full awareness of all conditions throughout the operations of all suppliers worldwide.

Subsequently, M&S were the subject of a major study by EIRIS for the Ecumenical Council for Corporate Responsibility (ECCR) as a way of fine-tuning that body's set of benchmarks against which ethical standards may be measured. Although the store chain cooperated with the study, it was unable to provide full answers as to how it monitors any use of child labour by suppliers. Now, not many companies could provide that information and so the study should not be read as critical of M&S – rather their cooperation with the work should indicate the company's underlying morality – but it does point to the problems that may arise if a company, even when it has nothing to hide, cannot demonstrate that fact.

Monitoring activities and identifying key information on ethical and environmental matters is an issue that might seem to require a whole new set of operating tools for business, which if it were the case would probably mean a great deal of expense. But there is already a well-established business practice that has provided the structure for a solution to this problem. When companies wish to know the full details of their financial and operational situation, they have an independent financial audit conducted by qualified accountants; indeed, an audit is the only way to unearth and be confident of the information that a business is required to include in the annual report, and it is an annual event. Financial and operational audit trails throughout the business trace and value every component and operation, confirm its place in the process of the business and record a clear understanding of its contribution to the bottom line. So it is logical that, when businesses wish to know the full details of their ethical, corporate governance and environmental situation, they should conduct another audit. Social auditing is the process by which companies can establish the ethical and environmental credentials of the enterprise, monitor activities against their own declared standards of decent behaviour and find the information needed to improve their social, ethical and environmental performance. You may come across other terms in this context: terms such as 'environmental impact', 'ethical and social accounting', 'social balances' and 'intellectual capital'. They all refer to the same principle.

In a similar vein, which supports the view that ethical concerns have now moved centre stage in business, the Institute of Chartered Accountants in England and Wales (ICAEW) called on companies in June 1998 to review their corporate governance guidelines thoroughly in the light of the requirement of the new Combined Code on corporate governance published by the Stock Exchange. This is the first structural change to the shape of annual reports for a number of years and provides companies with an opportunity to take stock and to check that their governance disclosures are cohesive, concise and informative. Sir Brian Jenkins, Chairman of the Institute's Corporate Governance Group, commented: 'In their reports on governance, companies should focus on the measures that they have taken to ensure that the right board is in place and that it is working effectively.'

These days, companies ignore the ethical and environmental dimensions of their operations at their peril. Size is no defence; indeed, the public often positively relishes the spectacle of a giant brought down. Corporate power cannot easily be deployed to limit the damage caused by revelations (whether proven or not, whether fair or not) of ethical or environmental shortcomings. McDonald's discovered that much when two campaigners distributed leaflets impugning the quality of the company's products. When the corporate giant won a lengthy court case, the financial cost had been enormous but that was not the worst cost the business incurred. The damage done to McDonald's image by two campaigners (apparently acting in accordance with honestly held principles and representing themselves in court) being crushed, albeit legally, by a global business was even more costly. The only way that a company can securely avoid such a situation arising in the first place is to establish its integrity beyond question through an independent report that addresses head on any concerns that are voiced about the way it conducts its business, the manner in which it treats employees, the sources from which it buys in materials and components or the integrity with which it sells its products and services.

While a few years ago it might have been regarded as unnecessary for a company to justify its ethical, environmental and social performance alongside that of its financial results, the world has changed and some very big players have had to respond. Businesses do not come much larger or better established than Shell. But the oil group found itself in environmental hot water over the way that it planned to dispose of life-expired rigs (the Brent Spar was the rig that brought this issue to the boil) and the perception that it made no effort at 'tidying up' behind its operations in Third World countries. From this, people drew the inference, fair or not, that the business did not consider those countries to matter. At the same time, there were ethical difficulties over its apparent indifference to the human rights of people in countries, such as Nigeria, where it does business. Shell defeated a shareholders' motion calling for audited social reports at the 1997 annual general meeting but has since gone on to publish a new statement of business principles committing the group to act 'with honesty and integrity and respect for people'. Fine words but how would one know whether or not they had translated into operation policy? To meet this requirement, Shell commissioned a social responsibility report and an audited environmental statement, both of which were first published in 1998. There will also be a separate health, safety and environment report on all the group's activities and all its operating companies. The report, to be produced by the group's financial auditors, includes verification of management statements down to the lowest levels. If any evidence were necessary to show that the mightiest companies are coming to realize that the ethical and environmental agenda is not one to be ignored, this would be it. Of course, since then, Shell has fallen foul of another ethical issue, that of overstating its reserves and thus creating a false price for the shares. This has incurred a hefty fine from the City regulator, the Financial Services Authority, and we have once more seen Shell promising to do better next time. Ethical investors may prefer to wait and see what actions support the fine words currently emanating from this global business.

Already, in the USA, ethical fund managers take a proactive stance, investing in businesses whose policies they wish to change, and that investment approach, known as 'engagement', is now available in the UK. It is the view of many leading lights of the ethical investment movement that such a policy would not only have a wider appeal but would also greatly increase both the profile of ethical funds and the notice that company boards took of them.

GENERALLY AGREED SOCIAL AND ETHICAL ACCOUNTABILITY

When a business publishes its financial accounts, performance measurements are taken at preordained points in the operation, which are the same for all businesses and will be presented in an agreed manner to which all accountants have to work. That way, observers and shareholders can compare the financial performances of different businesses knowing that they are comparing like with like. The problem with ethical or environmental standards and social responsibility is that, as with ethics itself, there could easily be as many standards as there are people and organizations practising them. An essential prerequisite for proper auditing is the establishment of generally agreed standards of social and ethical conduct and accountability that carry the same clout as the generally agreed accounting principles do for the financial aspects of an operation. Then, businesses that submit themselves to a social audit under the agreed rules know that they will be subjected to the same scrutiny as others. The outcome of the audit will be respected and will honestly tell them and potential investors how they are doing against generally recognized standards of social responsibility, against their own objectives and compared to the performance of other businesses. It will also provide a framework within which to set their own objectives and the information from which a socially accountable corporate policy may be formulated, implemented and maintained.

The New Economics Foundation, which promotes the inclusion of ethical standards in business and sustainable development, set up the Institute of Social and Ethical Accountability (ISEA) as long ago as 1996 for the purpose of clarifying and agreeing standards against which social audits could be judged. It is this structured and organized approach to social accountability in business, placing it alongside financial accountability, that will get things done. As ISEA puts it in a phrase that reflects long-established management practice, 'what gets measured gets managed'. Having agreed standards of measurement in a particular part of the operation removes any opportunities to hide behind phrases such as 'It depends what you mean by...' or 'It depends how you measure...' and other evasive terms with which we have become wearily familiar over the years. It also makes much easier the task of focusing on improvement and of reporting the degree of improvement achieved.

SO, WHAT IMPACT?

There is no doubt that the success of companies that practise corporate social responsibility reflects a growing awareness in the world of commerce that a policy that puts sustainable development, decent dealings and clean activities at the forefront of a company's mission will be a policy for long-term success. Among the pressures that have brought about this situation is the pressure of shareholders standing up at annual meetings and pointing out the financial risks and long-term costs of particular policies. Only the best-informed shareholders can do this effectively and they tend to be the managers of the large collective investment funds who have access to the research resources that can put a value on corporate activity using generally agreed standards. The more people who invest their own savings and capital through funds whose investment criteria single out companies that follow these policies, the more the policies and, more importantly, the good that they can do will take root in business culture.

The impact of green investment will be enormous and the strength of that impact will bear a direct relationship to the numbers of ordinary investors who express their views in this most effective of languages, the language of money.

11

The advantages of ethical investment

John Hancock

SACRIFICE? NO, THANK YOU!

There is something in our human psyche that conditions us to assume that, if what we are doing is good, then it must be at some sacrifice to our own best interests. Phrases such as 'doing the right thing' and 'taking advantage' express in a few words our whole hang-up concerning how we feel about the cost of acting correctly and the ethics of looking after our own best interests. And it's all rubbish, absolute rubbish. With the possible exception of acts of individual bravery, we do what we perceive as beneficial to ourselves. When calculating the benefit of our actions for others or ourselves we can make two cardinal mistakes.

The first mistake would be always to value that benefit in monetary terms, because some people get their sense of well-being from feeling that they have added something to the sum value of human life and some, it must be said, bask in the glory of their 'sacrifice'. The second mistake would be to ignore the tribal or species element in our psyche. We do not always act from individual motivations but may often act as the one member of the human race, or our 'tribe' (be that family, business, football team or any other grouping), able to do something right now.

So our self-interest may grow from different motivations at different times but we save and invest money in order to achieve a return and some growth. The specific purpose is usually so that, in the future, the accumulated savings or investment will be able to do a job for us such as redeem a mortgage, realize a long-cherished dream or provide for our increasing material needs in retirement and, perhaps, enable us to take that step earlier than might have ordinarily been the case. Given that, there is no sense in placing our money where it will be at any disadvantage or where its performance will cost us any sacrifice, not simply of the money itself but particularly of the purpose for which we are saving or investing it. Unfortunately, socially accountable investment (whether ethically or environmentally motivated or both) has, in the past, carried that aura of sacrifice, which goes a long way towards explaining why, until the mid-1990s, it remained a little-visited corner of the investment market. Equally, it may be the dawning realization that short-term gains are sometimes at the expense of long-term benefits that has begun to raise interest in the sector and seen more investors and, significantly, more fund managers explore the opportunity to think that way. Certainly, the improving performance of the sector as it matures will have influenced a number of people to look further into socially accountable investment. Much of the credit must go to pioneers such as Friends Provident, whose Stewardship Fund set the ball rolling, and to organizations such as Ethical Investment Research Services (EIRIS) and the UK Social Investment Forum (UKSIF), which have made available the information needed to achieve understanding. But do not discount self-interest as a perfectly good reason why investors should consider a socially responsible investment. There are many advantages in investing ethically and some of those advantages are financial.

ORDINARY INVESTORS CAN MAKE A DIFFERENCE

In one company's office, among the certificates and management buzz words on the wall behind the boss's desk, there hangs a framed motto that simply reads, 'The goldsmith's rule: He who has the gold makes the rules.' The love of money may well be at the root of all evil although power, lust and pious incompetence probably account for more of that condition, but money is also a significant engine for good and money certainly does talk. Indeed, it would be hard to imagine a human activity in which money (or the barter of goods and services) does not play a part nowadays. Communism was the only system that ever seriously advanced the notion that money was not required within a society but the system never lived up to its pious aspirations and ultimately paid the price of flying in the face of human nature. Any remaining outposts of the communist system that may still exist will be conspicuous by their failure to meet even the most basic human aspirations. Capitalism rules, OK! And in the capitalist system, the goldsmith's rule holds good.

Companies require capital in order to establish and equip their operation and, to raise that money beyond the pocket of the founder or the inclination of the bank manager, they issue shares in the business. Those shares are purchased by individuals or institutions with capital to invest, and capital is money. Capitalism relies on market forces: where people and institutions believe they can get the best value for their money, to attract capital investment to successful operations and deny it to failing ones. That is an oversimplification but crudely sums up the way the system works. Of course, once a company's shares have been initially issued and bought, the price that people are prepared to pay for them in future trading neither puts money into nor takes money from the business – not directly, at least. However, whether or not investors are prepared to buy the shares of a company reflects their calculation of the likely value of those shares in projected income and growth terms. So, if investors believe that the company has good prospects, they will wish to buy its shares and that will push up the price of those shares whereas, if they feel that the prospects for the business are not so good, they will not wish to buy and may even wish to sell any shares that they do hold, which will push down the share price. If the share price is high and/or rising, the company will have no trouble raising short-term capital (borrowing) or long-term capital (further issues of shares) to fund developments. On the other hand, a company whose share price is low and/or falling will find either that the bank is reluctant to help in the short term or that the price of that help is too high, while new share issues will either not be taken up or have to be sold at a discount to face value. Also, if the share price is low, competitors may be encouraged to make takeover bids. The system works because it tends to support the survival of the fittest in the long term. In this climate, and it is the one that has prevailed across most of the world, companies take decisions and structure their operations in a way that will ensure the share price stays high and rising.

Socially responsible, ethical and environmentally concerned investors can exploit this system to introduce their particular value system into the equation with a result that will be more powerfully effective in the long term than any number of protests. Traditionally, the way for companies to achieve high share valuations and thus, by implication, a high rating of the management team's competence and future prospects, has been to focus on the profit and the dividend that can be paid to shareholders in the short term. And the reason for that is because investors have always seemed to value short-term profit. But there has also been a longer-term consideration by which investors also expect growth in the value of their investment. However, that again has often been linked in investors' minds to an expectation that profits will continue to be high. Where ethical or socially accountable investment makes a difference is that investors do not simply look to this year's profit as a measure of how well the business is doing; they also weigh into the equation the performance and activities of the business in broader terms. So, even where the profit is high this year, if that has been earned wholly or partly from unethical activities – by reducing the value in a non-renewable resource, by making the cheapest rather than the best arrangements for disposing of waste, by poor treatment of employees or any other of the criteria by which socially responsible business practice is judged – socially aware investors who consider the whole picture will not wish to buy the company's shares. If enough investors take that view, then part of what management teams set out to achieve will be to operate in a manner that ensures the company's shares are wanted by socially responsible investors.

And we must not forget that the boards of directors who run companies have to face their shareholders each year at the annual general meeting to explain their actions in the past year and answer questions. Either as individual shareholders or, more likely, through the fund managers who control collective investments, socially responsible investors can raise the topics that relate to the long-term costs of any short-term gains and whether the broader implications of any policy have been considered or whether their implications are included in the strategy to implement that policy. In these ways, by influencing the price of shares with their support or otherwise and by raising issues of real concern at shareholders' meetings, socially concerned investors can make a difference to the priorities and activities of modern business.

At the Kyoto earth summit in 1997, former UK Minister for the Environment John Gummer told delegates that BP's share price had risen following the company's withdrawal from the Global Climate Coalition group of oil companies campaigning against an effective agreement on greenhouse gas emissions. Shell followed BP out of the coalition, a signal, if ever there was one, that large companies can certainly see the disadvantages of not listening to ethical investors and may even be seeing the advantages of listening.

KNOWLEDGE IS STRENGTH

Because of the high profile and extensive publicity given to lottery and competition winners today, we often forget that most success is born of knowledge and, even more importantly, the diligent application of that knowledge rather than luck, although even the most successful investor or fund manager would not be so arrogant as to exclude some contribution from luck in his or her success. This truth extends through life. It is true for the shopkeeper who monitors sales of all lines in order to arrange the display so that, to reach the popular lines, shoppers must pass the rest of the stock or who holds prices on the lines that sell well while loudly cutting prices on less popular lines. It is equally true for the politician who commissions research to find out what concerns the voters and then promulgates that concern as a key priority. And it is certainly true of the investment fund manager.

Successful fund managers use a technique of asset allocation and stock selection to identify companies, investment in which will meet the objectives that the fund has set for itself within the criteria that define it. Thus, if a fund is described as 'Far East Growth', shares will need to be in Far Eastern businesses whose share price looks undervalued in the long term or whose plans are considered likely to deliver an expansion of the business and therefore achieve growth. On the other hand, a 'UK Income' fund will seek shares in UK companies that are expected to return good profits and therefore pay good dividends in the future. This investment method works. Almost all investment fund managers who perform consistently well will cite their asset allocation and stock selection procedures as the grounds for their success. And how do these procedures work? Well, behind every successful fund manager there sits an investment analyst who in turn is backed up by a team of researchers.

In the first place, the asset allocation is not simply a matter of listing all of the shares in a particular region or sector. After all, within the Far East, say, there are many economies whose performances, although linked as are all world economies, are at different stages in the economic cycle, which have different strengths and weaknesses and which are, perhaps, constrained by different regulations, financial controls or cultural attitudes. Equally, within a particular sector, say energy, there will be extraction and delivery systems, even products, that are in the ascendant or are facing a barrage of disapproval, and this, if translated into legislation in the key economies, might affect the share performance of companies whose interests are committed to particular systems or products.

At the level of individual investments, the detailed research is even more important, for, while the broad sweep of information about a region or sector will be reported daily by the press and major investment analysis groups, individual company outlooks that are right for some investors will be wrong for others. If you were looking for income, a business with high growth prospects would not be the right one for your objectives even though it might well be an intrinsically sound investment. So the research that supports stock selection must investigate a number of issues. It is important to know the past record of the business and what trends might be discerned from that record. The fund manager will need to consider whether that record suggests the stock will meet the criteria set for the fund or whether the trend of results, if it continues, will meet those criteria. But, of course, investment success cannot be left to chance and so, even if the company's past record is in line with what the fund is seeking, there will need to be evidence that the management team has not neglected any area in the business that might create later problems and has plans in place to ensure control of events and outcomes in the future. There will also need to be evidence that there are no financial or other issues in subsidiary, parent or associate businesses that might later impact upon the proposed investment. This is very important because fund managers generally like to pick an investment and then stick with it to reap the reward of their own far-sightedness rather than chop and change their holdings. That would be costly because every investment, whether a success or not, starts out using the same amount of research resource, and share dealing costs are the same for good buys or bad.

But it is not enough to have plans. Fund managers will wish to be sure that the business has the resources – both human and financial as well as material and systems – to carry through those plans, which otherwise may be no more than fond hopes. For instance, where change is planned, investing fund managers will want to know that the training is arranged to ensure that personnel are able to get the best value out of the new situation and that the plans include the necessary actions to meet any legislative or market requirements. Then, given all of the above information together with some intuition and 'local' knowledge, a fund manager can put a value on the prospects for the business in terms that would meet the wishes of his or her investors.

That would be the requirement for any fund manager operating in the equity markets. However, for the manager of a socially responsible, ethical or environmentally concerned fund, there needs to be a further raft of information. He or she will need to know whether the business is involved in any products, services or trade that fall outside the fund's social, ethical or ecological criteria. The way in which the business is run with regard to its main stakeholder groups will also need to be well understood and documented. It will be important to know whether the business is likely to face any financial or legislative pressure that might cast a doubt on its ability to continue to operate within the social, ethical or environmental criteria of the fund.

But companies do not operate in isolation and so the research must include some very detailed consideration of the businesses of any subsidiary, parent or associate businesses, not just as to potential financial or litigation problems but also as to what they produce and how they measure up to the socially accountable standards of the fund. There will also be a need to check the conditions under which components are manufactured and the use to which the product is applied after sale. Information technology (IT) companies find this a particularly difficult issue as, while by and large their businesses are clean, sometimes their products are put to military or other repressive purposes. It all means that a great deal of research is needed to be sure that the potential investment is a business that, as far as is humanly possible, operates to socially responsible standards and is prepared to be socially accountable for its actions. Even if it is, fund managers concerned with the moral dimension will then apply exactly the same stringent financial criteria to a potential investment as any other fund manager because nobody would regard poor management of other people's money as ethical.

Much of this type of research is conducted by EIRIS, and many fund managers take advantage of that organization's independent resources to understand the true situation in respect of a potential investment. All in all, ethical and ecological fund managers use more research than others and, while the additional resources used may vary, estimates of 40 per cent more are not uncommon. Also, in the nature of socially responsible criteria, not all businesses will even get on to the list of potential investments. It all adds up to the fact that socially responsible, ethical and environmentally concerned fund mangers will know their investments better than most and that additional knowledge translates into greater investment strength.

IN TUNE WITH THE TIMES

Think what you will about the methods employed by some activists to draw our attention to particular matters, there can be no more sense in destroying the environmental balance on which we depend than in sawing off a tree branch on which we are sitting. And there can be no sense in treating people so badly that they ultimately look for deliverance to systems far more hostile than an investor with an ethical agenda. Just being pragmatic, it is dawning on most people that we need to change the way in which we run our system in order to be fairer to a broader group of people and for our processes to add value rather than simply mortgaging future value in order to live well today. It is called sustainable development, and socially responsible investment fund managers look for it as a sign of far-sighted management. The philosophy of decency and intelligent custodianship of resources is also in tune with thinking in the last years of the 20th and first years of the 21st centuries.

The facts, if nothing else, have driven a change in attitudes. In a 1998 British Chambers of Commerce and Alex Lawrie survey of 3,735 businesses (all sizes, all sectors), over half, 55 per cent, of those surveyed had suffered increased costs and 30 per cent had lost business as a result of road congestion. The survey also found that 'businesses are concerned about the effects of congestion on the environment and are taking action to combat the problem – including staggering staff times and changing the frequency and time of deliveries'. The awareness is there, and an understanding that investors who support the long-term strategy that usually goes with a 'green' agenda will actually help strengthen the arm of those managers who would rather do the right thing. Ethical investors can provide a valuable window on the world for management teams who would benefit from stepping back and seeing the full context in which their business operates.

Companies that look to their social, ethical and environmental responsibilities are generally well-managed companies. Just as fund managers need more information to understand companies in this group, so the management teams of those companies need to look properly at their business and, in so doing, will become aware of more than just these matters of conscience. For instance, if a business looks carefully at the way in which its waste is disposed of, it may turn out that toxic or non-degradable waste is being dumped in a manner that could potentially harm the environment and any people who come in contact with it. While the immediate issue may not be serious, managers might well conclude that future legislation could outlaw that particular disposal process and may even face the business with the cost of dismantling the dump and restoring it to a natural state or of compensating anyone who may have been harmed by the materials that have been dumped. Environmental health and trading standards officials are already able to close plants that are not disposing of their waste in an acceptable manner and insist on the restitution, at the business's expense, of any environmental damage. Also, as set out in the government's 'Waste Strategy 2000', further legislation on these matters can be expected. For instance, the landfill tax was planned to increase from its introductory rate of £2 per ton in 1996 to £15 per ton in 2004 plus the cost of safely transporting the waste to the landfill site. Also, the implementation into UK law of a number of EU directives will soon make environmental considerations part of normal business practice. Once again, examples would be the EU 'End of Life' directives that place the onus for safe disposal of products on their manufacturer, or the packaging waste regulations that charge companies for packaging not derived from recycled materials. So it is already financially as well as environmentally sensible to address the issue now when it is within the control of the company to decide what to do and the timescale in which to do it. That would be preferable to waiting until forced to do something in a timescale determined by someone else with little or no consideration of whether that suits the business or not. But a further bonus might be that, in seeking a better way to dispose of waste, the company might move to recycling waste as a useful material for another process or incineration in a plant that will meet its own costs and might even make a profit from energy production.

Treating workers well, as many companies have discovered, means that ideas for improvement to the process often come up from the workplace. Also, lower staff turnover means that training costs are lower, because fewer people need to go through the process, and then additional training becomes viable, which in turn will improve the running of the business still further. Treating suppliers and customers fairly means that the quality of inputs can more easily be controlled in the context of a long-established and mutually beneficial supplier/client relationship; similarly, customer loyalty takes some of the negative pressure away from the marketing effort so that, instead of working to overcome poor perceptions, the business can work to develop positive perceptions and grow its place in the market. All of this can be translated as quality and efficiency, which in turn mean more money to pay the workforce a fair return for their input and more money to reward shareholders for the use of their capital. Companies working with social, ethical and environmental components to their mission are companies in tune with the future and unlikely to be caught expensively on the hop by future changes in legislation or by changes dictated by common sense.

At the John Reynolds lecture in 1997, Terry Thomas, managing director of the Co-operative Bank, said: 'What shareholders or members want cannot be summed up in a simplistic statement "to enhance shareholder value", since it ignores the issues surrounding how to increase shareholder value across time, not just by the next reporting period.' That is the key: investors who wish to make a profit and those who wish to do the right thing need not have conflicting priorities.

THERE OUGHT TO BE A LAW ABOUT IT!

Most usually, society expresses its requirements as laws and there are a number of legislative programmes rolling forward that will cause expensive problems for businesses that have ignored their social responsibilities. Conversely, businesses that have acknowledged and addressed those issues will find themselves at an advantage. We cannot predict what laws will be enacted in various countries over the next few years but there are some obvious examples of the type of thing we might expect from the international, European and United Kingdom perspectives.

In the first place, the earth summits of recent years may not have changed much but they have begun to change attitudes by publicizing the issues that will impinge on the ecological balance that preserves not just life as we know it but life entire. The limits that have been placed on emissions may well owe much to the poker skills and negotiating powers of the various delegates but the fact that polluting emission limits have been quantified at all is a step forward that acknowledges that things cannot continue as they are. Of course, there is now a market in which countries can trade their emission allowances so that large industrial economies can continue to pollute using the allowances of smaller, less industrialized nations. But that does not change the fact that there is an overall target for emission levels. Far-sighted companies will start now to prepare for real reductions in the levels that are allowed either following the summit to negotiate the next group of reductions or, perhaps, following some environmental disaster. Where would it be best to invest? In a company that ignores all of these warnings, makes no effort to plan and implement cumulative measures to reduce its levels of polluting emissions steadily but consistently and will arrive at any major legislative event unprepared and needing to divert enormous resources to resolve the problem? Or would it be better to invest in a business that makes tackling the issue an integral part of quality management in the organization so that, come any major legislation requirements, the company will be able to continue with business as usual, delivering its normal product or service along with continuing improvements in its environmental performance?

In Europe there are a number of environmental and ethical areas in which the law is taking a stand. Some have been outlined above with regard to waste management issues. Water quality is a case in point where very strict standards for the purity and potability of water have been established, which the water businesses are meeting with steady but quite high levels of investment. Also, in Europe, there is a growing body of employment legislation that places on businesses the onus to work within the parameters of decent incomes for employees, reasonable holiday times, good standards of health and safety and equality of treatment regardless of race, sex or creed. For businesses that have always paid regard to these matters, the new legislation may mean little more than tweaking already sound systems to match the specific framing of the legislation. However, for those that have made no effort in this direction, compliance with the legislation may well require a major programme of rapid development with the costs concentrated over a short period of time and resources diverted from the usual purposes of the business. It is often during such a management crisis that market share and valued customers are lost so ignoring the trend towards more decent business practices is now likely to prove costly.

As regards the future legislative moves towards a better environment and more decent standards of business conduct, it would not take a genius to see the way the world is going and what it might cost those who try to swim against that tide. (The issue of legislation and its effect on business practice is examined further in Chapter 3.)

I FEEL GOOD!

This chapter has tried to set out some of the financial and business advantages for socially responsible, ethical and environmentally concerned investment but it would be remiss not to give space to the emotional advantages of doing the right thing. No matter how much people may be moved by issues related to ethics and the environment, with the exception of a few activists and committed people they will not be prepared to risk their savings, their family's security and their retirement on an emotionally strong but financially uncertain proposition. And this is quite understandable. But if you can see the sense of socially responsible business practice as simply being good business practice, then it is also good to realize that, in committing the voice of your money to that system, you may well be adding pressure to help today. You will be helping to create a business community in which today's added value is generated from skills applied in a quality workplace rather than from raiding the future and depleting at an unsustainable rate those resources that our children and grandchildren will need in order to enjoy their time on earth as much as we enjoy ours. And if that makes you feel good – good!

THE BOTTOM LINE

Socially responsible, ethically and environmentally based investment is not a sacrifice of your present well-being for some ill-defined future good. It is an investment made for all the reasons that one ever makes an investment with the added clear understanding that, in a world of finite resources and where communications are so efficient, sooner or later everybody will know if a company treats people badly or depletes finite resources for short-term profit. Also, in a world where governments are increasingly willing to prescribe standards in these critical areas and fine or tax those who do not meet those standards, doing the right thing is not only morally good but is also good business for everybody.

Appendix 1

Funds' ethical policies and processes[1]

Ethical Investment Research Services (EIRIS)

In order to know whether or not the investment policy of a particular ethical or socially responsible investment fund can closely match the concerns of a particular investor, it is necessary to know what are the funds' ethical and SRI policies. This appendix, supplied by Ethical Investment Research Services (EIRIS) does just that through a thorough survey to which the funds listed have responded. It covers not only the issues that funds consider when planning their investment, and which can be matched to the issues that a particular investor might wish to see reflected (use Appendix 3 to help define this), but also the operational policy of the fund, ie research resources, avoidance/support/engagement policy, voting policy, etc.

The information in this appendix is taken from information previously given to EIRIS through questionnaires sent to the funds. Each fund was given the chance to update or amend these details in early summer 2004. The funds varied in how fully they answered the questions, and this is reflected in their entries.

This section contains a number of funds of funds. These invest in a selection of other funds. Before investing in a fund of funds you should be happy with the ethical policies of all the underlying funds.

ABERDEEN ETHICAL WORLD FUND

Broad ethical aims of the fund

Investments are chosen on the basis of ethical ('socially responsible') criteria. These criteria include approximately 15 screens in such areas as the environment, employee relations, product quality, international operations and human rights.

Development and review of the fund's policy and criteria

The fund's policy has been developed, reviewed and approved by Aberdeen Asset Management's (AAM) SRI team (including the fund's manager, SRI analyst and senior managers). The policy is reviewed on an annual basis.

The fund's criteria have been developed, reviewed and approved by Aberdeen Asset Management's (AAM) SRI team (including the fund's manager, SRI analyst and senior managers).

Are in-house ethical/SRI resources used?	Yes
Is EIRIS research used?	Yes
Other external research resources used?	Yes

LexisNexis.

Positive criteria

Companies which have demonstrated:

- Truthful advertising.
- Ethical policies for employees.
- A contribution to communities and encouragement for staff to do the same.
- A balance of board members, including the presence of independent directors, minorities and women and the disclosure of member qualifications.
- Separation of chairman and CEO.
- Transparency on directors' and executives' total pay packages.
- Commitment to government codes and standards on the environment.
- Conservation of energy, water, materials.
- Disclosure of environmental policies and record.

- Support for the UN Declaration on Human Rights throughout global operations.
- Commitment to ILO standards.
- Existence of an equal opportunities policy.
- Hiring, training and promotion of women and minorities.
- Offering of overtime and fair pay.
- A policy on child and forced labour.
- The existence of a health and safety policy.
- Audits of international operations.
- Offering employee and family benefits.
- Transparency on products' health-related issues.
- Appropriate labelling of products.

Negative criteria

- No producers or sellers of alcohol permitted where more than 10 per cent of turnover comes from alcohol sales.
- No companies testing or commissioning animal tests.
- No companies with a three-year history of antitrust/monopolistic activity.
- No companies with a history of fraud.
- No companies with a pattern of non-compliance with local environmental regulations.
- No companies with significant breaches or heavy fines for water, air or soil pollution.
- No companies with more than 10 per cent turnover from gambling operations or the supply of gambling equipment.
- No companies with continued business in countries with human rights abuses without good cause.
- No companies demonstrating a pattern of engaging forced, compulsory or child labour.
- No companies with more than three instances (over three consecutive years) of discrimination, harassment or health and safety offences.
- No companies with more than 10 per cent turnover from military involvement or military sales.
- No companies with more than 10 per cent turnover from involvement with the nuclear power industry.
- No companies with more than 5 per cent turnover from pornography production or sale.

- No producers or sellers of tobacco products where this accounts for more than 10 per cent of turnover.
- No companies with more than 10 per cent annual turnover from the production/ sale of nuclear/conventional weapons or their manufacture.
- No companies where military servicing contracts account for more than 10 per cent of turnover.

Does the fund have an engagement policy?   Yes

Objectives of the engagement policy

If there is room for improvement in any area of importance to the fund then AAM will actively encourage the company to develop its policies in that domain.

Method of engagement

- Letters to key personnel, such as environmental managers and investor relation managers.
- Telephone dialogues.
- Meetings with staff with direct policy making and/or policy implementation authority regarding SRI/ethical issues.
- Collaboration with other shareholders.

Examples of recent engagement

AAM has engaged with a number of Asian, European and North American companies on SRI topics. No further details given.

Further steps taken when engagement is considered unsuccessful

AAM's policy is to engage continually with companies on important issues. There is no cut-off time period, generally, for companies to make or show improvement in areas of concern.

Does the fund have a voting policy?   Yes

Details of the voting policy

AAM have an arrangement with ISS, the proxy voting service, through which they vote their proxies on a set of well-defined criteria.

Are voting practices disclosed?   No

AEGON ETHICAL FUND

Broad ethical aims of the fund

The fund excludes companies on the basis of the activities they undertake and the products and services that they provide. The negative screening criteria that are applied capture current social, environmental and ethical concerns. The fund is positioned to appeal to investors with strong concerns on particular issues that they are unwilling to compromise on.

Development and review of the fund's policy and criteria

The Ethical Funds' policy and criteria are developed by the Corporate Governance and SRI Department with reference to current market developments. Policy changes would be reviewed and approved by the Aegon Asset Management Investment Management Committee.

Are in-house ethical/SRI resources used?	Yes
Is EIRIS research used?	Yes
Other external research resources used?	Yes

Positive criteria

None applicable.

Negative criteria

The fund is 'negatively screened' and excludes companies which undertake the following :

- **Alcohol:** companies which gain more than 10 per cent of their total business through involvement in brewing, distillation or sale of alcoholic drinks.
- **Animal welfare:** companies which provide animal testing services or which manufacture or sell animal-tested cosmetics or pharmaceuticals; have any involvement in intensive farming; who operate abattoirs/slaughterhouse facilities; are producers or retailers of meat, poultry, fish, dairy products or slaughterhouse by-products.

- **Banks:** companies which are corporate and/or international banks with exposure to large corporate and/or Third World debt.
- **Gambling:** companies which have investments in betting shops, casinos or amusement arcades which account for more than 10 per cent of their total business.
- **Tobacco:** companies which make 10 per cent or more of their business turnover from the growing, processing or sale of tobacco products.
- **Military:** companies which manufacture armaments or nuclear weapons or associated strategic products.
- **Nuclear power:** companies which provide critical services to or are owners or operators of nuclear power facilities.
- **Political donations:** companies which have made political donations greater than £25,000 in the last year.
- **Pornography:** companies which provide adult entertainment services.
- **Genetic engineering:** companies which have patented genes.
- **Environment:** companies which are involved in activities which are commonly held to be environmentally unsound – specifically covering the areas of PVC, ozone-depleting chemicals, hazardous pesticides or who have been convicted of serious pollution offences.
- **Oppressive regimes:** companies which are operating in countries with poor human rights records without established management policies on these issues with due regard to the nature of the activities that the company is undertaking.

Does the fund have an engagement policy?   No

Does the fund have a voting policy?   Yes

Details of the voting policy

Full details are available on the fund's website, www.abetterway.co.uk.

Are voting practices disclosed?   No
The funds disclose their voting practices and reasoning for decisions to clients.

Examples of recent voting activity

Environmental issues were a consideration in how Aegon Asset Management voted at the BP AGM in April 2002.

ALLCHURCHES AMITY FUND

Broad ethical aims of the fund

The Allchurches Amity Fund is an ethically screened fund, established to offer a positive emphasis for individuals, corporate bodies and charitable groups alike.

Development and review of the fund's policy and criteria

The policy has been approved by the directors and Advisory Panel and can be changed with their approval.

Are in-house ethical/SRI resources used?   Yes

Is EIRIS research used?   Yes

Other external research resources used?   Yes

Positive criteria

The manager aims to invest in companies which demonstrate a positive contribution to the quality of individual and community life and which respect the environment. Investments include companies involved in pollution control, waste management, energy conservation, housing, education, home safety, medical and health care.

Negative criteria

The principal areas which the managers seek to avoid are companies with material interests in countries with oppressive regimes, the production of alcohol, tobacco, gambling and producers of magazines or videos of an explicit or violent nature. The fund also avoids investing in companies involved in the manufacture of strategic arms and the use of animals for cosmetic research.

Does the fund have an engagement policy?   Yes

Method of engagement

- Letters to key personnel.
- Telephone calls to key personnel.

Does the fund have a voting policy?	Yes
Are voting practices disclosed?	No

AXA ETHICAL OEIC

Broad ethical aims of the fund

The fund will avoid investing in companies that contravene its ethical criteria (see below for details).

Development and review of the fund's policy and criteria

The investment policy was established at the inception of the fund, following discussions between AXA Fund Managers and AXA Investment Managers. Both parties would be reluctant to change the policy. Any change must be agreed by AXA Fund Managers and AXA Investment Managers, although both parties would be reluctant to make any substantive changes. Either party can initiate a discussion on a change and both parties' agreement would be required.

Are in-house ethical/SRI resources used?	Yes
Is EIRIS research used?	Yes
Other external research resources used?	Yes

Positive criteria

None applicable.

Negative criteria

The fund will avoid investing in companies that:

- Conduct animal testing.
- Derive more than 10 per cent of their reported annual turnover from gambling; or
- Are members of the National Lottery.

- Derive more than 33 per cent of their reported annual turnover from the fossil fuel industries; or
- Derive more than 33 per cent of their reported annual turnover from energy-intensive industries.
- Have subsidiaries or associate interests in five or more countries on the EIRIS Observer ex/Freedom House Category A list.
- Derive any turnover from intensive poultry farming or pig farming.
- Own or operate a fish farm.
- Own or operate an abattoir or poultry slaughterhouse.
- Derive more than 33 per cent of reported annual turnover from the sale of meat; or
- Derive more than 33 per cent of reported annual turnover from the sale of slaughterhouse by-products.
- Supply strategic services for military and/or nuclear bases.
- Are involved in major exports to military purchasers; or
- Have had contracts with the MOD worth more than £25 million in any one of the last three years.
- Derive any turnover from mining or quarrying.
- Own or operate any nuclear power stations; or
- Are members of a nuclear power industry association.
- Manufacture or supply high- or medium-rated ozone-depleting chemicals.
- Publish, print or wholesale pornographic magazines or newspapers; or
- Distribute 18-certificate films or videos.
- Derive more than 10 per cent of their reported annual turnover from the production or sale of tobacco or tobacco products; or
- Derive any turnover from the production of tobacco.
- Sell more than 2,000 cubic metres annually of uncertified tropical hardwood in products retailed by the company.
- Have been convicted or cautioned for water pollution offences more than once in the past three years.

Does the fund have an engagement policy?   No

Does the fund have a voting policy?   Yes

Details of the voting policy

AXA Investment Managers encourage companies in which they invest to place good corporate governance at the heart of their management philosophy; governance issues form part of their dialogue with them. This dialogue includes exercising votes at company general meetings. AXA test meeting resolutions against their policy, although they also expect companies to adhere to corporate governance 'best practice' in their own country. For UK companies, they draw upon standards set down by the Association of British Insurers.

Are voting practices disclosed?   Yes

AXA WORLD FUNDS II – GLOBAL ETHICAL EQUITY

Broad ethical aims of the fund

The fund will seek to invest in companies where ideally a minimum of 25 per cent of revenue is derived from environmentally friendly activities (see below for specific details) and will seek to avoid investing in companies which contravene its negative criteria.

Are in-house ethical/SRI resources used?   No

Is EIRIS research used?   No

Other external research resources used?   No

Positive criteria

The fund will seek to invest in companies where ideally a minimum of 25 per cent of revenue is derived from environmentally friendly activities, including the following:

- Pollution control.
- Waste treatment and disposal.
- Recycling.
- Alternative energy and clean power.
- Water treatment and resource management.
- Environmental consultancy.
- Manufacture and supply of environmentally friendly products.
- Equipment for environmental monitoring.

Negative criteria

The fund will seek to avoid companies which:

- Have infringed environmental legislation.
- Manufacture armaments.
- Manufacture environmentally damaging chemicals.
- Supply the nuclear power industry.
- Carry out animal testing.

Does the fund have an engagement policy?	No
Does the fund have a voting policy?	No
Are voting practices disclosed?	No

BANNER REAL LIFE FUND

Broad ethical aims of the fund

The fund aims to invest in companies which publicly profess their commitment to pro-life values, which supply the basic necessities of life, which provide products and services of long-term benefit to the community and the environment and those which avoid any significant involvement in armaments, alcohol, tobacco or gambling.

Development and review of the fund's policy and criteria

The ethical policy has been approved by the Reference Committee and it can be changed by contacting them. The Reference Committee decide on changes to any more detailed criteria.

Are in-house ethical/SRI resources used?	No
Is EIRIS research used?	No
Other external research resources used?	Yes

- Ethical Investors Group;
- SPUC;
- LIFE.

Positive criteria

It is intended that the trust will consider investing in companies which:

- Publicly profess their commitment to 'pro-life' values.
- Support or sponsor 'pro-life' agencies.
- Provide support for employees during pregnancy and make generous provision for maternity and paternity leave.
- Make special provision for disabled employees and in general provide a high standard of employee welfare.
- Supply the basic necessities of life.
- Provide products and services of long-term benefit to the community and the environment.
- Strive to avoid handling goods produced by exploited labour forces overseas.
- Act to conserve energy and natural resources, and to reduce waste and to control pollution.

Negative criteria

It is intended that the trust will not consider investing in companies which:

- Manufacture, sell, distribute or in any way promote the sale of abortion equipment or abortion-linked pharmaceuticals including RU486, the 'morning-after' pill, and any other pill described as 'emergency contraception'.
- Support or subsidize certain types of human embryo research or genetic engineering.
- Are involved in the provision of pharmaceuticals for or research into euthanasia.
- Are involved in the production, distribution or sale of pornographic material or have been subject to a complaint on the grounds of decency.
- Support oppressive regimes or companies which exploit labour in the Third World.
- Perform tests on animals for purposes other than the benefit of human health.
- Are involved in the manufacture of alcohol, or derive more than 10 per cent of turnover from the sale of alcohol.
- Are involved in the production of tobacco, or tobacco-related products, or derive more than 10 per cent of turnover from the sale of tobacco.
- Derive more than three per cent of turnover from gambling.
- Are involved in the manufacture or overseas sales of armaments.
- Have a poor environmental record.

Does the fund have an engagement policy?   No

Does the fund have a voting policy?   No

Are voting practices disclosed?   No

BARCHESTER BEST OF GREEN FUNDS

Broad ethical aims of the fund

The fund will retain a core investment in the Jupiter Ecology Fund and will support any divestments it makes where the Barchester Fund has a similar holding. Areas of support and avoidance for the fund are outlined below.

Are in-house ethical/SRI resources used?	Yes
Is EIRIS research used?	Yes
Other external research resources used?	Yes

Positive criteria

The fund managers will seek to invest in company groups which:

- Are involved in recycling and/or disposal of waste in a responsible way.
- Have a public environmental policy or produce an environmental report.
- Develop or use renewable energy sources in the UK.
- Have a public equal opportunities policy.
- Manufacture or sell products or provide services whose purpose is to save or protect human life.
- Have clear health and safety systems in place.
- Derive more than 33 per cent of their annual turnover from the sale or manufacture of food, clothing or housing.
- Show a clear commitment to community involvement or charitable causes.

Negative criteria

The fund will avoid investing in company groups which:

- Own or operate nuclear power stations, provide major nuclear-related products or services, or derive more than 5 per cent of turnover from the sale of nuclear-generated electricity or provision of nuclear-related services.
- Have been convicted of a serious pollution offence by the Environment Agency.
- Manufacture pesticide products.
- Are involved in the extraction or growing of commodities in developing countries (this is not an automatic exclusion and a considered view will be taken).

- Have broken the international code on marketing of breast-milk substitutes in developing countries.
- Are major exporters of military products to oppressive regimes or areas of conflict.
- Derive more than 5 per cent of turnover from the sale or production of weapons systems or provision of other services to the military.

Does the fund have an engagement policy?   No

Does the fund have a voting policy?   No

Are voting practices disclosed?   No

CAF SOCIALLY RESPONSIBLE FUND

Broad ethical aims of the fund

The fund invests in companies whose policies are consistent with the global trend towards environmentally and socially sustainable activity.

The fund invests in 'best-in-class' companies which demonstrate leadership in their approach to environmental management and positive response towards social needs and concerns.

This policy largely excludes:

- Companies which are responsible for casinos or gaming; landmine or arms manufacture; alcohol or tobacco production or sale; or serious violations of human rights.
- Electric utility companies generating nuclear power.
- Companies having a controlling interest in a company involved in uranium mining.

The fund adopts a 'triple return' approach, investing in companies which are judged as having sound financial prospects (financial return) and which are among the top 30 per cent in their approach to social and environmental issues within their industry sector.

An environmental return is delivered by companies judged as having superior eco-efficiency and eco-management policies, practices and systems which minimize the environmental impact from processes, products and services.

A social return is generated by companies where management demonstrate progressive attitudes towards their business and its stakeholders. The investment manager looks for a responsible and entrepreneurial culture that influences all aspects of corporate behaviour. These companies develop all aspects of their business, including those not recorded on a balance sheet, such as skilled and motivated employees and a trusted and respected reputation.

The fund may invest in companies making progress towards 'best-in-class' status. Continued investment is however subject to these companies continuing to progress to 'best-in-class' status. This rewards companies that are committed to achieving best practice, and encourages industry laggards to improve.

Development and review of the fund's policy and criteria

The fund's ethical/SRI policy is derived from Storebrand Investments, who carry out research and investment on behalf of CAF. The fund's criteria are developed by Storebrand. Policy and criteria are continuously monitored by Storebrand.

Are in-house ethical/SRI resources used?	Yes
Is EIRIS research used?	No
Other external research resources used?	Yes

Storebrand Investments.

Positive criteria

See above 'What are the broad social, environmental and/or ethical aims of the fund?'

Negative criteria

See above 'What are the broad social, environmental and/or ethical aims of the fund?'

Does the fund have an engagement policy?	No
Does the fund have a voting policy?	No
Are voting practices disclosed?	No

CIS ENVIRON TRUST

Broad ethical aims of the fund

The general rule is that, in order to qualify, companies must be involved wholly or in part in the manufacture of products, industrial processes or the provision of services associated with improving the environment and the enhancement of human health and safety. In addition, companies may qualify if they promote awareness of these issues amongst the general public or are likely to be beneficiaries, in the medium to long term, of changing attitudes in favour of a cleaner and safer environment. Consideration will also be given to companies seen to be making above-average efforts to minimize environmental damage caused by their activities. Furthermore, the Trust invests in companies engaged in certain activities which are considered to improve the quality of life of the population in general or a specific section of the population. This can include areas such as medical, scientific and educational publishing, education and training, electricity distribution, house purchase lending and telecommunications. Once a company has been selected on the basis of the positive criteria, it is screened to establish whether it is active in the areas which the Trust seeks to avoid: (a) animal testing (unless conducted for the benefit of the health or safety of humans or animals); (b) items with military applications; (c) countries where human rights are disregarded.

Development and review of the fund's policy and criteria

Specific matters of policy are developed, reviewed and approved by the external advisory committee. This applies also to the Society's Responsible Shareholding policy and approach to property investment. The Committee undertakes its work in this area with the assistance of reports produced by the Environ fund manager and CIS's Responsible Shareholding Unit.

Environ's criteria were originally drawn up by CIS and were subject to approval and amendment by the advisory committee. It has not been felt appropriate subsequently to introduce any amendments to the criteria, as this would alter the basis on which existing units have been purchased. There is no defined programme for reviewing Environ's policy or criteria. Policy is dealt with as and when issues of concern arise. Policy statements, based on accumulated experience, were published in 1999 and 2001 and a further edition is planned for the near future.

Are in-house ethical/SRI resources used?	Yes
Is EIRIS research used?	No
Other external research resources used?	Yes

Material is utilized from specialist SRI research providers, brokers, etc. General information from the media and other sources is also assimilated.

Positive criteria

See above 'What are the broad social, environmental and/or ethical aims of the fund?'

Negative criteria

See above 'What are the broad social, environmental and/or ethical aims of the fund?'

Does the fund have an engagement policy?   Yes

Objectives of the engagement policy

In its policy of engagement, Environ works in tandem with CIS's Responsible Shareholding policy, which applies to all of the Society's equity investments. It has always been the practice for Environ to raise issues of concern with its investee companies with the intention of obtaining a satisfactory explanation or an undertaking to improve matters. There is a clear overlapping of interests between Responsible Shareholding and Environ, in that both are concerned with good SEE performance; whereas Environ will be required within a short period to divest itself of shares in any companies that contravene its criteria, the application of Responsible Shareholding to all other CIS funds means in these cases that the Society will continue to engage with the aim of improving performance. Broadly, the aim of Responsible Shareholding is to increase social accountability on the part of companies in which CIS has shares, through engagement and by using the Society's voting rights at Annual General Meetings. One central line of approach is to establish which companies demonstrate best practice in a particular sector, and to encourage other companies in the sector to adopt similar practices. In Environ's case, companies that are found not to meet the criteria are removed from the list of companies approved for investment.

Method of engagement

Letters to chief executives, investor relations managers or managers concerned with specific interests. Telephone dialogue can take place as part of the same procedure.

Meetings occur with key personnel as part of the investigations conducted by the fund manager or as part of broader initiatives undertaken by the Responsible Shareholding Unit.

Through Responsible Shareholding, CIS supports joint investor initiatives on matters such as climate change and human rights. These joint initiatives entail collaboration with other SRI shareholders.

Examples of recent engagement

Examples include the following:

- Pfizer's investor relations manager was contacted after the company had been censured for marketing a drug in the UK before receiving regulatory approval.
- Contact was made with WH Smith's retail manager for information on the company's policy on material that is retailed.

Further steps taken when engagement is considered unsuccessful

In the case of Environ, it would be necessary for the company to be removed from the approved list.

Does the fund have a voting policy?   Yes

Details of the voting policy

Under Responsible Shareholding, CIS undertakes an extensive programme in relation to corporate governance, which applies to Environ as much as to other funds. From the outset of the policy, CIS undertook to play an active part as shareholder by exercising its vote on every motion at every general meeting of every company in which shares are held, and regards voting in a responsible, informed and consistent manner by institutional investors to be a fiduciary duty. In general CIS will vote FOR if the resolution is consistent with its guide-lines, accords with best practice and is in shareholders' long-term interests. It will, however, ABSTAIN if the resolution falls short of best practice, but the issue is not sufficiently material to oppose management. Votes AGAINST arise when the resolution is inconsistent with the CIS guidelines, does not accord with best practice and is not in shareholders' long-term interests. In applying these practices the Society takes full account of the Combined Code of Corporate Governance. As a matter of course, CIS informs companies in advance of all instances when it intends to vote against or abstain on any reso-lution proposed by the directors at a general meeting, and is prepared in all cases to explain its course of action. CIS does not necessarily regard voting against the receiving of the report and accounts as a vote of no confidence in the Board.

Most of the opportunities for voting on CSR matters arise through shareholder motions, which are rare in the UK but a regular feature at the AGMs of US companies. Generally, CIS feels that shareholder motions put forward by activist groups can constitute an unnecessarily confrontational and divisive way of raising issues and have more to do with attracting publicity to a campaigning issue than with encouraging the good governance of a company. CIS has tended to vote against the majority of such motions since they are, in its view, irrelevant (as management adequately addresses them already) or they are simply too prescriptive or poorly constructed. As a rule of thumb, they are rejected if they are likely to commit management to inappropriate, restrictive, costly or uncompetitive practices. Nevertheless, CIS does give such matters individual attention and, depending on the subject matter, support can represent a precursor to engagement. CIS has used shareholder resolutions in the past as a means to engage and establish a dialogue with companies such as BP, ExxonMobil and Bristol-Myers Squibb (none of which is approved for Environ). In its own engagement strategy, CIS views shareholder motions as the last resort for investors to make their views known to corporate managers and considers that non-public meetings with management are a more constructive approach to effecting change in a company's behaviour.

Are voting practices disclosed?   Yes
The voting practices and reasoning are published in a leaflet, 'UK Corporate Governance and Voting Policy', which is available on request. There is no detailed information on CSR voting at this stage.

Examples of recent voting activity

- Johnson & Johnson (2002): abstained on motion on drug pricing.
- Merck (2002): abstained on motion on drug pricing.

CITY FINANCIAL ETHICAL FUND

Broad ethical aims of the fund

The fund has a range of negative and positive criteria used in the selection of stocks. See below for further details.

Development and review of the fund's policy and criteria

Are in-house ethical/SRI resources used?   No

Is EIRIS research used?	No

Other external research resources used?	Yes

HSBC.

Positive criteria

The fund will seek to invest in companies which:

- Seek to improve the quality of life of those it interacts with.
- Seek to solve unmet medical needs.
- Have good employment practices.
- Improve the environment.

Negative criteria

The fund will exclude investment in companies which:

- Manufacture or distribute arms.
- Manufacture or distribute tobacco.
- Manufacture or distribute alcohol.
- Are involved in pornography.
- Are involved in gambling.
- Have production systems that cause environmental damage or pollution.
- Carry out unnecessary experimentation on animals.
- Trade with oppressive regimes for anything other than humanitarian reasons.
- Manufacture or distribute nuclear weapons.

Does the fund have an engagement policy?	No
Does the fund have a voting policy?	No
Are voting practices disclosed?	No

CREDIT SUISSE FELLOWSHIP FUND

Broad ethical aims of the fund

The fund has a range of negative and positive criteria used in the selection of stocks. See below for further details.

Are in-house ethical/SRI resources used?	Yes

Is EIRIS research used?	Yes
Other external research resources used?	Yes

Positive criteria

The Fellowship Fund seeks to invest in:

- Companies with a positive approach to the world's resources, with humane treatment of animals and natural food production methods.
- Companies with a positive approach to the environment – conserving energy, controlling pollution, recycling waste.
- Companies with a positive approach to social issues – good employment practices, investing in people, giving equal opportunities.
- Companies which pursue a policy of 'openness' about their activities.

Negative criteria

The Fellowship Fund avoids investing in:

- Companies whose business is the production and sale of weapons of destruction.
- Companies producing alcoholic or tobacco products.
- Companies which have a significant involvement in gambling.
- Companies which print, publish, wholesale or broadcast pornographic material.
- Companies with a poor track record on pollution and damage to the environment.

Does the fund have an engagement policy?	No
Does the fund have a voting policy?	No
Are voting practices disclosed?	No

FAMILY CHARITIES ETHICAL TRUST

Broad ethical aims of the fund

The fund avoids investment in companies which generate significant turnover from certain negative areas (see below for list of ethical criteria).

Development and review of the fund's policy and criteria

The policy is reviewed annually by Family Investment Management Limited – there have been no changes since 1996.

Are in-house ethical/SRI resources used?	No
Is EIRIS research used?	Yes
Other external research resources used?	Yes

Positive criteria

None applicable.

Negative criteria

The fund avoids investments in companies which generate significant turnover from:

- Alcohol or tobacco.
- Export of goods or services for military users.
- Supplying ozone-depleting chemicals.
- Testing of cosmetics or toiletries on animals.
- Using intensive farming methods.
- Extracting or importing tropical hardwood.
- Trade in prohibited pesticides.
- Activities which significantly pollute waterways.
- Ownership of registered companies in a significant number of countries identified as violating certain human rights.

Does the fund have an engagement policy?	No
Does the fund have a voting policy?	No
Are voting practices disclosed?	No

FAMILY PAVILION SRI FUND

Broad ethical aims of the fund

The fund operates a preference strategy utilizing both positive and negative criteria. The process is meant to be positive and inclusive by nature, while the initial screening results highlight specific areas for targeting Pavilion's engagement strategy (which is another component of the overall process).

Pavilion gives roughly equal weighting to the three screening processes applied to the stocks, which are taken largely from the FTSE 350, ie 1) basic business, 2) environmental policy and practices, and 3) social responsibility towards staff, community etc.

Development and review of the fund's policy and criteria

The policy has been approved by Pavilion Asset Management and the Ethical Advisory Committee. There are more detailed criteria available to investors. Pavilion Asset Management in consultation with investors and the Ethical Advisory Committee decides on changes to detailed criteria.

Are in-house ethical/SRI resources used?	Yes
Is EIRIS research used?	Yes
Other external research resources used?	Yes

Positive criteria

Detailed criteria are available to investors.

Negative criteria

Detailed criteria are available to investors.

Does the fund have an engagement policy?	Yes
Does the fund have a voting policy?	No
Are voting practices disclosed?	No

FRAMLINGTON HEALTH FUND

Broad ethical aims of the fund

The fund aims to invest primarily in companies providing health care and has certain avoidance criteria.

Development and review of the fund's policy and criteria

The policy has been approved and can be changed by the manager.

Are in-house ethical/SRI resources used?   No

Is EIRIS research used?   No

Other external research resources used?   No

Positive criteria

The fund seeks to invest in health care, including biotechnology, drugs, medical devices and services.

Negative criteria

Areas of avoidance are:

- Manufacture or sale of alcohol.
- Production or sale of tobacco products.
- Manufacture, distribution or sale of weapons.
- Gambling.
- Companies which do not observe the Animals (Scientific Procedures) Act 1986.
- Cosmetics companies which undertake animal testing.

Does the fund have an engagement policy?   No

Does the fund have a voting policy?   No

Are voting practices disclosed?   No

FRIENDS PROVIDENT/ISIS STEWARDSHIP FUNDS

Broad ethical aims of the fund

Stewardship applies ethical, social and environmental principles to the selection of investments and uses its influence as a shareholder to encourage more socially responsible and environmentally sustainable behaviour.

Development and review of the fund's policy and criteria

The fund policy is researched and reviewed by the ISIS Governance and Socially Responsible Investment (GSRI) Team with input and approval from an independent Committee of Reference.

The fund criteria are researched and reviewed by the GSRI Team with input and approval from an independent Committee of Reference.

Are in-house ethical/SRI resources used?	Yes
Is EIRIS research used?	Yes
Other external research resources used?	Yes

KLD and other European research partners are used on an ad hoc basis.

Positive criteria

- Provision of basic necessities.
- Provision of high-quality products and services that are of long-term benefit to the community.
- Conservation of energy or natural resources.
- Environmental improvements and pollution control.
- Good relations with customers and suppliers.
- Good employment practices.
- Training and education.
- Strong community involvement.
- Openness about company activities.
- A good equal opportunities record.

Negative criteria

- Manufacture and sale of weapons systems.
- Companies whose activities support oppressive regimes.
- Alcohol production (absolute) and significant involvement in retail.
- Tobacco production (absolute) and significant involvement in retail.
- Gambling.
- Pornography and violence.
- Nuclear power ownership and operation.
- Unnecessary exploitation of animals – animal testing/welfare.
- Environmental degradation and pollution.
- Exploitation of developing countries.

- Offensive or misleading advertising.

Does the fund have an engagement policy?   Yes

Objectives of the engagement policy

The fund has an engagement agenda, which aims to improve company activity in a range of social and environmental areas. This is integrated with ISIS's reo programme.

Method of engagement

- Letters to key personnel.
- Telephone dialogue with key personnel.
- Meetings with key personnel.
- Support for certain campaigns.
- Collaboration with other influential shareholders.

Examples of recent engagement

ISIS has engaged with over 1,000 companies in the past year. For full details on engagement activity, visit www.friendsprovident.co.uk/stewardship.

Does the fund have a voting policy?   Yes

Details of the voting policy

ISIS takes established codes of practice for corporate governance as its starting point, but recognizes that best practice will frequently evolve more quickly than any particular code. ISIS will seek to encourage best practice wherever it finds it and not be constrained by the recommendations of any particular code. As far as codes are concerned, ISIS takes as its starting point the Combined Code of the UK Listings Authority section of the FSA, but also guidelines such as those produced by the Organisation for Economic Co-operation and Development. National codes, such as those developed by the Association of British Insurers and the National Association of Pension Funds, are adopted and adapted for worldwide guidance.

Are voting practices disclosed?   Yes
Via the Friends Provident website, www.friendsprovident.co.uk/stewardship. This report shows voting disclosure on all of Friends Provident's fund holdings, which also include all Stewardship holdings.

Examples of recent voting activity

Between April 2003 and March 2004 social, environmental and ethical factors have influenced the way some of Stewardship's US shares have been voted. For full details, visit www.friendsprovident.co.uk/stewardship.

HALIFAX ETHICAL FUND

Broad ethical aims of the fund

The objective of the fund is to invest in companies whose activities are considered ethical both in terms of their primary activities and the means of achieving them.

Are in-house ethical/SRI resources used?	Yes
Is EIRIS research used?	Yes
Other external research resources used?	Yes

Positive criteria

The majority of the portfolio will be invested in the following areas:

- Pollution control.
- Environmental protection.
- Efficient utilization of material and energy resources.
- Clean fuels and alternative energy systems.
- Healthcare services and medical technology.
- Enabling technologies considered to be beneficial to society.

Negative criteria

The fund will strive to avoid investments in companies involved in any of the following areas:
- Alcohol.
- Animal testing.
- Armaments.
- Banking.
- Child labour.

- Fur trade.
- Gambling.
- Links with undemocratic regimes.
- Nuclear power production.
- Polluting the environment.
- Pornography.
- Tobacco.

Does the fund have an engagement policy?   Yes

Objectives of the engagement policy

Engagement activities are conducted as a house, rather than at an individual fund level. The cornerstones of Insight's Investor Responsibility Engagement activities are as follows:

- **Human rights:** working (in consultation with organizations such as Amnesty International) to ensure companies recognize their responsibility for upholding and promoting human rights.
- **Bribery and corruption:** encouraging companies to implement anti-corruption policies based on the OECD Convention on Combating Bribery of Foreign Public Officials, and to bring greater transparency to financial transactions between companies and Third World governments.
- **Climate change:** developing and supporting initiatives to encourage the rapid and effective implementation of the Kyoto Protocol and other international initiatives by the corporate sector.
- **Fair labour standards:** working to ensure that companies adopt fair working practices and employment standards within their own operations and across their supply chains, and thereby meeting ILO standards.
- **Access to medicines:** building on recent voluntary agreements to improve access to medicines in developing countries.

Method of engagement

- Letters to key personnel.
- Telephone dialogue with key personnel.
- Meetings with key personnel.
- Support for certain campaigns.
- Collaboration with other influential shareholders.

Examples of recent engagement

During the first quarter of 2003, ie from 1 January to 31 March, Insight held shares in 83 per cent of all the companies in the UK FTSE All-Share Index. Of those, during this time period Insight engaged with 22.4 per cent by number, which translates to 86.6 per cent by value.

Further steps taken when engagement is considered unsuccessful

Should engagement with a company bring to light information that is relevant to the screening criteria for this fund, then this could lead to divestment.

Does the fund have a voting policy?   Yes

Details of the voting policy

Insight Investment promotes compliance with the Combined Code of the Committee on Corporate Governance and refers to this document when making voting decisions on corporate governance.

Are voting practices disclosed?   No

Examples of recent voting activity

Resolutions raising social, ethical or environmental issues were not submitted to companies approved for this fund. If such resolutions were submitted to UK companies that were approved for the fund, then we would consider SEE issues when deciding on how to vote as a matter of policy.

HENDERSON ETHICAL FUND

Broad ethical aims of the fund

The Henderson Ethical Fund is committed to investing in company shares and other stocks that do not violate ethical principles. In particular, it will never knowingly invest in any company, activity or regime which has a significant involvement in the arms industry, the production or sale of alcohol or tobacco, gambling or pornography, the abuse of human and animal rights or harming the environment.

The fund will specifically seek to invest in companies whose track record has demonstrated concern for the environment and social issues, or whose business contributes positively to society.

Investments will only be made providing the fund's negative objectives are not contravened.

Development and review of the fund's policy and criteria

Are in-house ethical/SRI resources used?	Yes
Is EIRIS research used?	Yes
Other external research resources used? KLD.	Yes

Positive criteria

Areas where Henderson Ethical Fund will seek to invest:

- **Social (positive screens):**
  - Companies which aim to contribute in a positive way to society in general.
  - Companies which offer alternatives to products tested on animals or alternatives to animal testing, or who use humane food production methods.
  - Companies committed to their employees with equal opportunities policies toward gender, age, religion and sexual orientation.
  - Companies which contribute positively to the local community, for example via gifts in kind or community projects.
  - Companies with a high level of openness on all aspects of their business activities and good corporate governance.

- **Environmental (positive screens):**
  - Companies with a proactive approach and a consistently sound record on environmental issues.
  - Companies which are sustainable resource users or are improving their energy efficiency, including a responsible attitude to climate change.
  - Companies promoting the use of renewable energy.
  - Companies with an exceptional policy on genetically modified organism (GMO) avoidance and labelling.
  - Companies involved in reducing overall waste through recycling, effective waste management or energy conservation.

- Companies improving the standard of drinking water or who are involved in the protection of rivers and seas.
- Companies involved in sustainable forest management and timber extraction, such as those recognized by the Forest Stewardship Council (FSC).
- Companies that grow and sell organic produce.

Negative criteria

Areas where Henderson Ethical Fund will not seek to invest:

- **Social (negative screens):**
  - Companies deriving any turnover from the production of alcohol, or more than a third of their annual turnover from the sale of alcohol.
  - Companies deriving any turnover from gambling, excluding spot-the-ball and other prize competitions, such as the National Lottery, which are run mainly in shops or newspapers. We will not invest in providers of the National Lottery.
  - Companies deriving any turnover from the production of tobacco or more than a third of their turnover from the sale of tobacco products.
  - Companies which publish, print or wholesale pornography, including newspapers with page 3 topless women.
  - Companies which distribute cut 18 films or provide adult entertainment television.
  - Companies providing animal testing services, or which test products on animals, even for pharmaceuticals. Companies producing cosmetics and toiletries, including 'own brand', must have a fixed cut-off date policy which includes their ingredients' suppliers.
  - Companies with substantial economic presence in a country where human rights have been abused, unless the company's operations are deemed to be having a positive effect.
  - Companies with a poor track record on any of the following: health and safety, employee relations and working conditions, and advertising standards.
  - Companies who exploit disparity around the world in employment regulations or safety procedures.
  - Companies producing goods or services vital to military operations, weapons manufacturers or the managers of a military base – including combat, communication and training equipment.

- Companies classified as major arms traders by Campaign against the Arms Trade.
- Companies involved in nuclear military activities.
- Companies which irresponsibly market breast-milk substitutes or pharmaceuticals in the developing world.

- **Environmental (negative screens):**
  - Companies which exploit disparity in environmental standards around the world.
  - Companies involved with intensive farming, fish farms or abattoirs.
  - Companies which derive more than a third of turnover from the sale or processing of meat and slaughterhouse by-products.
  - Companies involved in genetic engineering and gene patenting, including medical applications and industrial uses in a contained setting.
  - Companies with poor genetically modified organism (GMO) avoidance or labelling policy.
  - Companies manufacturing ozone-depleting chemicals and companies seen to be taking insufficient action to stop using ozone-depleting chemicals in their own products.
  - Companies within industries which are major contributors to climate change unless they show responsible attempts to address their impact.
  - Companies with a poor track record on pollution (for example, repeated offences or fines according to conviction records received in the last three years).
  - Companies which pollute water supplies, and water companies which do not have an acceptable record regarding water leakage rates, water quality standards and sewage discharge consents.
  - Companies which make PVC or phthalates.
  - Companies which derive more than a third of their turnover from road building.
  - Companies which derive more than a third of their turnover from manufacturing cars or private commercial vehicles.
  - Companies involved in nuclear energy production, or manufacturers of equipment which is needed in nuclear energy production (excluding safety equipment and essential services such as food catering).
  - Companies involved in unsustainable timber extraction, growing or trading;
  - Companies producing pesticides that are banned in more than five countries or which are irresponsibly marketed in the developing world.

Does the fund have an engagement policy?   Yes

Objectives of the engagement policy

At Henderson, engagement is a structured process of dialogue with a company that aims to ensure continuous improvement in the integration of sustainability and corporate responsibility into its overall strategic planning, risk management and corporate governance systems.

Priorities for engagement are selected in various ways:

- Through the ongoing process of company analysis, which will highlight areas in need of improvement for particular companies.
- Through the identification of important sustainability themes, eg climate change or human rights.
- In response to incidents affecting a company, the emergence of new issues, through non-governmental organization campaigns, etc.
- In response to shareholder resolutions on sustainability issues. Such resolutions are common at US companies and are now also being used increasingly by campaigners in the UK; and
- Through the implementation of the corporate governance policy that applies to all Henderson's funds.

Henderson's engagement and thus its expectations of companies are shaped by extensive dialogue with external specialists and its Advisory Committee, and are based on the SRI team's own analysis and judgement.

Method of engagement

Direct engagement is usually preceded by a phase of focused research into a company's approach to the issue in question. Engagement is then initiated in order to encourage specific improvements in company practice. Engagement consists of face-to-face meetings with companies, as well as communication by e-mail and letter. Specific objectives are set for each engagement activity: these may include, for example, the introduction of a formal policy statement and management systems on a specified issue or improved reporting on sustainability or corporate responsibility matters. Progress in each engagement activity is reviewed periodically and reported regularly to clients.

Examples of recent engagement

In quarter 4 2003, the SRI team carried out SRI evaluations of 151 stocks, 85 of which were new companies and 66 where we were updating our assessments. They also met with 52 companies to discuss social responsibility, corporate governance and investment performance issues. A major focus was on the banking sector with the completion of a survey of nearly 40 leading European banks.

Company engagement: Hewlett Packard (HP): the team hosted a conference call with the US IT hardware company involving discussions with key company individuals responsible for directing and implementing the company's corporate responsibility strategy as well as investor relations. This increased Henderson's understanding of the company's strategy on corporate responsibility. Marks & Spencer: the Chairman invited Henderson and a small number of corporate responsibility specialists to discuss its performance and progress. Unilever: Henderson met a main board director to discuss the measurement of corporate responsibility performance.

Research: In November, Henderson presented at a DTI workshop on 'Investing in Sustainable Developments'. Bringing together practitioners from construction, property and investment, the workshop built on previous work by the Sustainable Construction Task Force. The event sought to identify the barriers to, and the drivers for, investments in sustainable developments and also how best to demonstrate the business case to property investors. In December 2003, the SRI team contributed to a public consultation on the ethics of using animals in research. This was organized by the Nuffield Council on Bioethics, which was set up in 1991 to identify, examine and report on the ethical questions raised by recent advances in biological and medical research. The consultation ended in December and the Council expects to report the findings early in 2005.

In quarter 1 2004, 76 companies were evaluated, and Henderson's programme of company meetings also continued with the team meeting the management of 38 companies since the beginning of the year. Henderson's focus in Q1 was on the media and mining sectors, completing a mining sector review where they assessed the sustainability and responsibility performance of UK listed companies.

On the engagement front, there is increasing interest in corporate governance as companies and investors prepare for the 2004 AGM season. Henderson is also leading a collaborative engagement initiative where numerous institutional investors are seeking to improve standards of disclosure by companies on social, ethical and environmental risks.

Further steps taken when engagement is considered unsuccessful

In the event of continuing failure by the company to make the changes they are seeking, votes may be exercised against directors, or in favour of a shareholder resolution on a relevant issue. If a company held in an SRI fund does not demonstrate a willingness to make progress, the SRI team will divest from the company.

Does the fund have a voting policy?   Yes

Details of the voting policy

Henderson expects UK companies to comply with the Combined Code, including the Turnbull Guidance on Internal Control, or to provide adequate explanation of areas in which they fail to comply. Henderson expect companies to follow the principles and spirit of the Combined Code, and they evaluate each instance of non-compliance on its own merits. Where adequate explanation of breaches is provided, Henderson will support management. However, where they judge that insufficient assurance has been given that the arrangements adopted are in the best interests of shareholders, they will vote against management, for example on the appointment of directors or the adoption of the report and accounts.

Henderson expects all companies in which it invests to adopt standards, policies and management processes covering the corporate responsibility issues affecting them. These should be based wherever possible on internationally recognized instruments such as the UN Global Compact; the UN Universal Declaration of Human Rights and the related covenants and conventions; International Labour Organization conventions on labour standards; the OECD Guidelines for Multinational Enterprises; and the Draft Norms on Responsibilities of Transnational Corporations and Other Business Enterprises with Regard to Human Rights. Henderson expects companies to comply with the ABI Disclosure Guidelines on Social Responsibility so as to achieve a reasonable level of credibility.

Henderson believes the Global Reporting Initiative (GRI) is the leading global standard for voluntary corporate responsibility reporting. They also encourage companies to take part in sector and issue-specific disclosure initiatives, such as the Carbon Disclosure Project and the framework set out in the Investor Statement on Pharmaceutical Companies and the Public Health Crisis in Emerging Markets.

Are voting practices disclosed?   Yes
This information is disclosed to clients and their advisers through the reporting process.

Examples of recent voting activity

Henderson abstained on a shareholder resolution at the BP AGM on the management of environmental and social risks and on political lobbying.

At Home Depot Henderson voted in favour of a resolution calling on the company to adopt a more detailed policy on compliance with international labour standards in its supply chains.

HENDERSON GLOBAL CARE FUNDS

Broad ethical aims of the fund

The funds aim to invest in companies that contribute to, benefit from and adapt best to the shift to an environmentally sustainable and socially responsible economy. 'Industry of the Future' companies provide the strategic backbone of the funds. Here, investment managers aim to spot and exploit long-term trends, such as the renewable energy sector. The funds also seek out corporate responsibility leaders.

Development and review of the funds' policy and criteria

The funds' ethical and socially responsible policy is developed by the SRI research and investment team and approved by the SRI Advisory Committee.

The funds' ethical and socially responsible investment criteria were developed by the Global Care team and were approved by the SRI fund managers and analysts in the research team, and reviewed and approved by the SRI Advisory Committee. The investment philosophy and policy towards sustainability is always open to review though there are no 'formal dates' for doing so. Changes to the criteria, however, are only undertaken after careful consideration of the issues and consultation with investors and the Advisory Committee. The criteria of the Global Care funds have been amended in the past to reflect the latest developments in areas of public concern, for example a number of years back criteria were introduced with respect to GMOs.

Are in-house ethical/SRI resources used?	Yes
Is EIRIS research used?	Yes
Other external research resources used? KLD.	Yes

Positive criteria

The following inclusion policy applies for each of the Henderson Global Care Funds including Henderson Global Care Growth, Henderson Global Care Income Fund and Henderson Global Care Managed Fund. They also apply to funds held within the following investment wrappers: NPI Pension Global Care Fund, NPI Pension Global Care Managed Fund, NPI SRI With Profits Fund, NPI Life Global Care Fund and NPI Life Global Care Managed Fund.

Note: these wrappers are closed to new business. Their assets are 100 per cent invested into one or more of the Henderson Global Care Funds, which are OEIC funds that remain open through Henderson. See www.npi.co.uk/globalcare for more information.

Positive criteria

- **Community involvement:** companies active in the community with programmes that may include staff secondment, support of Business in the Community, the Per Cent Club or charitable giving and fund-raising.
- **Education and training:** companies supplying education or training services to enhance the quality of life and opportunity in the workplace.
- **Healthcare services:** companies supplying medical equipment, nursing services, care for the elderly or holistic therapies.
- **Health and safety equipment:** stricter legislation and corporate focus on employee safety has created a demand for equipment that minimizes the risk of industrial accidents and improves workplace conditions. We look for companies supplying specialist equipment or devices that have a health, safety or environmental application.
- **Good employee relations:** companies with good industrial relations records and policies that include, for example, measures to encourage employee participation, support for women and minorities, and employee share ownership plans.
- **Policy statements, audits and openness:** companies with clear policies and systems of accountability, for example those that publish a statement of business ethics or code of conduct, have environmental management systems (such as EMAS) or conduct social audits and make them publicly available, and respond fully to external enquiries.
- **Progressive relationships and strategy:** companies that clearly outline and explain their corporate strategy, environmental implications. Companies which actively promote the interests of staff, such as maternity/paternity leave, counselling services, pension schemes or other welfare services; customers, for example those with eco-labelling of products; suppliers, such as those implementing audits for environmental performance and fair trade; and the public, such as those which contribute to community activities.
- **Effective corporate governance:** companies which demonstrate accountability to their investors and are seeking compliance with the recommendations of the Cadbury Committee on Corporate Governance.

Benefits to the environment:

- **Energy conservation:** companies engaged in the supply of energy conservation services such as domestic or industrial insulation, or electronic energy efficiency devices.
- **Mass transit systems:** companies engaged in the provision of bus and rail services, or manufacture of bicycles, buses and trains.
- **Multimedia and telecommunications:** companies which are directly involved in transforming the use of information, communication or ways of working, including developments in the internet, CD ROMs, teleworking and mobile telephony.
- **Pollution monitoring/pollution control equipment:** companies engaged in the manufacture, supply or operation of pollution control equipment or monitoring devices.
- **Process control equipment:** companies engaged in the manufacture or supply of efficiency improvement devices that provide water, energy or materials savings.
- **Recycling services:** companies engaged in the collection and recycling of waste or which use a high proportion of recycled waste in their products.
- **Water management:** companies involved in the protection and provision of water supplies, or providing water purification services or equipment.
- **Benefit to animals:** companies active in processing or retailing vegetarian foods, or developing alternative textiles to leather.

Negative criteria

The following negative criteria apply only to Henderson Global Care Growth, NPI Life Global Care Fund and NPI Pension Global Care Fund (both of which invest 100 per cent into Henderson Global Care Growth Fund).

Impact on people:

- **Alcohol:** companies involved in the production of alcoholic drinks or which generate more than 10 per cent of their turnover from its sale.
- **Gambling:** companies with activity related to gambling, including the National Lottery and ownership or operation of betting shops, horse and greyhound racing tracks, licensed bingo halls, casinos or gaming clubs.
- **Irresponsible marketing:** companies that have consistently had public complaints upheld against them by the Advertising Standards Authority (ASA) or have irresponsibly marketed products, such as breast-milk substitutes, to developing countries.

- **Armaments:** companies involved in the sale or production of strategic goods or services for military weapons or operations.
- **Oppressive regimes:** companies with subsidiaries or associated interests which support the activities of oppressive regimes, or companies which use forced labour are avoided.
- **Pornography:** companies that publish, print or distribute newspapers or magazines or distribute films or videos classed as pornographic.
- **Tobacco:** companies that engage in activities related to the production of tobacco products or generate more than 10 per cent of turnover from tobacco sales.

Impact on the environment:

- **Greenhouse gases:** companies generating high emissions of carbon dioxide, the main greenhouse gas, including the extraction, refining or distribution of fossil fuels except natural gas, oil exploration and distribution and fossil fuel power stations that use coal or oil.
- **Mining:** companies directly involved in mining or quarrying.
- **Nuclear power:** companies which are involved in the uranium fuel cycle, treat radioactive waste or supply nuclear-related equipment or services for constructing or running nuclear plant or facilities.
- **The ozone layer:** companies that make or sell ozone-depleting chemicals, or users of ozone-depleting chemicals that have yet to set dates for their phase-out.
- **Pesticides:** companies which manufacture, store, wholesale or retail pesticide products in the UK which are on the Department of the Environment Red List, which have been restricted in five or more countries or which have been implicated in incidents investigated by the Health and Safety Executive.
- **Road builders:** companies generating more than 10 per cent of turnover from road building.
- **Tropical hardwood:** companies active in the extraction, clearing, processing or import of tropical hardwood products.
- **Water pollution:** companies consistently exceeding discharge consents.

Impact on animals:

- **Animal testing:** companies which manufacture pharmaceuticals, medicines, vitamins, cosmetics, soaps or toiletries, unless they make it clear that their products and ingredients are not animal tested.
- **Fur:** companies involved in the sale or manufacture of animal fur products.

- **Meat/dairy production:** any companies involved in the production or processing of meat/poultry or dairy products or eggs, or whose primary activity involves their sale are avoided.
- **Genetic engineering:** companies whose primary activity is research into life forms involving the transfer of genes across species and alteration of plant or animal genes for commercial use.

The following statement regarding the negative screening criteria applies only to Henderson Global Care Income Fund, the SRI With Profits Fund, Henderson Global Care Managed Fund, NPI Life Global Care Managed Fund and NPI Pension Global Care Managed Fund: 'Investments will not be made in companies in contentious industries such as mining, oil, chemicals or in companies using animal testing, unless the company can show an outstandingly positive response towards public concerns.'

Do the funds have an engagement policy?   Yes

Objectives of the engagement policy

At Henderson, engagement is a structured process of dialogue with a company that aims to ensure continuous improvement in the integration of sustainability and corporate responsibility into its overall strategic planning, risk management and corporate governance systems.

Priorities for engagement are selected in various ways:

- Through the ongoing process of company analysis, which will highlight areas in need of improvement for particular companies.
- Through the identification of important sustainability themes, eg climate change or human rights.
- In response to incidents affecting a company, the emergence of new issues through non-governmental organization campaigns, etc.
- In response to shareholder resolutions on sustainability issues. Such resolutions are common at US companies and are now also being used increasingly by campaigners in the UK; and
- Through the implementation of the corporate governance policy that applies to all Henderson's funds.

Henderson's engagement and thus our expectations of companies are shaped by extensive dialogue with external specialists and our Advisory Committee, and are based on the SRI team's own analysis and judgement.

Method of engagement

Direct engagement is usually preceded by a phase of focused research into a company's approach to the issue in question. Engagement is then initiated in order to encourage specific improvements in company practice. Engagement consists of face-to-face meetings with companies, as well as communication by e-mail and letter. Specific objectives are set for each engagement activity: these may include, for example, the introduction of a formal policy statement and management systems on a specified issue or improved reporting on sustainability or corporate responsibility matters. Progress in each engagement activity is reviewed periodically and reported regularly to clients.

Examples of recent engagement

In quarter 4 2003, the SRI team carried out SRI evaluations of 151 stocks, 85 of which were new companies and 66 where we were updating our assessments. They also met with 52 companies to discuss social responsibility, corporate governance and investment performance issues. A major focus was on the banking sector with the completion of a survey of nearly 40 leading European banks.

Company engagement: Hewlett Packard (HP): the team hosted a conference call with the US IT hardware company involving discussions with key company individuals responsible for directing and implementing the company's corporate responsibility strategy as well as investor relations. This increased Henderson's understanding of the company's strategy on corporate responsibility. Marks & Spencer: the Chairman invited Henderson and a small number of corporate responsibility specialists to discuss its performance and progress. Unilever: Henderson met a main board director to discuss the measurement of corporate responsibility performance.

Research: In November, Henderson presented at a DTI workshop on 'Investing in Sustainable Developments'. Bringing together practitioners from construction, property and investment, the workshop built on previous work by the Sustainable Construction Task Force. The event sought to identify the barriers to, and the drivers for, investments in sustainable developments and also how best to demonstrate the business case to property investors. In December 2003, the SRI team contributed to a public consultation on the ethics of using animals in research. This was organized by the Nuffield Council on Bioethics, which was set up in 1991 to identify, examine and report on the ethical questions raised by recent advances in biological and medical research. The consultation ended in December and the Council expects to report the findings early in 2005.

In quarter 1 2004, 76 companies were evaluated and Henderson's programme of company meetings also continued with the team meeting the management of 38 companies since the beginning of the year. Henderson's focus in Q1 was on the media and mining sectors, completing a mining sector review where they assessed the sustainability and responsibility performance of UK listed companies.

On the engagement front, there is increasing interest in corporate governance as companies and investors prepare for the 2004 AGM season. Henderson is also leading a collaborative engagement initiative where numerous institutional investors are seeking to improve standards of disclosure by companies on social, ethical and environmental risks.

Further steps taken when engagement is considered unsuccessful

In the event of continuing failure by the company to make the changes they are seeking, votes may be exercised against directors, or in favour of a shareholder resolution on a relevant issue. If a company held in an SRI fund does not demonstrate a willingness to make progress, the SRI team will divest from the company.

Does the fund have a voting policy?   Yes

Details of the voting policy

Henderson expects UK companies to comply with the Combined Code, including the Turnbull Guidance on Internal Control, or to provide adequate explanation of areas in which they fail to comply. Henderson expect companies to follow the principles and spirit of the Combined Code, and they evaluate each instance of non-compliance on its own merits. Where adequate explanation of breaches is provided, Henderson will support management. However, where they judge that insufficient assurance has been given that the arrangements adopted are in the best interests of shareholders, they will vote against management, for example on the appointment of directors or the adoption of the report and accounts.

Henderson expects all companies in which it invests to adopt standards, policies and management processes covering the corporate responsibility issues affecting them. These should be based wherever possible on internationally recognized instruments such as the UN Global Compact; the UN Universal Declaration of Human Rights and the related covenants and conventions; International Labour Organization conventions on labour standards; the OECD Guidelines for Multinational Enterprises; and the Draft Norms on Responsibilities of Transnational Corporations and Other Business Enterprises with Regard to Human Rights. Henderson expects companies to comply with the ABI Disclosure Guidelines on Social Responsibility. as to achieve a reasonable level of credibility.

Henderson believes the Global Reporting Initiative (GRI) is the leading global standard for voluntary corporate responsibility reporting. They also encourage companies to take part in sector and issue-specific disclosure initiatives, such as the Carbon Disclosure Project and the framework set out in the Investor Statement on Pharmaceutical Companies and the Public Health Crisis in Emerging Markets.

Are voting practices disclosed?	Yes

This information is disclosed to clients and their advisers through the reporting process.

Examples of recent voting activity

Henderson abstained on a shareholder resolution at the BP AGM on the management of environmental and social risks and on political lobbying.

At Home Depot Henderson voted in favour of a resolution calling on the company to adopt a more detailed policy on compliance with international labour standards in its supply chains.

HOMEOWNERS FRIENDLY SOCIETY FTSE4GOOD FUND

Broad ethical aims of the fund

Homeowners FTSE4Good Fund aims to track the FTSE4Good UK index, which is independently calculated and based on those FTSE All-Share stocks which meet the FTSE4Good criteria.

Are in-house ethical/SRI resources used?	No
Is EIRIS research used?	No
Other external research resources used?	No

Positive criteria

Aspects of a company's activities that will be taken into account include:

- Working towards environmental sustainability.
- Developing a positive relationship with stakeholders and employees.
- Upholding and supporting universal human rights.

Negative criteria

FTSE4Good exclusions include:

- Tobacco producers.
- Manufacturers of weapons systems.
- Owners/operators of nuclear power stations.
- Those who mine/process uranium.

Does the fund have an engagement policy?   No

Does the fund have a voting policy?   No

Are voting practices disclosed?   No

HSBC AMANAH FUND

Broad ethical aims of the fund

The fund's ethical aims are based on an interpretation of Islamic Shariah.

Development and review of the fund's policy and criteria

The policy has been approved by the fund's Shariah Supervisory Committee and can only be changed with its approval.

Are in-house ethical/SRI resources used?   Yes

Is EIRIS research used?   No

Other external research resources used?   Yes
KLD Associates.

Positive criteria

None applicable.

Negative criteria

The fund will not invest in companies whose primary business activities are the following:

- Arms.
- Alcohol.
- Tobacco.
- Pork.
- Gambling.
- Financial institutions.
- Biotechnology.
- Leisure/media.

In addition, the fund will not invest in companies which exhibit the following characteristics:

- Debt/assets ratio exceeds 30 per cent.
- Interest income exceeds 5 per cent of gross revenues.
- Amounts receivable and cash represent more than 50 per cent of total assets.

Does the fund have an engagement policy?   No

Does the fund have a voting policy?   No

Are voting practices disclosed?   No

IMPAX ENVIRONMENTAL MARKETS

Broad ethical aims of the fund

The fund seeks to invest in companies that provide, utilize, implement or advise upon technology-based systems, products or services that provide solutions to environmental problems particularly the energy, water and waste sections ('Environmental Markets').

Development and review of the fund's policy and criteria

The ethical policy has been approved by Impax Asset Management in consultation with ASN Bank. Changes to the ethical criteria will be decided by the portfolio management team.

Are in-house ethical/SRI resources used?	Yes
Is EIRIS research used?	No
Other external research resources used?	No

Positive criteria

The fund positively includes 'Environmental Markets' companies. For a company to be included in the Environmental Markets universe it has to pass two criteria:

- The technology/activity has an environmental benefit.
- More than 60 per cent of revenues or invested capital is dedicated to Environmental Markets.

Negative criteria

None applicable.

Does the fund have an engagement policy?	Yes
Does the fund have a voting policy?	Yes
Are voting practices disclosed?	Yes

INSIGHT INVESTMENT EUROPEAN ETHICAL FUND

Broad ethical aims of the fund

The fund invests in a range of companies that make a positive contribution to society, carry out good employment practices, protect the environment and make sustainable use of natural resources.

Development and review of the fund's policy and criteria

Are in-house ethical/SRI resources used?	Yes
Is EIRIS research used?	Yes
Other external research resources used?	Yes

Positive criteria

The fund seeks to invest in companies with good human rights and environmental policies.

Negative criteria

The fund seeks to avoid companies that:

- Derive 5 per cent or more of turnover from the production and/or sale of tobacco.
- Derive 5 per cent or more of total turnover from gambling.
- Produce or supply armaments or strategic parts of armaments.
- Own or operate nuclear power stations.
- Provide strategic parts and/or services to nuclear power stations.
- Produce, distribute or sell pornography.
- Have a high negative impact on the environment.
- Harvest or sell unsustainable timber or timber products.
- Test cosmetics or household products on animals.
- Sell non-medical products tested on animals.
- Are involved in the supply of fur.
- Operate in countries with particularly problematic human rights records, unless those companies can demonstrate that they have sufficient human rights policies and procedures in place.

Does the fund have an engagement policy?   Yes

Objectives of the engagement policy

Engagement activities are conducted as a house, rather than at an individual fund level.

    The cornerstones of Insight's investor responsibility engagement activities are as follows:

- **Human rights:** working (in consultation with organizations such as Amnesty International) to ensure companies recognize their responsibility for upholding and promoting human rights.
- **Bribery and corruption:** encouraging companies to implement anti-corruption policies based on the OECD Convention on Combating Bribery of Foreign Public Officials, and to bring greater transparency to financial transactions between companies and Third World governments.

- **Climate change:** developing and supporting initiatives to encourage the rapid and effective implementation of the Kyoto Protocol and other international initiatives by the corporate sector.
- **Fair labour standards:** working to ensure that companies adopt fair working practices and employment standards within their own operations and across their supply chains, and thereby meeting ILO standards.
- **Access to medicines:** building on recent voluntary agreements to improve access to medicines in developing countries.

Method of engagement

- Letters to key personnel.
- Telephone dialogue with key personnel.
- Meetings with key personnel.
- Support for certain campaigns.
- Collaboration with other influential shareholders.

Examples of recent engagement

During the first quarter of 2003, ie from 1 January to 31 March, Insight held shares in 83 per cent of all the companies in the UK FTSE All-Share Index. Of those, during this time period Insight engaged with 22.4 per cent by number, which translates to 86.6 per cent by value.

Further steps taken when engagement is considered unsuccessful

Should engagement with a company bring to light information that is relevant to the screening criteria for this fund, then this could lead to divestment.

Does the fund have a voting policy?   Yes

Details of the voting policy

Insight Investment promotes compliance with the Combined Code of the Committee on Corporate Governance and refers to this document when making voting decisions on corporate governance.

Are voting practices disclosed?   No

Examples of recent voting activity

Resolutions raising social, ethical or environmental issues were not submitted to companies approved for this fund. If such resolutions were submitted to UK companies that were approved for the fund, then we would consider SEE issues when deciding on how to vote as a matter of policy.

INSIGHT INVESTMENT EVERGREEN FUND

Broad ethical aims of the fund

The fund aims to invest in companies whose products, processes or services contribute to the restoration and renewal of the earth's ecology or to a cleaner and healthier environment.

Are in-house ethical/SRI resources used?	Yes
Is EIRIS research used?	Yes
Other external research resources used?	Yes

Positive criteria

Investments considered appropriate for the Evergreen Fund will typically be involved in one or more of the following areas:

- Air quality/emissions control.
- Drinking water purification.
- Energy conservation.
- Environmental assessment.
- Geothermal energy.
- Natural gas.
- Pollution analysis.
- Recycling.
- Site remediation.
- Waste reduction/disposal.
- Waste water treatment.
- Wind power.

Negative criteria

The fund seeks to avoid companies that:

- Produce tobacco products.
- Provide gambling services.
- Manufacture or provide armaments.
- Produce or distribute pornography.
- Manufacture ozone-depleting chemicals (CFCs and halons).
- Manufacture or distribute harmful pesticides.

- Harvest or sell unsustainable timber or timber products.
- Produce, sell or distribute products that have been tested on animals.
- Produce, sell or distribute fur products.
- Produce, process or sell meat products.
- Operate in countries with particularly problematic human rights records, unless those companies can demonstrate that they have sufficient human rights policies and procedures in place.

Does the fund have an engagement policy?   Yes

Objectives of the engagement policy

Engagement activities are conducted as a house, rather than at an individual fund level. The cornerstones of Insight's investor responsibility engagement activities are as follows:

- **Human rights:** working (in consultation with organizations such as Amnesty International) to ensure companies recognize their responsibility for upholding and promoting human rights.
- **Bribery and corruption:** encouraging companies to implement anti-corruption policies based on the OECD Convention on Combating Bribery of Foreign Public Officials, and to bring greater transparency to financial transactions between companies and Third World governments.
- **Climate change:** developing and supporting initiatives to encourage the rapid and effective implementation of the Kyoto Protocol and other international initiatives by the corporate sector.
- **Fair labour standards:** working to ensure that companies adopt fair working practices and employment standards within their own operations and across their supply chains, and thereby meeting ILO standards.
- **Access to medicines:** building on recent voluntary agreements to improve access to medicines in developing countries.

Method of engagement

- Letters to key personnel.
- Telephone dialogue with key personnel.
- Meetings with key personnel.
- Support for certain campaigns.
- Collaboration with other influential shareholders.

Examples of recent engagement

During the first quarter of 2003, ie from 1 January to 31 March, Insight held shares in 83 per cent of all the companies in the UK FTSE All-Share Index. Of those, during this time period Insight engaged with 22.4 per cent by number, which translates to 86.6 per cent by value. More detailed information on this engagement activity can be found in Insight's bulletins, which are published quarterly and can be found at http://www.insightinvestment.com/responsibility.

Further steps taken when engagement is considered unsuccessful

Should engagement with a company bring to light information that is relevant to the screening criteria for this fund, then this could lead to its divestment.

Does the fund have a voting policy?   Yes

Details of the voting policy

Insight Investment promotes compliance with the Combined Code of the Committee on Corporate Governance and refers to this document when making voting decisions on corporate governance.

Are voting practices disclosed?   No

Examples of recent voting activity

Resolutions raising social, ethical or environmental issues were not submitted to companies approved for this fund. If such resolutions were submitted to UK companies that were approved for the fund, then we would consider SEE issues when deciding on how to vote as a matter of policy.

ISIS UK ETHICAL FUND

Broad ethical aims of the fund

The fund avoids investing in companies that do particular harm, and balances the positive and negative aspects of a company's operations.

Development and review of the fund's policy and criteria

The socially responsible policy was developed by the ISIS Governance and Socially Responsible (GSRI) Team, with advice from the clients and approved by the independent Committee of Reference. This policy is reviewed and updated by the GSRI Team, with guidance from the Committee of Reference and approval of the existing clients.

The criteria of the fund were developed by the GSRI Team with advice from the clients and approved by the independent Committee of Reference. The criteria are reviewed and updated by the GSRI Team, with guidance from the Committee of Reference and approval of the existing clients.

The policy and criteria are reviewed on an ongoing basis and as new and significant social, environmental and ethical issues emerge.

Are in-house ethical/SRI resources used?   Yes

Is EIRIS research used?   Yes

Other external research resources used?   Yes
KLD and other European research partners on an ad hoc basis.

Positive criteria

The fund actively seeks to support companies involved in/with:

- Provision of basic necessities.
- Provision of high-quality products and services that are of long-term benefit to the community.
- Conservation of energy or natural resources.
- Environmental improvement.
- Good stakeholder relations.
- Good employment practices.
- Training and education.
- Strong community involvement.
- Transparency.

Negative criteria

The fund aims to avoid companies significantly involved in:

- Manufacture of weapons/defence systems or strategic parts.
- Oppressive regimes.

- Environmental damage.
- Exploitation of developing countries.
- Offensive advertising.
- Nuclear power/production/irresponsible disposal or transport of waste.
- Pornography.
- Alcohol production and retail.
- Tobacco production or retail.
- Gambling.
- Animal testing of cosmetics (applies to manufacturers of end products only).

Does the fund have an engagement policy?   No

Method of engagement

- Letters to key personnel.
- Telephone dialogue with key personnel.
- Meetings with key personnel.
- Support for certain campaigns.
- Collaboration with other influential shareholders.

Examples of recent engagement

For full details on engagement activity, visit www.isisam.com.

Does the fund have a voting policy?   Yes

Details of the voting policy

ISIS takes established codes of practice for corporate governance as its starting point, but recognizes that best practice will frequently evolve more quickly than any particular code. ISIS will seek to encourage best practice wherever it finds it, and not be constrained by the recommendations of any particular code. As far as codes are concerned, ISIS takes as its starting point the Combined Code of the UK Listings Authority section of the FSA, but also guidelines such as those produced by the Organisation for Economic Co-operation and Development. National codes, such as those developed by the Association of British Insurers and the National Association of Pension Funds, are adopted and adapted for worldwide guidance.

Are voting practices disclosed?   Yes

Examples of recent voting activity

Between April 2002 and March 2003 social, environmental and ethical factors have influenced the way some of Stewardship's US shares have been voted. For full details visit www.isisam.com.

JUPITER ECOLOGY FUND

Broad ethical aims of the fund

The fund invests in companies that either provide products and services which contribute to social and environmental improvements or act in a way that reduces the adverse external impacts of their operation or both. The fund will not invest in companies that derive more than 10 per cent of turnover from certain activities. See below for further details.

Are in-house ethical/SRI resources used?	Yes
Is EIRIS research used?	No
Other external research resources used?	Yes

Positive criteria

The fund invests in companies that either provide products or services which contribute to social and environmental improvements or act in a way that reduces the adverse external impacts of their operations, or both. Examples of beneficial products or services include:

- Environmental technologies and services.
- Healthcare products and services.
- Public transport.
- Telecommunication and information technologies.

Examples of beneficial practices include:

- Adherence to health, safety and environmental policy standards.
- Management of operations to ensure minimal environmental impact.
- Publication of social and environmental performance reports.
- Worldwide implementation of codes of conduct for labour standards.

The fund may exceptionally invest in a company that meets the negative but not the positive criteria if the Research Unit believes it can influence the company to improve its environmental or social performance. The Research Unit will answer all questions about the criteria.

Negative criteria

The fund will not invest in companies which derive over 10 per cent of turnover from:

- The manufacture or sale of alcoholic drinks.
- The manufacture or trade of armaments.
- The operation of gambling facilities.
- The generation of nuclear power or the construction of nuclear power plants.
- The publication or distribution of pornographic material.
- The manufacture of tobacco products.

Any company which derives less than 10 per cent of turnover from any one of these activities may be invested in, but only if the Jupiter Environmental Research Unit believes that it makes an outstanding contribution to sustainable development in other respects.

The fund will also not invest in any company which conducts or commissions animal tests carried out for cosmetic and toiletry purposes. A company involved in animal testing on other products, and their ingredients, will only be suitable for investment if the Research Unit believes it has made a substantial commitment to minimize animal testing, and in other respects makes an outstanding contribution to sustainable development.

Does the fund have an engagement policy?   Yes

Objectives of the engagement policy

Jupiter's approach to responsible shareholding is to integrate social and environmental issues into its corporate governance policy, through a programme of constructive dialogue and engagement.

Method of engagement

Most of the Research Unit's engagement is with UK companies through one-to-one meetings with company management or through written communication. From time to time, we may also work alongside other investment managers to take advantage of the combined influence of a wider shareholder group.

Examples of recent engagement

Jupiter engaged extensively with companies during this period and continue to do so.

Further steps taken when engagement is considered unsuccessful

Engagement is considered to be an ongoing process. However, on a case-by-case assessment, a company may be unapproved and subsequently divested from the screened fund.

Does the fund have a voting policy?   No

Are voting practices disclosed?   No

JUPITER ENVIRONMENTAL OPPORTUNITIES FUND

Broad ethical aims of the fund

The fund invests in companies that are responding positively to and profiting from the challenge of environmental sustainability and are making a positive contribution to social well-being. The fund may invest in companies that lead their competitors in respect to environmental and social performance. These are referred to as 'best-in-class' companies. The fund will not invest in companies that derive more than 10 per cent of turnover from certain activities. See below for further details.

Are in-house ethical/SRI resources used?   Yes

Is EIRIS research used?   No

Other external research resources used?   Yes

Positive criteria

The fund invests in companies that either provide products or services which contribute to social and environmental improvements or act in a way that reduces the adverse external impacts of their operations, or both. Examples of beneficial products and services which fall into favoured investment themes include:

- Environmental technologies, most notably in the energy and water sector.
- Waste recycling and waste minimization.

- Public transport.
- The quality of food manufacture.

Examples of beneficial practices include:

- Adherence to health, safety and environmental policy standards.
- Management of operations to ensure minimal environmental impact.
- Publication of social and environmental performance reports.
- Worldwide implementation of codes of conduct for labour standards.

Companies may be rated 'best in class' if they provide products or services that are compatible with sustainable development or lead the way amongst their peer group of companies in addressing the environmental and social impacts of the processes that they operate.

Negative criteria

The fund will not invest in companies which derive over 10 per cent of turnover from:

- The manufacture or sale of armaments.
- The manufacture or sale of tobacco products.
- The generation of nuclear power.

Any company which derives less than 10 per cent of turnover from any one of these activities may be invested in, but only if the Jupiter Environmental Research Unit believes that it makes an outstanding contribution to sustainable development in other respects. The fund will also not invest in any company which conducts or commissions animal tests carried out for cosmetic and toiletry purposes. A company involved in animal testing on other products, and their ingredients, will only be suitable for investment if the Research Unit believes it has made a substantial commitment to minimize animal testing, and in other respects makes an outstanding contribution to sustainable development.

Does the fund have an engagement policy?   Yes

Objectives of the engagement policy

Jupiter's approach to responsible shareholding is to integrate social and environmental issues into its corporate governance policy, through a programme of constructive dialogue and engagement.

Method of engagement

Most of the Research Unit's engagement is with UK companies through one-on-one meetings with company management or through written communication. From time to time, we may also work alongside other investment managers to take advantage of the combined influence of a wider shareholder group.

Examples of recent engagement

Jupiter engaged extensively with companies during this period and continue to do so.

Further steps taken when engagement is considered unsuccessful

Engagement is considered to be an ongoing process. However, on a case-by-case assessment, a company may be unapproved and subsequently divested from the screened fund.

Does the fund have a voting policy?	No
Are voting practices disclosed?	No

JUPITER GLOBAL GREEN INVESTMENT TRUST

Broad ethical aims of the fund

The fund invests in companies that are responding positively to and profiting from the challenge of environmental sustainability and are making a positive contribution to social well-being. The fund may invest in companies that lead their competitors in respect to environmental and social performance. These are referred to as 'best-in-class' companies. The fund will not invest in companies that derive more than 10 per cent of turnover from certain activities. See below for further details.

Are in-house ethical/SRI resources used?	Yes
Is EIRIS research used?	No
Other external research resources used?	No

Positive criteria

The fund invests in companies that either provide products or services which contribute to social and environmental improvement or act in a way that reduces the adverse external impacts of their operations, or both. Examples of beneficial products and services which fall into favoured investment themes include:

- Environmental technologies, most notably in the energy and water sector.
- Waste recycling and waste minimization.
- Public transport.
- The quality of food manufacture.

Examples of beneficial practices include:

- Adherence to health, safety and environmental policy standards.
- Management of operations to ensure minimal environmental impact.
- Publication of social and environmental performance reports.
- Implementation of codes of conduct for labour standards.

Companies may be rated 'best in class' if they provide products or services that are compatible with sustainable development or lead the way amongst their peer group of companies in addressing the environmental and social impacts of the processes that they operate.

Negative criteria

The fund will not invest in companies which derive over 10 per cent of turnover from:

- The manufacture or sale of armaments.
- The manufacture or sale of tobacco products.
- The generation of nuclear power.

The fund will also not invest in any company which conducts or commissions animal tests carried out for cosmetic and toiletry purposes. A company involved in animal testing on other products, and their ingredients, will only be suitable for investment if the Research Unit believes it has made a substantial commitment to minimize animal testing, and in other respects makes an outstanding contribution to sustainable development.

Does the fund have an engagement policy?   Yes

Objectives of the engagement policy

Jupiter's approach to responsible shareholding is to integrate social and environmental issues into its corporate governance policy, through a programme of constructive dialogue and engagement.

Method of engagement

Most of the Research Unit's engagement is with UK companies through one-on-one meetings with company management or through written communication. From time to time, we may also work alongside other investment managers to take advantage of the combined influence of a wider shareholder group.

Examples of recent engagement

Jupiter engaged extensively with companies during this period and continue to do so.

Further steps taken when engagement is considered unsuccessful

Engagement is considered to be an ongoing process. However, on a case-by-case assessment, a company may be unapproved and subsequently divested from the screened fund.

Does the fund have a voting policy?   No

Are voting practices disclosed?   No

LEGAL & GENERAL ETHICAL TRUST

Broad ethical aims of the fund

The objective of the Ethical Trust is to invest in a portfolio of securities of companies whose business conforms to a range of ethical and environmental guidelines. All social, environmental and ethical criteria are included within our benchmarks.

Development and review of the fund's policy and criteria

Legal & General Retail initially developed the Ethical Trust's policy through the use of questionnaires. The criteria on which the investment decisions of the Ethical

Trust are based were originally designed by investors expressing their commonly held beliefs. These views were obtained by conducting extensive research, involving both focus groups and in-depth interviews. The Ethical Trust's policy and criteria are reviewed once every four years.

Are in-house ethical/SRI resources used?	Yes
Is EIRIS research used?	Yes
Other external research resources used? ABI.	Yes

Positive criteria

None applicable.

Negative criteria

The Ethical Trust has been designed to track the FTSE 350 Index, excluding any company that is substantially involved in or causes any of the following criteria:

- Animal testing.
- Gambling.
- Health and safety convictions.
- Human rights.
- Intensive farming.
- Military.
- Nuclear power.
- Ozone-depleting chemicals.
- Pornography and adult films.
- Tobacco.
- Tropical hardwood.
- Water pollution.

In addition, the Investment Trusts, which form part of the FTSE 350, are also excluded as their investment objectives may include companies that fail to meet our criteria.

Does the fund have an engagement policy?	Yes

Objectives of the engagement policy

L&G engage with companies regarding share schemes, remuneration and performance conditions, as well as SRI issues including health and safety and environmental risks.

Method of engagement

- Letters to investor relations personnel.
- Telephone dialogue with CSR management personnel.
- Meetings with CSR management personnel.
- Support for certain campaigns.
- Collaboration with other influential shareholders.

Examples of recent engagement

Thirty-three meetings were held with companies to discuss the risks and opportunities from CSR.

Further steps taken when engagement is considered unsuccessful

If engagement is considered to be unsuccessful, further meetings are held with the company, together with institutions and ABI.

Does the fund have a voting policy?   Yes

Details of the voting policy

L&G vote at all meetings, for which they use the ABI's guidelines on remuneration and SRI disclosure.

Are voting practices disclosed?   Yes
Voting actions are reported on a quarterly basis to pension clients.

LINCOLN GREEN FUND

Broad ethical aims of the fund

This fund invests in the Jupiter Ecology Fund as well as directly in equities. Lincoln has appointed Jupiter Asset Management as fund managers of the Lincoln Green Fund. Jupiter manages the fund with the same ethical criteria as the Jupiter Ecology Fund; therefore see the Jupiter Ecology Fund entry for full details of policy, criteria and engagement approach.

Are in-house ethical/SRI resources used?	No
Is EIRIS research used?	No
Other external research resources used?	No

Positive criteria

See above 'What are the broad social, environmental and/or ethical aims of the fund?'

Negative criteria

See above 'What are the broad social, environmental and/or ethical aims of the fund?'

Does the fund have an engagement policy?	No
Does the fund have a voting policy?	No
Are voting practices disclosed?	No

M&G/SCOTTISH AMICABLE/PRUDENTIAL ETHICAL FUNDS

Broad ethical aims of the fund

The funds managed by M&G are managed according to a specific set of ethical and environmental criteria. It is intended to meet the investment requirements of those investors who, although concerned about investment returns and appropriate levels of risk, feel that social responsibility should play a significant part in their choice of investments. The funds are described as 'light green'.

Development and review of the fund's policy and criteria

The ethical policy has been approved by the team of fund managers in consultation with scheme members. The criteria will be continually reviewed in the light of developing public opinion. For example, a development in recent years has been the exclusion on companies which develop genetically modified crops.

Are in-house ethical/SRI resources used?	No
Is EIRIS research used?	Yes
Other external research resources used?	Yes

Positive criteria

None applicable.

Negative criteria

The investment criteria target first-round 'offenders' through the exclusion of manufacturers rather than second-round distributors of 'unethical' goods. For example, tobacco producers are excluded, but not supermarkets that sell cigarettes.

M&G have aimed to exclude from the fund's investment universe companies which, according to information held in the EIRIS database, fall into the categories below:

- Environment and pollution.
- Health and safety convictions.
- Genetic engineering.
- Tobacco production.
- Exploitation of animals.
- Military.
- Pornography.
- Third World exploitation.

Does the fund have an engagement policy?	No

Method of engagement

While M&G does have an active engagement policy it is focused on corporate governance rather than SRI, although at times the line between the two will blur.

Does the fund have a voting policy?	Yes

Details of the voting policy

M&G always vote on resolutions. These can range from issues such as the adoption of the annual accounts and remuneration of the auditors to far-reaching plans for the reconstruction of a company in which they have a shareholding. M&G consider the issues, meet the management if necessary and vote accordingly.

In instances where M&G vote against a board's recommendation they seek to ensure that management understand the reasons for their opposition and on occasion they will attend a general meeting in person.

Are voting practices disclosed? No

MERCHANT INVESTORS ASSURANCE ETH. CAUTIOUS MANAGED FUND

Broad ethical aims of the fund

Companies eligible for the fund must demonstrate a responsible attitude to the environment and community, both local and global, and practise good worker/management relations and fair treatment for their employees. Organizations associated with certain negative areas will be excluded (see below for further details).

Development and review of the fund's policy and criteria

The policy has been approved by senior management and can be changed by the Ethical Committee.

Are in-house ethical/SRI resources used? Yes

Is EIRIS research used? No

Other external research resources used? Yes

Positive criteria

None applicable.

Negative criteria

Organizations associated with the following will be excluded:

- Armaments.
- Nuclear processing.
- Oppressive regimes.
- Tobacco production.
- Alcohol production.
- Experimentation on animals.
- Environmental damage.

Does the fund have an engagement policy?	No
Does the fund have a voting policy?	No
Are voting practices disclosed?	No

MINERVA GREEN FUNDS

Broad ethical aims of the fund

These funds are funds of funds and therefore the ethical policy is derived from underlying ethical funds in which the funds invest.

The funds invest in any unit trusts listed in the EIRIS publication *Choosing an Ethical Fund* except Framlington Health Fund and Scottish Widows Environmental Investor Fund. The Minerva Green Protector Portfolio also invests in the Gartmore Govett UK Blue Chip Fund or the UK Equity Bear Fund.

Development and review of the fund's policy and criteria

The policy has been approved by Minerva Fund Managers Ltd and is influenced by participating IFA feedback.

Are in-house ethical/SRI resources used?	No
Is EIRIS research used?	No
Other external research resources used?	No

Positive criteria

None applicable.

Negative criteria

None applicable.

Does the fund have an engagement policy?	No
Does the fund have a voting policy?	No
Are voting practices disclosed?	No

MORLEY SUSTAINABLE FUTURE / NU UK EQUITY ETHICAL

Broad ethical aims of the fund

The Morley Sustainable Future Funds' investment philosophy is based on the concept – and goal – of global sustainable development. The Sustainable Future Funds will seek out investment in companies whose core business and operational processes address environmental and social problems such as resource shortage, climate change, world health and human rights abuses. Consequently Morley will seek to invest in sectors such as renewable or low-emission energies, health care, education and waste recycling. At the same time the funds will not invest in those companies or sectors which Morley believe to be in conflict with environmental and social sustainability, such as tobacco or nuclear power. In addition to core business, the investment philosophy also focuses on management vision, process and practice.

Specifically, each company is awarded an SRI rating based on an analysis of both core business and management practices. These ratings define a company's positioning within the Morley Sustainability Matrix, and the matrix itself, through specific cut-off points, defines the range of companies eligible for inclusion within the Sustainable Future Funds.

Development and review of the fund's policy and criteria

The overall SRI investment criteria were developed by the Sustainable Future Investment Team at Morley Fund Management. Each company's SRI rating is updated on a regular basis, with each rating to be ratified by an additional member of the SRI research team. Criteria on individual policy areas are regularly reviewed internally by Morley's in-house research team, but also with the Advisory Committee that consists of three internal and four external members, of whom only one is a member of the SRI team. The advisory committee meets three times a year to consider and review engagement efforts in addition to SRI criteria.

All policy criteria are regularly reviewed by the SRI research team in conjunction with the SRI advisory committee. Sector-by-sector criteria are reviewed by the in-house SRI research team, and three times a year in conjunction with the advisory committee.

Are in-house ethical/SRI resources used?   Yes

Is EIRIS research used?   No

Other external research resources used?   Yes

Positive criteria

See above for a description of the Sustainability Matrix.

Negative criteria

The Sustainable Future Funds' specific SRI criteria are based on Morley's Sustainability Matrix. Each company is awarded an SRI rating, based on an analysis of the company's core business (what it does) and the processes and practices employed (how they do it). This process was developed by the Morley SRI team to provide a clear link between the definition of their investable universe and their SRI criteria. This method also promotes transparency by providing investors a clear vision of which companies are eligible for inclusion in our portfolios.

The matrix approach rates core business on an A–E scale, with an A rating likely to be given to a company whose core business provides a sustainability solution, such as renewable energies, health care or education. Companies likely to be graded E would include those involved in nuclear energy, tobacco or armaments.

Policy and practices are graded 1–5. A grade of 1 would be awarded to those companies displaying the highest standards in areas such as environmental management, human rights and supply chain issues and corporate governance.

Morley's investable universe includes those companies graded A1 to A4, B1 to B4, and C1, C2 and C3.

Issue-specific positioning papers and industry-level sector blueprints are available on request or from our websites www.morleyfm.com/sri or at www.norwichunion.com/sri.

Does the fund have an engagement policy?   Yes

Objectives of the engagement policy

The aims of Morley's engagement policy are to press for improved environmental, social and corporate governance policies. More specifically, the main engagement themes for this year are climate change, human rights, environment and safety, transparency and globalization.

Method of engagement

- Letters to key personnel.
- Telephone dialogue.
- Meetings.
- Support for certain campaigns.
- Collaboration with other shareholders.

Does the fund have a voting policy?   Yes

Details of the voting policy

The funds apply the Morley Fund Management corporate governance policy. This policy requires adherence to the best-practice codes of conduct on composition of the board, tenure of director appointments, and remuneration structures. In addition, the corporate governance voting policy requires UK FTSE 100 companies, and those mid-cap companies in environmentally sensitive areas to publish a robust environmental report as part of the company's annual report and accounts. If such a report is not forthcoming, Morley will vote against accepting that company's report and accounts at their AGM. This leading voting policy applies to all funds under management, extending beyond merely the assets held in the SRI funds. Morley also maintain the right to vote against environmentally or socially damaging proposals where they believe the company is exposing itself to unnecessary risk.

Are voting practices disclosed?   Yes
Through the press and through key contacts with investor relations teams in the companies in which the fund invests.

OLD MUTUAL ETHICAL FUND

Broad ethical aims of the fund

The fund seeks to invest in companies which are responding positively to the challenges of environmental sustainability and are making a positive commitment to social issues which are to the long-term benefit of the community, and those which avoid any significant involvement in armaments, animal testing, pornography, gambling, tobacco or any other activities which are considered to have an adverse effect on health, the environment or human dignity.

Are in-house ethical/SRI resources used?	Yes
Is EIRIS research used?	Yes
Other external research resources used?	Yes

Positive criteria

It is intended that the fund will consider investing in companies:

- Committed to a positive approach to social issues, particularly concerning employee rights and equal opportunities.
- Which support and work with local communities and charitable causes.
- With a consistently positive environmental policy and record.
- Committed to recycling waste products, reducing waste in their manufacturing processes and energy conservation.
- Which offer alternatives to animal-tested goods, or use humane food production methods.
- Which are involved in public transport activities.
- Which offer safety and security products beneficial to the environment and to the community.
- Which invest in the training and development of employees.
- Which provide products or services identified as being basic necessities.

Negative criteria

It is intended that the fund will not consider investing in:

- Producers of alcoholic drinks or companies whose principal activity is the sale of alcoholic drinks.

- Producers of tobacco or companies who derive more than 10 per cent of their turnover from the sale of tobacco.
- Companies which are involved in the production and sale of armaments or products intended to endanger life.
- Companies which manufacture or sell environmentally harmful chemical substances, and those which have a poor environmental record.
- Companies which exploit labour in the Third World and developing countries or trade with suppliers who do so.
- Companies which support oppressive regimes or whose goods or services are to the detriment of the general population in countries with a poor human rights record.
- Companies encouraging degrading or addictive activities.
- Companies which test on animals.

Does the fund have an engagement policy?	No
Does the fund have a voting policy?	No
Are voting practices disclosed?	No

QUADRIS ENVIRONMENTAL FUND

Broad ethical aims of the fund

The fund exclusively invests in forestry projects. The ethical policy embodies the principles and criteria of the Forest Stewardship Council (FSC).

Investments are made in accordance with positive selection criteria, ensuring that they are: ethical, sustainable, environmentally sound and socially pro-active.

Development and review of the fund's policy and criteria

The policy has been approved by Quadris's board of directors and board of advisers. Changes can only be effected with the approval of both boards.

Are in-house ethical/SRI resources used?	Yes
Is EIRIS research used?	No
Other external research resources used?	Yes

Investments are regularly monitored by SGS (Forestry), Oxford, to ensure that they continue to meet the necessary criteria.

Positive criteria

See above 'What are the broad social, environmental and/or ethical aims of the fund?'

Negative criteria

See above 'What are the broad social, environmental and/or ethical aims of the fund?'

Does the fund have an engagement policy?	Yes
Does the fund have a voting policy?	No
Are voting practices disclosed?	No

RATHBONE ETHICAL BOND FUND

Broad ethical aims of the fund

Bond-issuing companies involved in any of the activities outlined by the negative criteria will not be considered for inclusion in the fund universe. Bond-issuing companies demonstrating well-developed policies and practices in at least one of the positive areas will be included in the fund universe, providing they are not involved in any areas of negative concern.

Development and review of the fund's policy and criteria

The fund's policy is reviewed at six-monthly meetings between the Ethical Screening Committee (including co-heads of the Ethical Team) and an external panel representing unit holders.

Are in-house ethical/SRI resources used?	Yes
Is EIRIS research used?	Yes
Other external research resources used?	Yes

Positive criteria

To qualify for inclusion in the fund's universe, companies issuing bonds should demonstrate progressive or well-developed policies in one of the following key areas:

- **Management of environmental impacts.** Companies should have a clearly defined and published policy for managing their environmental impact. This should include: having a nominated board member with responsibility for environmental issues; and monitoring and reporting on progress against key performance indicators (KPIs) in areas such as waste disposal and recycling, consumption of water and fuel, emissions to air, and discharges to land and water.
- **Human rights.** Companies should comply with local and national standards in accordance with minimums set by the International Labour Organization (ILO) and UN Universal Declaration of Human Rights (UDHR). Alternatively, companies may implement their own codes of conduct to ensure compliance with local laws covering child labour, working conditions and health and safety.
- **Provision of beneficial products and services.** Companies should be involved in designing or manufacturing products that have social and environmental benefits. These might include companies which make industrial processes cleaner or more efficient; companies involved in enabling compliance with health and safety legislation; companies engaged in supplying educational products or services; or companies involved in waste recycling or acceptable forms of waste management (excluding energy-from-waste incineration).
- **Corporate community investment.** Companies should demonstrate long-term giving programmes of benefit to the community, either via cash donations or gifts in kind (eg staff time, use of buildings or office facilities). Membership of corporate giving benchmarking groups such as Business in the Community's Per Cent Club or the London Benchmarking Group.
- **Employment.** Companies should demonstrate a commitment to workplace diversity and equal opportunities, as well as facilitating employee work/life balance by offering flexible working, carer's leave and/or childcare facilities.

Negative criteria

The fund shall exclude bonds issued by companies involved in the following activities:

- **Armaments.** Manufacturers or vendors of strategic weapon systems, ordnance or combat vehicles.
- **Environmentally unsustainable or high-impact activities.** Companies involved in mineral extraction, fossil fuel exploration and production, quarrying, agrochemical production, production of genetically modified seeds or foodstuffs, sale of hardwood products from non-sustainable sources, motor car manufacturing, or road building. Also, those companies with convictions for serious or persistent pollution offences.
- **Animal testing.** Companies providing animal testing facilities, or those which use animals in the discovery or development of pharmaceutical or healthcare products; manufacturers or retailers not adopting a fixed cut-off date policy with regard to the testing of cosmetic or household products (and their ingredients) on animals.
- **Tobacco.** Manufacturers or wholesalers of tobacco or tobacco products.
- **Nuclear power.** Companies involved in the construction of nuclear power plants, the generation of electricity from nuclear power, or the handling or reprocessing of radioactive waste.
- **Alcohol.** Companies involved in the production of alcoholic beverages.
- **Pornography.** Companies involved in the production or sale of pornographic material.
- **Gambling.** Companies operating betting or gaming facilities (including casinos, betting shops and internet-based services).

Does the fund have an engagement policy?	No
Does the fund have a voting policy?	No
Are voting practices disclosed?	No

SCOTTISH LIFE UK ETHICAL FUND

Broad ethical aims of the fund

The fund has a range of negative and positive criteria used in the selection of stocks. See below for further details.

Development and review of the fund's policy and criteria

The policy has been approved by the independent Committee of Reference. Fundamental changes are likely to be infrequent, being made in order to reflect any widespread changes in public opinion. Such changes would have to be approved by the Committee of Reference.

Are in-house ethical/SRI resources used?	Yes
Is EIRIS research used?	Yes
Other external research resources used?	Yes

Positive criteria

The fund will favour those companies:

- With good corporate environmental policy, management and reporting systems.
- Making use of wind, wave, solar or geothermal energy sources in the UK.
- With good equal opportunities policies.
- Deriving more than 33 per cent of turnover from the provision of goods or services which aid pollution control or conserve natural resources.
- Deriving more than 33 per cent of turnover from the operation of bus, coach or train services or the manufacture of buses, coaches, rail rolling stock, components and systems, or bicycles.
- Which have met the requirements of the Investors in People scheme.
- Which have at least one woman director on the board of the parent company.

Negative criteria

The fund will avoid those companies:

- Involved in the testing of cosmetics on animals.
- Deriving any turnover from the sale of animal fur products.
- Involved in the research and development of genetically modified food products and ingredients.
- Deriving more than 33 per cent of turnover from high-energy-use industry sectors.
- With significant malign involvement in countries with poor human rights records.
- Deriving any turnover from intensive poultry and pig farming or supply intensive farming equipment.
- Which own or operate a fish farm.
- Which own or operate at least one abattoir, poultry slaughterhouse or poultry-processing plant.
- Involved in the sale or production of weapons systems, including nuclear weapons, or which are major arms traders.

- Which operate nuclear power stations.
- Which manufacture or supply ozone-depleting chemicals.
- Which manufacture pesticide products.
- With pollution convictions.
- Which manufacture PVC or phthalates.
- Which are banks holding Third World debt.
- Which market tobacco products in the Third World.
- Deriving any turnover from the production of tobacco or tobacco products.
- Which import, use or retail tropical hardwood from uncertified sources.
- Which breached discharge consents for a Red List substance.

Does the fund have an engagement policy?   Yes

Objectives of the engagement policy

Constructive dialogue is a central theme of the fund. Efforts are concentrated on those companies where pressure from ethical investors is most likely to have an effect. For example, there seems little benefit to be had from trying to persuade a tobacco company to stop making cigarettes, but there may be more to be gained from persuading a clothing retailer to improve working practices in its overseas factories.

Does the fund have a voting policy?   No

Are voting practices disclosed?   No

SCOTTISH WIDOWS ENVIRONMENTAL INVESTOR FUND

Broad ethical aims of the fund

The fund's investment universe is drawn from companies benchmarked against a broad range of ethical criteria.

Development and review of the fund's policy and criteria

The fund's policy has been approved by the Trustees, the Conservation Foundation Fund Committee and Scottish Widows. Changes to the policy would be the decision of the Committee.

Are in-house ethical/SRI resources used?	Yes
Is EIRIS research used?	Yes
Other external research resources used?	Yes

Positive criteria

The fund will actively seek to invest in the following:

- Companies which use sustainably managed forests to supply wood as raw material.
- Companies which have taken steps to stop the use of CFCs in aerosols or foam packaging, or which have controlled CFC emissions from refrigeration plants.
- Companies which have taken initiatives in the following areas: recycled paper or cardboard, bottle banks/refundable glass bottles, recycling waste, biodegradable packaging, use of reverse vending machines.
- Companies which demonstrate leadership in use of derelict inner-city land, screening of sites, reinstatement of the environment after extraction or development.
- Companies which make efforts to reduce significantly sulphur dioxide emissions, actively prevent or clean up acid rain, look for new production methods to avoid the problem.
- Companies that have achieved a significant reduction in fuel bills by efficient energy conservation, and those who are involved in producing goods involving efficient use of energy, ie insulation materials or solar heating – this could range from the use of lead-free petrol in company cars to companies involved in the production and/or retail of more energy-efficient or more environmentally friendly transport.
- Companies involved in control of emissions of nitrates, oil, chemicals, etc into waterways or the atmosphere; control use of bleaches for paper products; water or sewage treatments.
- Companies which actively avoid the use of endangered species as raw materials, eg for jewellery or cosmetics.
- Companies which take steps to preserve the natural habitats of flora and fauna threatened by developments of that company and others.
- Companies involved in growing, producing or retailing organic produce (to Soil Association standard).

- Companies which actively avoid production or use of drugs or hormones used to promote yields through intensive farming.
- Companies which sponsor environmental projects or have evidence of comprehensive employee health and safety initiatives.

Negative criteria

None applicable.

Does the fund have an engagement policy?   No

Does the fund have a voting policy?   Yes

Details of the voting policy

SWIP's normal practice is to vote on all resolutions put forward at company meetings, whether annual or extraordinary, for the companies in which they invest. Their policy is to support a company's management as long as they are satisfied with its corporate governance standards and its business conduct.

Are voting practices disclosed?   No

SCOTTISH WIDOWS ETHICAL FUND

Broad ethical aims of the fund

The fund's investment universe is drawn from companies benchmarked against a broad range of ethical criteria. Such criteria are agreed with the fund's advisory body from time to time.

Development and review of the fund's policy and criteria

The policy and criteria are agreed between the independent Ethical Trust Advisory Board (ETAB) and Scottish Widows Investment Partnership (SWIP). SWIP meet quarterly with ETAB to review policy and criteria.

Are in-house ethical/SRI resources used?   Yes

Is EIRIS research used?   Yes

Other external research resources used?   Yes

Positive criteria

The fund will seek to emphasize investment in companies involved in the following positive areas:

- Health care.
- Care for the elderly.
- Healthy eating.
- Environmental protection and control.
- Safety and security.
- Third World projects.
- Education.
- Relaxation and family leisure.

Negative criteria

The fund will not, to the best of its knowledge, invest in companies with operations in the following negative areas:

- Armaments.
- Nuclear processing.
- Alcohol and tobacco production.
- Animal experimentation for cosmetics.
- Gambling.
- Sale of fur.
- Pornography.

Companies with strong positive criteria may have a small involvement in the following:

- Sale of alcohol.
- Sale of tobacco products.
- Involvement in oppressive regimes.
- Exploitation of scarce resources.
- Provision of gambling facilities.
- Genetic engineering of crops.

Does the fund have an engagement policy?   No

Does the fund have a voting policy?   Yes

Details of the voting policy

SWIP's normal practice is to vote on all resolutions put forward at company meetings, whether annual or extraordinary, for the companies in which they invest. Their policy is to support a company's management as long as they are satisfied with its corporate governance standards and its business conduct.

Are voting practices disclosed?   Yes

SKANDIA ETHICAL

Broad ethical aims of the fund

The Skandia Ethical is a screened fund that will not invest in companies involved in a range of negative ethical issues. Examples of these issues are environmental damage, human rights and armaments (see below for a full list of criteria).

Whilst the negative screen is generally dominant, positive issues are included in a number of ways. Where a number of companies are under consideration for investment that have passed the negative screen, the positive assessment may be used to influence the direction of the fund (ie to direct investment into the more positive company from the point of view of social issues, environmental management and employee relations).

Environmental issues are examined from both a positive and negative point of view, producing a balanced assessment. In a general sense a 'best-in-sector' approach is used.

Banks are excluded if they have significant corporate lending activities, unless they can meet a range of positive criteria. In practice this means that they must be best in sector on at least two areas from environmental, social and employee relations.

Development and review of the fund's policy and criteria

The policy is formed by an independent committee, which has advisory, approval and veto powers over stocks. There are 10 members of the committee, which meets monthly.

The screening criteria for the direct equity portion of the portfolio are constantly under review and the fund will react to changing circumstances. Criteria changes will be made after discussion between Skandia, the management company and the screening company.

Are in-house ethical/SRI resources used?   No

Is EIRIS research used?   No

Other external research resources used?   Yes
The fund uses Ethical Screening (the trading name of Ethical & Environmental Screening Services Ltd).

Positive criteria

The following positive criteria are used to distinguish between companies IF THE NEGATIVE CRITERIA ARE PASSED. The positive criteria do not override the negative. Every effort is made to assess companies for their positive social and environmental impact.

- **Employee relations:** companies that operate equal opportunities policies or abide by codes of conduct regarding labour standards throughout their operations.
- **Social issues:** companies that provide socially beneficial products and services such as social housing, home care and nursing, etc, or demonstrate outstanding commitment to the communities in which they operate.
- **Environmental management:** companies that apply a systematic approach to the management of their environmental impact through, for example, environmental management systems, auditing and reporting.
- **Environmental products and services:** companies whose products and services produce environmental benefit, such as pollution control systems, waste management and recycling services, renewable energy and public transport.

Negative criteria

Companies will be excluded according to the following criteria:

- **Alcohol:** companies whose primary activity is the manufacture or sale of alcoholic drinks.
- **Animal testing:** companies which manufacture animal-tested cosmetics, industrial or household chemicals, pharmaceutical or healthcare products, or provide animal testing services.

- **Factory farming:** companies involved in the rearing of animals in intensive conditions.
- **Armaments:** companies that manufacture or sell weapons or weapons systems, or provide strategic components or services specifically for military use.
- **Banks:** companies that operate substantial commercial lending operations will be excluded, unless they can demonstrate significant positive initiatives (see positive criteria). For the time being, privatized building societies will be acceptable investments.
- **Gambling:** companies whose primary activity is the operation of gambling facilities.
- **Nuclear:** companies that are involved in the generation of nuclear power, or provide nuclear services to the military.
- **Pornography:** companies involved in the production of pornographic material or distribution via print.
- **Environment:** companies will be excluded where their activities have a significant negative environmental impact, such as mineral extraction, oil and gas production and chemicals, unless those companies can demonstrate positive responses to these impacts (see positive criteria).
- **Human rights:** the fund will avoid companies with operations in developing countries and countries regarded as having oppressive regimes where evidence is held of their involvement, either by collusion or complacency, in abuses of human rights.
- **Tobacco:** companies whose primary activity is the production or manufacture of tobacco products.

Does the fund have a voting policy?   Yes

Details of the voting policy

The fund does not have a separate corporate governance voting policy in its own right, but rather votes in accordance with the corporate governance voting policy governing all JP Morgan Fleming's investments.

The fund and JP Morgan Fleming do not have a specific policy on CSR, but rather encompass this within the JP Morgan Fleming SRI voting policy. Included within this definition of SRI are social, environmental and ethical issues. In accordance with its view of having a positive engagement approach to these important issues, JP Morgan Fleming engages with company management on specific environmental and sustainability issues either at company meetings or by coordinated use of votes.

Are voting practices disclosed?   No

SOVEREIGN ETHICAL FUND

Broad ethical aims of the fund

The investment policy will avoid, as far as is practicable, companies whose activities contravene the negative criteria listed below.

Development and review of the fund's policy and criteria

The fund's policy is developed, reviewed and approved by the Committee of Reference, the Sovereign Unit Trust Managers Board of Directors and the fund manager.

Are in-house ethical/SRI resources used?	Yes
Is EIRIS research used?	Yes
Other external research resources used?	Yes

Positive criteria

The fund will seek to invest in companies:

- Whose products or business activities contribute to the improvement of the environment.
- Which display an awareness of environmental issues and are taking steps to reduce their negative impact on the environment.
- Which have a good employment record, including human rights.
- Which contribute to society generally by supporting local community, national or worldwide projects or charities.

Negative criteria

As far as is practicable, the fund will avoid companies whose activities include links with:

- Oppressive regimes.
- The manufacture or supply of armaments.
- The production of alcohol or tobacco.
- The promotion of gambling.
- Nuclear processing.
- Unnecessary exploitation of animals.

Does the fund have an engagement policy?   No

While there is no written policy, engagement will be considered on a case-by-case basis.

Method of engagement

- Telephone dialogue with key personnel.
- Meetings with key personnel.

Examples of recent engagement

The fund has engaged with companies on employment conditions in the developing world, reducing pollution incidents, improving health and safety records, involvement in defence contracts, involvement in the nuclear cycle.

Further steps taken when engagement is considered unsuccessful

This is considered on a case-by-case basis. Ultimately the stock could be sold.

Does the fund have a voting policy?   No

Details of the voting policy

No policy; voting is carried out on a case-by-case basis.

Are voting practices disclosed?   No

Examples of recent voting activity

The fund has voted on remuneration, acquisition strategy, political donations and lack of pre-emption rights.

STANDARD LIFE ETHICAL FUNDS

Broad ethical aims of the fund

The fund aims to avoid investing in companies which could seriously harm the environment, the planet or its inhabitants. The fund has a range of negative and positive criteria used in the selection of stocks. See below for further details.

Are in-house ethical/SRI resources used?	Yes
Is EIRIS research used?	Yes
Other external research resources used?	No

Positive criteria

The funds seek to invest in companies which:

- Make a positive contribution to the environment.
- Promote good employment practices.
- Promote products and services which benefit the environment or human life, or which are basic necessities.
- Donate to charities or are strongly involved in the community.

Negative criteria

The funds will not invest in those companies:

- Which supply ozone-depleting chemicals.
- Which manufacture pesticide products.
- Which have been convicted for environmental pollution.
- Whose products or their ingredients have been tested on animals.
- Which carry out genetic engineering of crops or animals or which patent genes.
- Which use intensive farming methods, produce intensive farming equipment or own or operate a fish farm.
- Which operate in two or more countries with poor human rights records, unless they have policies on human rights.
- Which publish, print, distribute or wholesale pornographic magazines or films.
- Which produce or sell weapons, including nuclear weapons.
- Which own or operate nuclear power stations.
- Which derive 10 per cent or more of turnover from alcohol production.
- Which derive 10 per cent or more of turnover from gambling.

Does the fund have an engagement policy?	Yes

Objectives of the engagement policy

The fund has the same engagement policy that applies to all Standard Life funds. The aim of the policy is to encourage best practice standards in the management of social and environmental issues.

Method of engagement

Company meetings and correspondence.

Examples of recent engagement

Standard Life recently engaged with clothing retailers to encourage the adoption of standards, which were developed by the Ethical Trading Initiative for management of labour standards in the supply chains.

Further steps taken when engagement is considered unsuccessful

If a company does not conform to the ethical policy the holding is sold.

Does the fund have a voting policy?   Yes

Details of the voting policy

All shares are voted – see below.

Are voting practices disclosed?   Yes

Examples of recent voting activity

Standard Life (SL) voted the funds' shares in favour of most resolutions at shareholder meetings during the year ending 29 February 2004. At BP and Surfcontrol, however, SL voted against resolutions to approve the remuneration report. SL also voted against the re-election of a director at BG and abstained on a resolution seeking approval to incur political expenditure.

Note

[1]   © Copyright EIRIS, October 2004.

Appendix 2

The performance of ethical, environmental and SRI funds

Standard & Poor's

"Value at 1 October 2004 of £1,000.00 invested on..." 1/10/2001

	General Sector	Launch Date	Fund Size £ million	1/9/2004 £ Value	1/9/2004 % Chg	1/9/2004 Rank	2/8/2004 £Value	2/8/2004 % Chg	2/8/2004 Rank	1/7/2004 £ Value	1/7/2004 % Chg	1/7/2004 Rank	1/4/2004 £ Value	1/4/2004 % Chg	1/4/2004 Rank	1/10/2003 £ Value	1/10/2003 % Chg	1/10/2003 Rank	1/10/2002 £Value	1/10/2002 % Chg	1/10/2002 Rank	1/10/2001 £ Value	1/10/2001 % Chg	1/10/2001 Rank	1/10/1999 £ Value	1/10/1999 % Chg	1/10/1999 Rank	1/10/1997 £ Value	1/10/1997 % Chg	1/10/1997 Rank	3/10/1994 £Value	3/10/1994 % Chg	3/10/1994 Rank	1/10/2004 Volatility
UK SRI Unit Trusts/OEICs																																		
Aberdeen Ethical World Inc	Ethical Global	21/5/1999	29.58	1020.80	2.08	28	1039.10	3.91	23	1005.00	0.50	22	1037.30	3.73	10	1129.50	12.95	14	1310.30	31.03	18	1109.00	10.90	12	878.50	−12.15	18	–	N/A	–	–	N/A	–	4.50
AEGON Ethical A	Ethical UK	17/4/1989	45.44	1036.00	3.60	6	1051.40	5.14	2	1017.20	1.72	9	1027.40	2.74	19	1155.30	15.53	4	1395.80	39.58	4	1148.50	14.85	7	932.20	−6.78	13	1124.70	12.47	9	1815.70	81.57	8	4.89
AEGON Ethical Income Inc	Fixed Income GBP-Corporate	28/4/2000	19.09	1016.20	1.62	35	1037.00	3.70	25	1040.70	4.07	2	1028.10	2.81	18	1059.70	5.97	32	1125.40	12.54	35	1197.20	19.72	3	–	N/A	–	–	N/A	–	–	N/A	–	1.43
Allchurches Amity A	Ethical UK	10/2/1988	1.11	1029.70	2.97	13	1043.60	4.36	14	1015.30	1.53	11	1032.80	3.28	14	1144.30	14.43	5	1318.80	31.88	15	1158.20	15.82	5	1073.30	7.33	3	1153.40	15.34	8	1855.00	85.50	6	4.09
AXA Ethical B	Ethical UK	5/5/1998	25.53	1037.00	3.70	4	1046.40	4.64	8	996.00	−0.40	30	1000.40	0.04	32	1132.50	13.25	11	1314.90	31.49	16	1021.30	2.13	24	864.30	−13.57	21	–	N/A	–	–	N/A	–	5.62
Banner Real Life A Acc	Ethical UK	22/9/1998	3.67	1027.90	2.79	18	1040.50	4.05	19	1013.10	1.31	13	1033.90	3.39	13	1121.00	12.10	19	1336.30	33.63	12	1080.90	8.09	15	1065.60	6.56	4	–	N/A	–	–	N/A	–	4.60
CF Ethical Inc	Ethical Global	16/11/1988	1.52	1049.70	4.97	1	1040.30	4.03	20	978.10	−2.19	40	981.60	−1.84	39	1028.20	2.82	38	1103.10	10.31	39	955.70	−4.43	31	1011.00	1.10	8	960.30	−3.97	15	1406.30	40.63	12	3.80
CIS Environ	Ecology Global	28/5/1990	96.27	1040.30	4.03	3	1047.20	4.72	7	1014.00	1.40	12	1046.00	4.60	4	1131.90	13.19	12	1303.80	30.38	19	1005.50	0.55	28	801.80	−19.82	24	966.10	−3.39	14	1487.60	48.76	11	4.08
CIS UK FTSE4Good Tracker	Equity United Kingdom	29/9/2003	17.35	1032.40	3.24	8	1049.30	4.93	5	1029.40	2.94	6	1054.40	5.44	3	1085.00	8.50	26	–	N/A	–	–	N/A	–	–	N/A	–	–	N/A	–	–	N/A	–	N/A
Credit Suisse Fellowship Rtl	Ethical UK	7/7/1986	71.34	1036.70	3.67	5	1049.80	4.98	4	1015.50	1.55	10	1038.80	3.88	8	1133.30	13.33	10	1321.90	32.19	14	1092.60	9.26	14	915.60	−8.44	15	1047.40	4.74	10	1929.40	92.94	5	4.70
Family Charities Ethical	Ethical UK	31/3/1982	17.21	1030.70	3.07	11	1039.20	3.92	22	991.20	−0.88	33	967.20	−3.28	40	1052.90	5.29	36	1243.00	24.30	27	1020.00	2.00	25	866.50	−13.35	20	1220.20	22.02	7	1847.60	84.76	7	4.28
Halifax Ethical A	Ethical Global	4/1/1994	39.99	1017.30	1.73	34	1020.90	2.09	42	973.90	−2.61	42	999.70	−0.03	34	1056.80	5.68	34	1245.10	24.51	26	981.10	−1.89	29	995.90	−0.41	11	1316.90	31.69	3	1724.50	72.45	9	4.91
Henderson Ethical A	Ethical Global	23/1/1995	54.46	1016.10	1.61	36	1027.70	2.77	37	976.80	−2.32	41	956.00	−4.40	42	1010.40	1.04	42	1118.40	11.84	37	847.50	−15.25	36	690.10	−30.99	28	958.10	−4.19	16	–	N/A	–	4.79
Henderson Glbl Care Grth Rtl	Ethical Global	1/8/1991	191.10	1019.00	1.90	31	1031.90	3.19	33	981.60	−1.84	37	958.90	−4.11	41	1015.00	1.50	41	1144.80	14.48	34	857.80	−14.22	34	699.20	−30.08	27	856.60	−14.34	18	1375.10	37.51	13	4.88
Henderson Glbl Care Inc Rtl	Equity United Kingdom Income	3/7/1995	100.57	1032.20	3.22	9	1049.90	4.99	3	1029.60	2.96	5	1081.20	8.12	1	1137.70	13.77	7	1334.90	33.49	13	1067.20	6.72	18	1021.30	2.13	6	1437.10	43.71	2	–	N/A	–	4.05
Henderson Glbl Care Mgd Rtl	Asset Alloc Global Dynamic	29/7/2002	427.97	1026.10	2.61	21	1041.10	4.11	18	1011.30	1.13	15	1030.00	3.00	16	1068.10	6.81	30	1194.30	19.43	30	–	N/A	–	–	N/A	–	–	N/A	–	–	N/A	–	N/A
Insight Inv Eur Ethical Rtl	Ethical UK	1/11/2000	35.98	1029.10	2.91	15	1042.80	4.28	16	1004.60	0.46	24	1028.10	2.81	17	1127.40	12.74	15	1313.60	31.36	17	1149.80	14.98	6	–	N/A	–	–	N/A	–	–	N/A	–	4.30
Insight Inv Evergreen Rtl	Ecology Global	10/2/1990	24.74	1022.00	2.20	26	1025.50	2.55	38	979.80	−2.02	39	1000.80	0.08	31	1063.10	6.31	31	1260.40	26.04	24	1031.80	3.18	22	1012.50	1.25	7	946.20	−5.38	17	1224.00	22.40	15	4.75
ISIS Stewardship Gth SC1 Inc	Ethical UK	1/6/1984	540.80	1028.10	2.81	17	1042.50	4.25	17	1004.50	0.45	25	1037.90	3.79	9	1178.00	17.80	1	1439.70	43.97	1	1188.10	18.81	4	1005.40	0.54	9	1250.20	25.02	6	2002.00	100.20	4	4.37
ISIS Stewardship Inc SC1 Inc	Equity United Kingdom Income	13/10/1987	139.90	1011.70	1.17	40	1035.70	3.57	29	1011.90	1.19	14	1042.00	4.20	6	1170.90	17.09	3	1422.20	42.22	2	1432.70	43.27	1	1443.90	44.39	1	1761.60	76.16	1	2270.60	127.06	1	3.02
ISIS Stewardship Intl SC1 Inc	Ethical Global	13/10/1987	73.50	1019.10	1.91	29	1032.30	3.23	32	994.40	−0.56	31	1036.50	3.65	11	1094.90	9.49	24	1271.00	27.10	23	1008.90	0.89	26	791.50	−20.85	25	–	N/A	–	–	N/A	–	4.64
ISIS UK Ethical SC2 Inc	Ethical UK	14/10/1996	29.10	1026.80	2.68	19	1047.80	4.78	6	1023.70	2.37	7	1045.00	4.50	5	1136.20	13.62	8	1290.90	29.09	21	961.00	−3.90	30	831.90	−16.81	23	990.50	−0.95	13	–	N/A	–	4.93
Jupiter Ecology	Ecology Global	31/3/1988	115.23	1030.20	3.02	12	1022.30	2.23	41	986.80	−1.32	35	992.20	−0.78	36	1058.80	5.88	33	1115.50	11.55	38	857.40	−14.26	35	835.90	−16.41	22	1040.80	4.08	11	1602.10	60.21	10	5.09
Jupiter Environmental Opps	Ecology UK	22/11/1999	19.73	1026.30	2.63	20	1031.40	3.14	34	1010.40	1.04	16	1002.70	0.27	30	1095.80	9.58	23	1272.90	27.29	22	1068.40	6.84	17	–	N/A	–	–	N/A	–	–	N/A	–	4.33
L&G Ethical Inc	Ethical UK	5/7/1999	33.59	1023.50	2.35	23	1045.90	4.59	12	1008.00	0.80	19	1024.00	2.40	23	1144.00	14.40	6	1369.30	36.93	5	1113.30	11.33	11	866.60	−13.34	19	–	N/A	–	–	N/A	–	5.33
Morley SF Absolute Growth	Asset Alloc Global Flexible	19/2/2001	9.12	1023.40	2.34	25	1030.60	3.06	36	983.00	−1.70	36	981.70	−1.83	38	1091.90	9.19	25	1303.80	30.38	20	1033.20	3.32	21	–	N/A	–	–	N/A	–	–	N/A	–	5.98
Morley SF Corporate Bond	Fixed Income GBP-Corporate	19/2/2001	77.74	1015.00	1.50	37	1035.90	3.59	28	1042.30	4.23	1	1031.70	3.17	15	1070.40	7.04	29	1183.00	18.30	31	1241.50	24.15	2	–	N/A	–	–	N/A	–	–	N/A	–	1.42
Morley SF European Growth	Equity Europe ex UK	19/2/2001	34.99	1044.80	4.48	2	1066.40	6.64	1	1021.60	2.16	8	1068.60	6.86	2	1171.00	17.10	2	1349.20	34.92	7	1077.30	7.73	16	–	N/A	–	–	N/A	–	–	N/A	–	4.72
Morley SF Global Growth	Ethical Global	19/2/2001	13.76	1005.10	0.51	42	1024.80	2.48	39	981.60	−1.84	38	984.30	−1.57	37	1027.80	2.78	39	1124.30	12.43	36	826.40	−17.36	37	–	N/A	–	–	N/A	–	–	N/A	–	4.51
Morley SF Managed	Asset Alloc Global Dynamic	19/2/2001	84.99	1018.40	1.84	33	1036.00	3.60	27	1003.10	0.31	26	998.70	−0.13	35	1077.50	7.75	27	1228.00	22.80	28	1027.60	2.76	23	–	N/A	–	–	N/A	–	–	N/A	–	3.78
Morley SF UK Growth	Ethical UK	19/2/2001	46.99	1024.70	2.47	22	1035.00	3.50	30	999.50	−0.05	27	1002.80	0.28	29	1101.40	10.14	22	1354.00	35.40	6	1107.40	10.74	13	–	N/A	–	–	N/A	–	–	N/A	–	4.82
Norwich UK Ethical	Ethical UK	10/5/1999	69.38	1028.70	2.87	16	1034.40	3.44	31	996.70	−0.33	29	999.80	−0.02	33	1121.50	12.15	18	1399.10	39.91	3	1133.20	13.32	9	1118.70	11.87	2	#VALUE!	N/A	–	–	N/A	–	5.02
Old Mutual Ethical A Inc	Ethical UK	31/3/1998	5.58	1023.40	2.34	24	1043.50	4.35	15	1005.00	0.50	23	1024.70	2.47	21	1135.20	13.52	9	1339.10	33.91	11	1058.50	5.85	20	1040.50	4.05	5	#VALUE!	N/A	–	–	N/A	–	4.78
Rathbone Ethical Bd Fd Acc	Fixed Income GBP-Corporate	13/5/2002	38.63	1012.50	1.25	39	1031.10	3.11	35	1031.10	3.11	3	1015.90	1.59	25	1025.80	2.58	40	1078.30	7.83	40	–	N/A	–	–	N/A	–	#VALUE!	N/A	–	–	N/A	–	N/A
Scot Amicable Ethical	Ethical UK	5/4/1999	13.28	1029.40	2.94	14	1046.30	4.63	10	1008.00	0.80	20	1022.70	2.27	24	1125.90	12.59	16	1342.90	34.29	9	1132.30	13.23	10	886.30	−11.37	17	#VALUE!	N/A	–	–	N/A	–	4.83
Sovereign Ethical	Ethical UK	2/5/1989	32.10	1034.50	3.45	7	1046.40	4.64	9	1029.60	2.96	4	1008.70	0.87	27	1124.50	12.45	17	1341.60	34.16	10	1060.10	6.01	19	1000.10	0.01	10	1264.00	26.40	5	2205.30	120.53	3	4.65
St James's Pl Ethical Inc	Ethical Global	6/4/1999	21.98	1021.50	2.15	27	1045.50	4.55	13	1008.80	0.88	18	1039.30	3.93	7	1130.10	13.01	13	1256.50	25.65	25	937.70	−6.23	32	755.40	−24.46	26	–	N/A	–	–	N/A	–	4.94
Std Lf UK Ethical Rtl	Ethical UK	16/2/1998	52.68	1019.10	1.91	30	1038.30	3.83	24	991.30	−0.87	32	1006.90	0.69	28	1118.70	11.87	20	1343.10	34.31	8	1146.70	14.67	8	986.30	−1.37	12	–	N/A	–	–	N/A	–	4.31
SW Environmental Investor A	Ecology UK	29/6/1989	177.09	1013.30	1.33	38	1036.80	3.68	26	996.70	−0.33	28	1010.00	1.00	26	1041.70	4.17	37	1164.50	16.45	33	928.70	−7.13	33	931.30	−6.87	14	1287.70	28.77	4	2266.00	126.6	2	4.03
SW Ethical A Acc	Ethical UK	12/9/1987	41.11	1018.70	1.87	32	1040.10	4.01	21	1005.20	0.52	21	1024.80	2.48	20	1075.80	7.58	28	1165.10	16.51	32	1008.10	0.81	27	914.40	−8.56	16	1020.30	2.03	12	1353.20	35.32	14	3.94
SWIP Global SRI A	Equity Global	23/7/2002	20.15	1006.80	0.68	41	1023.40	2.34	40	990.80	−0.92	34	1024.20	2.42	22	1056.50	5.65	35	1204.00	20.40	29	–	N/A	–	–	N/A	–	–	N/A	–	–	N/A	–	N/A
SWIP Pan-European SRI Eq A	Equity Europe	16/5/2002	43.57	1031.60	3.16	10	1045.90	4.59	11	1009.20	0.92	17	1035.10	3.51	12	1111.80	11.18	21	#VALUE!	N/A	–	–	N/A	–	–	N/A	–	–	N/A	–	–	N/A	–	N/A
Average				**1025.10**	**2.51**		**1039.10**	**3.91**		**1005.10**	**0.51**		**1018.20**	**1.82**		**1098.50**	**9.85**		**1268.60**	**26.86**		**1056.00**	**5.60**		**937.00**	**−6.30**		**1144.60**	**14.46**		**1757.60**	**75.76**		**4.41**
UK SRI Investment Trusts																																		
Impax Enviromental Markets	Spec: Alt Energy	22/2/2002	34.09	1060.30	6.03	1	1033.60	3.36	2	1020.70	2.07	1	1029.30	2.93	2	1118.20	11.82	1	1337.00	33.70	2	–	N/A	–	–	N/A	–	–	N/A	–	–	N/A	–	N/A
Jupiter Global Green - Ord	Global Growth	19/3/2001	32.74	995.70	−0.43	3	979.00	−2.10	3	979.00	−2.10	2	1068.80	6.88	1	1044.80	4.48	2	1151.80	15.18	3	814.20	−18.58	1	–	N/A	–	–	N/A	–	–	N/A	–	6.86
Merrill Lynch New Energy Tech	Spec: Alt Energy	31/10/2000	49.35	1034.90	3.49	2	1059.50	5.95	1	908.20	−9.18	3	936.80	−6.32	3	1034.90	3.49	3	1459.00	45.90	1	483.70	−51.63	2	–	N/A	–	–	N/A	–	–	N/A	–	10.24
Average				**1030.30**	**3.03**		**1024.00**	**2.40**		**969.30**	**−3.07**		**1011.60**	**1.16**		**1065.90**	**6.59**		**1315.90**	**31.59**		**649.00**	**−35.10**		**1000.00**	**0**		**1000.00**	**0**		**1000.00**	**0**		**8.55**
UK SRI Individual Pensions																																		
Abbey Life Ethical	(ABI) UK All Companies	30/3/1988	28.84	1017.20	1.72	39	1041.60	4.16	19	1007.80	0.78	18	1028.70	2.87	16	1080.60	8.06	36	1168.80	16.88	46	1034.90	3.49	35	968.30	−3.17	15	1120.30	12.03	11	1597.70	59.77	9	3.80
Clerical Med PP Ethical Fund	(ABI) UK All Companies	1/11/2000	15.16	1030.60	3.06	14	1043.40	4.34	17	1006.00	0.60	19	1030.60	3.06	15	1133.20	13.32	17	1326.00	32.60	20	1164.60	16.46	6	–	N/A	–	–	N/A	–	–	N/A	–	4.32

Ethical funds performance table (continued). Column groups show, for successive periods, the fund value, percentage growth and quartile/rank; the final column is the annual yield. Where data is not available the source shows "N/A" or a dash. Fund size "N/S" = not stated.

Fund	ABI Classification	Date	Size	V/%/Rank	V/%/Rank	V/%/Rank	V/%/Rank	V/%/Rank	V/%/Rank	V/%/Rank	V/%/Rank	V/%/Rank	V/%/Rank	Yield
Clerical Med PP UK Eq Tracker	(ABI) UK All Companies	1/12/2000	38.50	1028.60 2.86 15	1049.10 4.91 10	1026.00 2.60 6	1046.40 4.64 6	1133.40 13.34 16	1310.10 31.01 25	1054.70 5.47 30	1067.30 6.73 7	1270.10 27.01 6	N/A N/A N/A	4.29
Eagle Star Environ Opps 1	(ABI) UK All Companies	1/1/1991	6.44	1032.70 3.27 13	1055.30 5.53 6	1027.10 2.71 5	1050.60 5.06 5	1142.40 14.24 11	1323.30 32.33 22	1105.00 10.50 22	1118.60 11.86 5	1359.70 35.97 5	2109.30 110.93 1	3.90
Eagle Star Environ Opps 2	(ABI) UK All Companies	1/1/1996	4.91	1033.50 3.35 11	1057.10 5.71 3	1029.70 2.97 4	1055.40 5.54 4	1153.80 15.38 6	1350.20 35.02 18	1138.60 13.83 9	– – –	– – –	– – –	3.91
FP Conscience (ex NM)	(ABI) UK All Companies	1/9/1987	10.80	1018.10 1.81 34	1034.40 3.44 30	998.70 -0.13 32	1033.60 3.36 9	1173.70 17.37 3	1429.90 42.99 3	1165.40 16.54 5	980.90 -1.91 13	1209.40 20.94 8	1860.20 86.02 4	4.33
Friends Provdnt Mgd Stew'ship	(ABI) Balanced Managed	1/11/1998	74.00	1011.70 1.17 49	1029.40 2.94 38	1000.00 0 25	1028.40 2.84 19	1111.00 11.10 29	1296.00 29.60 28	1109.90 10.99 21	981.60 -1.84 12	– – –	– – –	3.57
Friends Provdnt Stewardship	(ABI) UK All Companies	1/6/1984	705.40	1019.50 1.95 31	1036.60 3.66 29	1000.00 0 25	1033.50 3.35 10	1170.90 17.09 4	1432.40 43.24 2	1196.30 19.63 3	1017.70 1.77 11	1277.10 27.71 11	2064.50 106.45 2	4.31
GE Pens Ethical	(ABI) UK All Companies	31/8/2000	1.80	1018.20 1.82 33	1031.30 3.13 34	1000.00 0 25	1022.50 2.25 24	1125.60 12.56 19	1305.80 30.58 27	1075.60 7.56 27	– – –	– – –	– – –	4.77
Halifax Lf 2000 Ethical Pen	(ABI) Global	6/3/2000	4.25	1017.30 1.73 37	1020.90 2.09 53	975.10 -2.49 53	994.90 -0.51 45	1050.10 5.01 44	1228.00 22.80 37	970.20 -2.98 40	– – –	– – –	– – –	4.85
Halifax Lf Ethical	(ABI) Global Equities	4/1/1994	25.06	1017.80 1.78 36	1021.30 2.13 52	975.10 -2.43 52	996.60 -0.34 40	1054.00 5.40 43	1236.90 23.69 39	976.90 -2.31 39	969.90 -3.01 14	1278.40 27.84 3	1653.30 65.33 8	4.86
L&G Ex Ethical	(ABI) UK All Companies	22/10/1999	8.37	1023.90 2.39 23	1046.30 4.63 14	1009.40 0.94 17	1022.60 2.26 23	1145.50 14.55 9	1359.00 35.97 9	1117.20 11.72 20	– – –	– – –	– – –	5.10
Lincoln Green	(ABI) Global Equities	26/6/1992	15.60	1034.80 3.48 8	1030.50 3.05 36	996.80 -0.32 36	1006.90 0.69 32	1055.70 5.57 42	1153.80 15.38 48	932.10 -6.79 46	895.00 -10.50 22	1165.40 16.54 9	1725.30 72.53 6	4.50
Norwich Union SF Absol Gth 2^	(ABI) Global Equities	6/4/2001	4.14	1014.20 1.42 44	1024.60 2.46 47	983.80 -1.62 45	986.30 -1.37 47	1111.90 11.19 27	1333.80 33.38 19	1073.00 7.30 28	– – –	– – –	– – –	5.88
Norwich Union SF Absol Gth 3	(ABI) Global Equities	6/4/2001	0.17	1013.40 1.34 45	1022.90 2.29 50	981.30 -1.87 47	981.30 -1.87 49	1100.80 10.08 32	1308.30 30.83 26	1039.70 3.97 33	– – –	– – –	– – –	5.89
Norwich Union SF Corp Bd 2 ^	(ABI) UK Fixed Interest	6/4/2001	31.55	1018.00 1.80 35	1039.60 3.96 23	1049.10 4.91 1	1037.40 3.74 7	1080.30 8.03 37	1234.30 23.43 35	1245.60 24.56 1	– – –	– – –	– – –	1.46
Norwich Union SF Corp Bd 3	(ABI) UK Fixed Interest	6/4/2001	0.78	1017.20 1.72 38	1037.80 3.78 26	1046.50 4.65 2	1032.40 3.24 12	1069.40 6.94 40	1210.00 21.00 41	1208.90 20.89 2	– – –	– – –	– – –	1.46
Norwich Union SF Euro Gth 2^	(ABI) Europe Excluding UK	6/4/2001	5.03	1041.20 4.12 1	1056.30 5.63 4	1019.80 1.98 11	1072.50 7.25 1	1192.50 19.25 1	1380.10 38.01 14	1122.00 12.20 19	– – –	– – –	– – –	4.58
Norwich Union SF Euro Gth 3	(ABI) Europe Excluding UK	6/4/2001	0.48	1040.40 4.04 2	1054.70 5.47 7	1017.20 1.72 12	1067.10 6.71 2	1180.60 18.06 2	1352.60 35.26 17	1088.00 8.80 25	– – –	– – –	– – –	4.58
Norwich Union SF Glo Gth 2 ^	(ABI) Global Equities	6/4/2001	5.06	1001.90 0.19 53	1024.30 2.43 48	979.40 -2.06 48	990.80 -0.92 46	1042.80 4.28 48	1150.80 15.08 49	863.90 -13.61 48	– – –	– – –	– – –	4.44
Norwich Union SF Glo Gth 3	(ABI) Global Equities	6/4/2001	0.37	1001.20 0.12 54	1022.50 2.25 51	976.80 -2.32 50	985.80 -1.42 48	1032.40 3.24 49	1127.70 12.77 50	836.70 -16.33 50	– – –	– – –	– – –	4.44
Norwich Union SF Managed 2 ^	(ABI) Balanced Managed	6/4/2001	62.58	1010.80 1.08 50	1030.80 3.08 35	999.40 -0.06 31	1000.50 0.05 37	1086.60 8.66 35	1256.20 25.62 31	1049.50 4.95 31	– – –	– – –	– – –	3.71
Norwich Union SF Managed 3	(ABI) Balanced Managed	6/4/2001	1.87	1009.90 0.99 51	1029.00 2.90 39	996.90 -0.31 35	995.40 -0.46 44	1075.70 7.57 39	1231.20 23.12 36	1016.70 1.67 36	– – –	– – –	– – –	3.72
Norwich Union SF UK Growth 2^	(ABI) UK All Companies	6/4/2001	12.17	1016.10 1.61 40	1028.60 2.86 40	996.10 -0.39 37	1004.50 0.45 33	1113.70 11.37 26	1388.70 38.87 26	1123.20 12.32 18	– – –	– – –	– – –	4.60
Norwich Union SF UK Growth 3	(ABI) UK All Companies	6/4/2001	0.69	1015.30 1.53 43	1026.90 2.69 46	993.70 -0.63 40	999.40 -0.06 38	1102.60 10.26 31	1361.40 36.14 31	1088.30 8.83 24	– – –	– – –	– – –	4.60
Norwich Union UK Equity Eth 1	(ABI) UK All Companies	10/5/1999	4.71	1020.10 2.01 27	1028.50 2.85 41	994.10 -0.59 39	997.20 -0.28 39	1119.10 11.91 20	1401.30 40.13 8	1135.10 13.51 11	1128.20 12.82 2	– – –	– – –	4.97
Norwich Union UK Equity Eth 2	(ABI) UK All Companies	10/5/1999	14.17	1020.80 2.08 25	1029.80 2.98 37	996.00 -0.40 38	1000.80 0.08 36	1127.50 12.75 18	1423.20 42.32 4	1160.00 16.02 7	1160.90 16.09 1	– – –	– – –	4.97
Norwich Union UK Equity Eth 3	(ABI) UK All Companies	10/5/1999	1.30	1019.90 1.99 30	1028.00 2.80 44	993.50 -0.65 43	995.80 -0.42 43	1116.20 11.62 25	1394.90 39.49 12	1125.20 12.52 17	1108.20 10.82 6	– – –	– – –	4.97
Norwich Union UK Equity Eth 4	(ABI) UK All Companies	10/5/1999	1.36	1019.90 1.99 28	1028.00 2.80 42	993.60 -0.64 42	995.90 -0.41 41	1116.20 11.64 23	1395.80 39.58 10	1131.80 13.18 6	1126.20 12.62 3	– – –	– – –	4.96
NPI Global Care	(ABI) Global Equities	1/3/1994	N/S	1019.20 1.92 32	1032.10 3.21 33	982.90 -1.71 46	963.80 -3.62 46	1017.70 1.77 51	1154.70 15.47 47	847.40 -15.26 49	691.50 -30.85 27	921.40 -7.86 13	1690.70 69.07 7	4.85
NPI Global Care Managed	(ABI) Balanced Managed	1/3/1996	N/S	1026.50 2.65 18	1040.90 4.09 21	1011.70 1.17 16	1028.50 2.85 18	1068.90 6.89 41	1220.60 22.06 39	962.20 -3.78 41	895.00 -10.50 21	1277.40 27.74 4	– – –	3.92
NPI New App Global Care	(ABI) Global Equities	1/1/1998	N/S	1020.50 2.05 26	1033.50 3.35 31	984.60 -1.54 44	967.50 -3.25 50	1025.20 2.52 50	1174.50 17.45 45	870.50 -12.95 47	721.50 -27.85 26	– – –	– – –	4.86
NPI New App Global Care Mgd	(ABI) Balanced Managed	1/1/1998	N/S	1028.30 2.83 16	1043.40 4.34 13	1015.20 1.52 13	1033.30 3.33 11	1078.80 7.88 38	1242.80 24.28 32	987.60 -1.24 38	934.70 -6.53 17	– – –	– – –	3.94
NU Ethical UK (Pre 10.00)	(ABI) UK All Companies	11/5/1999	6.42	1036.10 3.61 4	1028.00 2.80 42	993.60 -0.64 41	995.90 -0.41 41	1116.40 11.64 23	1395.80 39.58 10	1131.80 13.18 14	1126.20 12.62 3	– – –	– – –	4.96
Pru (ex DSF PP) Ethical	(ABI) UK All Companies	31/8/2004	N/S	– – –	– – –	– N/A –	1026.70 2.67 9	N/A N/A N/A	N/A N/A N/A	N/A N/A N/A	– – –	– – –	– – –	N/A
Pru(ScotAm) Ethical A Pen	(ABI) UK All Companies	6/4/1999	N/S	1035.90 3.59 5	1059.10 5.91 5	1022.80 2.28 9	– – –	1139.80 13.98 13	1408.40 40.84 6	1130.30 13.03 16	896.70 -10.33 20	– – –	– – –	5.02

(Continued)

Source: Standards & Poor's

Appendix 2 continued

"Value at 1 October 2004 of £1,000.00 invested on..." 1/10/2001

	General Sector	Launch Date	Fund Size £ million	1/9/2004 £ Value	% Chg	Rank	2/8/2004 £ Value	% Chg	Rank	1/7/2004 £ Value	% Chg	Rank	1/4/2004 £ Value	% Chg	Rank	1/10/2003 £ Value	% Chg	Rank	1/10/2002 £ Value	% Chg	Rank	1/10/2001 £ Value	% Chg	Rank	1/10/1999 £ Value	% Chg	Rank	1/10/1997 £ Value	% Chg	Rank	3/10/1994 £ Value	% Chg	Rank	1/10/2004 Volatility	Rank
Pru(ScotAm) Ethical Pen	(ABI) UK All Companies	6/4/1999	N/S	1035.70	3.57	6	1058.60	5.86	2	1022.60	2.26	10	1026.50	2.65	21	1140.30	14.03	12	1411.50	41.15	5	1133.90	13.39	12	902.30	-9.77	19	N/A	-	-	N/A	-	-	5.02	-
Prudential 1 Soc Responsible	(ABI) UK All Companies	13/3/2000	3.53	1033.30	3.33	12	1052.90	5.29	9	1023.70	2.37	8	1025.10	2.51	22	1146.20	14.62	8	1408.30	40.83	7	1132.80	13.28	13	-	N/A	-	N/A	-	-	N/A	-	-	5.20	-
Prudential 3 Soc Responsible^	(ABI) UK All Companies	6/4/2001	1.30	1034.30	3.43	10	1055.70	5.57	5	1025.50	2.55	7	1030.90	3.09	14	1144.50	14.45	10	1435.40	43.54	1	1170.90	17.09	4	-	N/A	-	N/A	-	-	N/A	-	-	5.15	-
Scot Eq Ethical	(ABI) UK All Companies	7/4/1988	N/S	1034.90	3.49	7	1047.90	4.79	11	1014.40	1.44	14	1028.70	2.87	17	1153.70	15.37	7	1395.90	39.59	9	1156.50	15.65	8	947.60	-5.24	16	1122.70	12.27	10	1824.70	82.47	5	4.72	5
Scot Eq Soc Resp Equity	(ABI) UK All Companies	1/9/1998	N/S	1024.80	2.48	20	1033.50	3.35	32	998.40	-0.16	33	1001.80	0.18	35	1099.80	9.98	33	1289.90	28.99	29	1038.20	3.82	34	839.80	-16.02	24	N/A	-	-	N/A	-	-	4.41	-
Scot Life UK Ethical	(ABI) UK All Companies	1/11/1999	3.90	1027.30	2.73	17	1053.30	5.33	8	1032.70	3.27	3	1064.70	6.47	3	1163.50	16.35	5	1270.10	27.01	30	1005.10	0.51	37	-	N/A	-	N/A	-	-	N/A	-	-	3.86	-
Scot Widows Environmental	(ABI) UK All Companies	9/5/2000	36.96	1012.00	1.20	48	1038.50	3.85	8	1000.00	0	25	1015.10	1.51	27	1048.20	4.82	45	1180.40	18.04	42	950.60	-4.94	42	-	N/A	-	N/A	-	-	N/A	-	-	4.10	-
SJP Ethical	(ABI) Global Equities	2/11/1998	3.40	1015.60	1.56	41	1039.40	3.94	24	1006.00	0.60	20	1031.70	3.17	13	1111.80	11.18	28	1222.90	22.29	38	942.00	-5.80	45	782.40	-21.76	25	N/A	-	-	N/A	-	-	4.55	-
Skandia Ethical	(ABI) Stock-market Managed	17/2/1992	23.45	1023.60	2.36	22	1040.10	4.01	20	1002.50	0.25	24	1011.90	1.19	30	1108.70	10.87	30	1219.10	21.91	40	1056.70	5.67	29	1023.60	2.36	10	1238.10	23.81	7	1892.90	89.29	3	4.02	3
Skandia Professional Eth'l	(ABI) Stock-market Managed	1/5/1997	2.66	1024.10	2.41	21	1041.20	4.12	20	1003.80	0.38	23	1015.40	1.54	26	1117.20	11.72	22	1237.10	23.71	33	1080.50	8.05	26	1062.20	6.22	8	1304.60	30.46	2	# VALUE!	N/A	-	4.01	-
Skandia/Ethical Portfolio SP	(ABI) Stock-market Managed	1/9/2003	23.45	1024.60	2.46	21	1041.80	4.18	18	1004.30	0.43	21	1015.70	1.57	25	1117.40	11.74	21	-	N/A	-	-	N/A	-	-	N/A	-	N/A	-	-	N/A	-	-	N/A	-
Skandia/Henderson Ethical SP	(ABI) Global Equities	1/9/2003	0.17	1002.50	0.25	52	1023.00	2.30	49	972.10	-2.79	53	950.20	-4.98	53	998.80	-0.12	52	-	N/A	-	-	N/A	-	-	N/A	-	N/A	-	-	N/A	-	-	N/A	-
Standard Life Ethical	(ABI) Balanced Managed	1/7/1998	92.90	1026.10	2.61	19	1044.00	4.40	15	1003.90	0.39	22	1010.90	1.09	31	1099.00	9.90	31	1322.50	32.25	23	1135.70	13.57	10	1058.00	5.80	9	N/A	-	-	N/A	-	-	3.84	-
Sun Life Ethical	(ABI) UK All Companies	5/5/1998	10.24	1037.90	3.79	3	1047.50	4.75	13	997.80	-0.22	34	1003.30	0.33	34	1137.10	13.71	14	1325.50	32.55	21	1041.50	4.15	32	893.30	-10.67	23	1316.10	31.61	1	N/A	-	-	5.54	-
SW Environmental 2	(ABI) UK All Companies	29/7/2000	36.96	1012.20	1.22	46	1037.40	3.74	27	1000.00	0	25	1013.70	1.37	28	1047.20	4.72	46	1177.00	17.70	43	947.30	-5.27	43	-	N/A	-	N/A	-	-	N/A	-	-	4.10	-
SW Environmental 3 ^	(ABI) UK All Companies	6/4/2001	36.96	1012.20	1.22	46	1037.40	3.74	27	1000.00	0	25	1013.70	1.37	28	1047.20	4.72	46	1177.00	17.70	43	947.30	-5.27	43	-	N/A	-	N/A	-	-	N/A	-	-	4.71	-
Winterthur C Suisse Fellowship	(ABI) Corporate Fellowship	1/5/1996	1.130	1034.60	3.46	9	1047.90	4.79	12	1014.30	1.43	15	1037.40	3.74	8	1137.00	13.70	15	1317.50	31.75	24	1095.40	9.54	23	914.70	-8.53	18	1042.20	4.22	12	N/A	-	-	4.71	-
Zurich Henderson Ethical	(ABI) Global Equities	13/11/2003	0	1015.60	1.56	42	1027.40	2.74	45	977.00	-2.30	49	956.90	-4.31	52	-	N/A	-	-	N/A	-	-	N/A	-	-	N/A	-	N/A	-	-	N/A	-	-	N/A	-
Average				1022.30	2.23		1038.00	3.80		1003.40	0.34		1014.40	1.44		1105.10	10.51		1297.20	29.72		1062.30	6.23		970.80	-2.92		1199.00	19.9		1824.30	82.43		4.41	
UK SRI Insurance Funds																																			
Abbey Life Ethical	(ABI) UK All Companies	1/4/1991	3.24	1017.00	1.70	29	1040.00	4.00	18	1006.10	0.61	18	1032.90	3.29	10	1082.80	8.28	25	1182.60	18.26	32	1051.10	5.11	22	977.70	-2.23	11	1120.20	12.02	10	1506.50	50.65	9	3.47	9
Allied Dunbar Henderson Ethic	(ABI) Stock-market Managed	11/2/2000	0.90	1013.70	1.37	35	1027.70	2.77	36	975.60	-2.44	47	952.30	-4.77	47	1003.90	0.39	47	1106.60	10.66	40	835.70	-16.43	42	-	N/A	-	N/A	-	-	N/A	-	-	4.82	-
AXA Ethical	(ABI) UK All Companies	10/5/2002	8.26	1037.10	3.71	4	1046.50	4.65	12	996.80	-0.32	30	1000.00	0	31	1131.30	13.13	9	1311.50	31.15	11	-	N/A	-	-	N/A	-	N/A	-	-	N/A	-	-	N/A	-
Clerical Med Ethical Fund	(ABI) UK All Companies	1/11/2000	2.38	1022.90	2.29	22	1034.10	3.41	25	1002.40	0.24	23	1021.60	2.16	18	1103.90	10.39	15	1226.60	22.66	24	1103.90	10.39	12	-	N/A	-	N/A	-	-	N/A	-	-	3.67	-
Eagle Star Environ Opps 1	(ABI) Stock-market Managed	8/10/1990	2.59	1032.90	3.29	8	1054.80	5.48	5	1026.50	2.65	8	1049.20	4.92	6	1139.00	13.90	5	1313.50	31.35	9	1105.20	10.52	11	1075.90	7.53	4	1251.30	25.13	4	1918.30	91.83	1	3.85	-
Eagle Star Environ Opps 2	(ABI) Stock-market Managed	29/8/1995	6.76	1033.60	3.36	7	1056.80	5.68	3	1029.40	2.94	6	1055.60	5.56	2	1153.00	15.30	3	1345.90	34.59	3	1148.60	14.86	6	1116.20	11.62	1	1316.10	31.61	1	N/A	-	-	3.86	-
Family Utd Chrties	(ABI) Friendly Societies	1/7/1996	3.73	1026.80	2.68	17	1034.40	3.44	24	986.90	-1.31	39	967.80	-3.22	44	1060.00	6.00	37	1267.80	26.78	14	1063.10	6.31	19	874.60	-12.54	16	1178.40	17.84	8	1740.00	74.00	4	4.26	-
FP Conscience (ex NM)	(ABI) Friendly Societies	1/9/1987	2.10	1015.20	1.52	34	1028.90	2.89	34	998.40	-0.16	27	1026.40	2.64	15	1149.50	14.95	4	1367.60	36.76	4	1194.50	19.45	1	1042.40	4.24	6	1266.30	26.63	6	N/A	-	-	3.73	4
Friends Provdnt Mgd Stew'ship	(ABI) UK All Companies	1/11/1998	36.10	1012.20	1.22	40	1029.60	2.96	31	997.20	-0.28	28	1028.60	2.86	13	1117.00	11.70	11	1317.50	31.75	7	1107.80	10.78	10	973.80	-2.62	12	N/A	-	-	N/A	-	-	3.75	-
Friends Provdnt Stewardship	(ABI) Friendly Societies	1/6/1984	258.40	1017.70	1.77	28	1033.90	3.39	26	998.70	-0.13	26	1034.10	3.41	9	1175.80	17.58	1	1436.80	43.68	1	1161.60	16.16	4	1014.80	1.48	8	1216.60	21.66	5	1812.40	81.24	2	4.30	2
Halifax Lf Ethical	(ABI) Global Equities	4/1/1994	3.76	1015.30	1.53	33	1018.80	1.88	44	977.30	-2.27	45	996.60	-0.34	37	1046.50	4.65	40	1198.00	19.80	30	1000.00	0	31	1007.60	0.76	10	1268.60	26.86	2	1607.00	60.70	6	3.87	6
HIFS FTSE4Good	(ABI) Stock-market Managed	10/3/1999	0.10	1036.60	3.66	5	1055.20	5.52	4	1028.30	2.83	7	1052.30	5.23	4	1096.10	9.61	18	1290.50	29.05	12	1046.60	4.66	23	786.80	-21.32	20	N/A	-	-	N/A	-	-	4.66	-
HIFS FTSE4Good Exempt	(ABI) Stock-market Managed	17/6/1998	3.40	1039.10	3.91	1	1058.50	5.85	1	1031.50	3.15	5	1057.10	5.71	1	1105.20	10.52	13	1317.30	31.73	8	1063.80	6.38	18	784.30	-21.57	21	N/A	-	-	N/A	-	-	4.84	-
HIFS Green Chip - Exempt	(ABI) Friendly Societies	6/2/1991	0	1026.70	2.67	18	1043.50	4.35	15	1032.30	3.23	3	1036.50	3.65	8	1062.30	6.23	35	1159.60	15.96	39	1100.30	10.03	13	1012.30	1.23	9	1215.90	21.59	6	1653.30	65.33	5	2.08	-
HIFS Green Chip 2 - Exempt	(ABI) Friendly Societies	9/10/1991	14.80	1030.00	3.00	15	1047.10	4.71	10	1031.60	3.16	4	1041.70	4.17	7	1073.80	7.38	31	1200.60	20.06	29	1090.00	9.00	15	943.10	-5.69	13	1155.30	15.53	9	1584.20	58.42	8	2.80	8
Lincoln Green	(ABI) Global Equities	26/6/1992	11.90	1037.80	3.78	2	1033.10	3.31	27	996.90	-0.31	29	1012.10	1.21	23	1060.50	6.05	36	1097.00	9.70	41	863.00	-13.70	38	779.50	-22.05	23	947.70	-5.23	13	1318.40	31.84	10	4.65	10
Norwich Union SF Absol Gth 1	(ABI) Global Equities	25/6/2001	0.28	1012.50	1.25	38	1019.40	1.94	43	982.00	-1.80	41	981.40	-1.86	42	1074.30	7.43	30	1233.20	23.32	22	1020.90	2.09	27	-	N/A	-	N/A	-	-	N/A	-	-	4.60	-

Norwich Union SF Absol Gth 3	(ABI) Global Equities	25/6/2001	0.06	1012.10	1.21	41	1018.60	1.86	45	980.70	−1.93	43	978.90	−2.11	43	1068.90	6.89	32	1220.70	22.07	26	1004.90	0.49	29	–	N/A	–	–	N/A	–	–	N/A	–	4.60
Norwich Union SF Corp Bd 1	(ABI) UK Fixed Interest	25/6/2001	7.32	1013.20	1.32	36	1029.20	2.92	32	1035.90	3.59	1	1022.20	2.22	17	1046.40	4.64	41	1188.40	18.84	31	1188.60	18.86	2	–	N/A	–	–	N/A	–	–	N/A	–	1.43
Norwich Union SF Corp Bd 3	(ABI) UK Fixed Interest	25/6/2001	1.94	1012.80	1.28	37	1028.30	2.83	35	1034.70	3.47	2	1019.70	1.97	19	1041.20	4.12	42	1176.50	17.65	34	1170.80	17.08	3	–	N/A	–	–	N/A	–	–	N/A	–	1.43
Norwich Union SF Euro Gth 1	(ABI) Europe Excluding UK	25/6/2001	1.35	1032.60	3.26	9	1044.70	4.47	13	1012.20	1.22	13	1052.40	5.24	3	1135.60	13.56	7	1262.70	26.27	15	1056.80	5.68	21	–	N/A	–	–	N/A	–	–	N/A	–	3.71
Norwich Union SF Euro Gth 3	(ABI) Europe Excluding UK	25/6/2001	0.16	1032.30	3.23	10	1043.80	4.38	14	1010.90	1.09	15	1049.80	4.98	5	1130.00	13.00	10	1250.00	25.00	18	1040.50	4.05	25	–	N/A	–	–	N/A	–	–	N/A	–	3.71
Norwich Union SF Glo Gth 1	(ABI) Global Equities	25/6/2001	0.98	1000.30	0.03	46	1017.60	1.76	46	977.90	−2.21	44	984.70	−1.53	40	1014.60	1.46	45	1083.30	8.33	42	859.30	−14.07	39	–	N/A	–	–	N/A	–	–	N/A	–	3.57
Norwich Union SF Glo Gth 3	(ABI) Global Equities	25/6/2001	0.09	999.90	−0.01	47	1016.80	1.68	47	976.80	−2.32	46	982.20	−1.78	41	1010.00	1.00	46	1072.80	7.28	43	845.70	−15.43	41	–	N/A	–	–	N/A	–	–	N/A	–	3.58
Norwich Union SF Managed 1	(ABI) Balanced Managed	25/6/2001	5.80	1009.00	0.90	44	1026.50	2.65	37	996.30	−0.37	33	994.80	−0.52	38	1056.90	5.69	38	1178.30	17.83	33	1011.80	1.18	28	–	N/A	–	–	N/A	–	–	N/A	–	3.02
Norwich Union SF Managed 3	(ABI) Balanced Managed	25/6/2001	0.89	1008.60	0.86	45	1025.50	2.55	38	995.10	−0.49	35	992.30	−0.77	39	1051.60	5.16	39	1166.40	16.64	37	996.30	−0.37	32	–	N/A	–	–	N/A	–	–	N/A	–	3.02
Norwich Union SF UK Growth 1	(ABI) UK All Companies	25/6/2001	2.25	1012.30	1.23	39	1023.30	2.33	39	993.20	−0.68	37	999.30	−0.07	34	1081.70	8.17	27	1271.50	27.15	13	1095.60	9.56	14	–	N/A	–	–	N/A	–	–	N/A	–	3.74
Norwich Union SF UK Growth 3	(ABI) UK All Companies	25/6/2001	0.25	1011.90	1.19	42	1022.50	2.25	40	992.00	−0.80	38	996.90	−0.31	36	1076.30	7.63	29	1258.50	25.85	16	1078.30	7.83	16	–	N/A	–	–	N/A	–	–	N/A	–	3.74
Norwich Union UK Eq Ethical 1	(ABI) UK All Companies	10/5/1999	6.30	1015.60	1.56	32	1021.70	2.17	42	994.50	−0.55	36	998.60	−0.14	35	1091.40	9.14	20	1249.00	24.90	19	1058.20	5.82	20	1077.80	7.78	3	–	N/A	–	–	N/A	–	3.68
Norwich Union UK Eq Ethical 2	(ABI) UK All Companies	10/5/1999	0.06	1015.90	1.59	31	1022.20	2.22	41	995.10	−0.49	34	999.90	−0.01	33	1094.10	9.41	19	1255.20	25.52	17	1066.30	6.63	17	1088.90	8.89	2	–	N/A	–	–	N/A	–	3.68
NPI Glb Care Mgd (P Bond)	(ABI) Balanced Managed	1/7/1999	N/S	1024.00	2.40	19	1038.40	3.84	21	1005.00	0.50	20	1015.00	1.50	21	1065.70	6.57	34	1215.30	21.53	27	947.40	−5.26	34	820.00	−18.00	19	–	N/A	–	–	N/A	–	4.02
NPI Global Care	(ABI) Global Equities	1/10/1997	N/S	1019.00	1.90	26	1031.60	3.16	28	983.00	−1.70	40	961.50	−3.85	45	1021.80	2.18	43	1168.00	16.80	35	866.10	−13.39	37	678.10	−32.19	25	789.50	−21.05	14	#VALUE!	N/A	–	4.95
NPI Global Care (P Bond)	(ABI) Global Equities	1/7/1999	N/S	1018.70	1.87	27	1031.60	3.16	29	982.00	−1.80	42	960.30	−3.97	46	1018.70	1.87	44	1162.10	16.21	38	859.20	−14.08	40	669.70	−33.03	26	#VALUE!	N/A	–	–	N/A	–	4.94
NPI Global Care Managed	(ABI) Balanced Managed	1/10/1997	N/S	1023.30	2.33	21	1038.80	3.88	20	1005.20	0.52	19	1015.80	1.58	20	1067.50	6.75	33	1222.40	22.24	25	953.60	−4.64	33	829.80	−17.02	18	1015.80	1.58	12	#VALUE!	N/A	–	4.03
Pru Ethical Fnd S2	(ABI) UK All Companies	1/7/2003	N/S	1030.60	3.06	14	1051.80	5.18	6	1012.20	1.22	12	1011.30	1.13	24	1085.70	8.57	22	–	N/A	–	–	N/A	–	–	N/A	–	–	N/A	–	–	N/A	–	N/A
Pru Ethical Fnd S3	(ABI) UK All Companies	1/7/2003	N/S	1030.70	3.07	13	1050.80	5.08	9	1011.30	1.13	14	1009.40	0.94	27	1083.70	8.37	24	–	N/A	–	–	N/A	–	–	N/A	–	–	N/A	–	–	N/A	–	N/A
Pru Ethical Fnd S4	(ABI) UK All Companies	1/7/2003	N/S	1029.70	2.97	16	1050.90	5.09	8	1010.30	1.03	17	1009.40	0.94	26	1082.70	8.27	26	–	N/A	–	–	N/A	–	–	N/A	–	–	N/A	–	–	N/A	–	N/A
Pru Ethical Fnd S5	(ABI) UK All Companies	1/7/2003	N/S	1030.90	3.09	12	1051.10	5.11	7	1010.40	1.04	16	1007.50	0.75	28	1078.70	7.87	28	–	N/A	–	–	N/A	–	–	N/A	–	–	N/A	–	–	N/A	–	N/A
Pru(ScotAm) Ethical	(ABI) UK All Companies	6/4/1999	N/S	1034.20	3.42	6	1056.90	5.69	2	1022.50	2.25	10	1023.80	2.38	16	1137.90	13.79	6	1396.60	39.66	3	1123.80	12.38	8	907.80	−9.22	15	–	N/A	–	–	N/A	–	4.98
Scot Eq Eth Care Caut	(ABI) Cautious Managed	1/9/1998	N/S	1022.80	2.28	23	1037.60	3.76	22	1025.70	2.57	9	1026.70	2.67	14	1098.50	9.85	17	1228.40	22.84	23	1122.90	12.29	9	1051.90	5.19	5	–	N/A	–	–	N/A	–	2.31
Scot Eq Eth Care Eqty	(ABI) UK All Companies	1/9/1998	N/S	1021.20	2.12	24	1029.10	2.91	33	996.40	−0.36	31	1004.70	0.47	30	1083.70	8.37	23	1247.50	24.75	20	1001.50	0.15	30	781.50	−21.85	22	–	N/A	–	–	N/A	–	4.30
Scot Eq Ethical	(ABI) UK All Companies	1/8/1989	N/S	1031.00	3.10	11	1042.10	4.21	16	1014.30	1.43	11	1029.50	2.95	12	1156.00	15.60	2	1408.40	40.84	2	1160.10	16.01	5	925.60	−7.44	14	1074.60	7.46	11	1596.50	59.65	7	4.62
Scot Widows Environmental	(ABI) UK All Companies	9/5/2000	16.48	1011.20	1.12	43	1030.00	3.00	30	1000.00	0	24	1014.10	1.41	22	1100.80	10.08	16	1236.70	23.67	21	942.50	−5.75	35	–	N/A	–	–	N/A	–	–	N/A	–	4.10
SJP Ethical	(ABI) Global Equities	2/11/1998	10.43	1016.00	1.60	30	1039.60	3.96	19	1004.00	0.40	21	1031.20	3.12	11	1104.50	10.45	14	1206.00	20.60	28	908.10	−9.19	36	707.90	−29.21	24	–	N/A	–	–	N/A	–	4.87
Skandia Ethical Portfolio	(ABI) Stock-market Managed	17/2/1992	41.53	1023.80	2.38	20	1041.20	4.12	17	1003.00	0.30	22	1010.50	1.05	25	1090.10	9.01	21	1167.60	16.76	36	1042.30	4.23	24	1015.10	1.51	7	1184.80	18.48	7	1741.40	74.14	3	3.47
Standard Life Ethical	(ABI) UK All Companies	10/5/2000	16.06	1020.30	2.03	25	1035.90	3.59	23	999.00	−0.10	25	1007.40	0.74	29	1108.10	10.81	12	1329.10	32.91	6	1135.90	13.59	7	–	N/A	–	–	N/A	–	–	N/A	–	3.71
Sun Life Ethical	(ABI) UK All Companies	5/5/1998	7.95	1037.50	3.75	3	1046.60	4.66	11	996.40	−0.36	32	1000.00	0	31	1132.20	13.22	8	1312.80	31.28	10	1020.90	2.09	26	857.60	−14.24	17	–	N/A	–	–	N/A	–	5.59
Average				**1021.90**	**2.19**		**1036.30**	**3.63**		**1003.70**	**0.37**		**1011.80**	**1.18**		**1086.20**	**8.62**		**1239.70**	**23.97**		**1036.00**	**3.60**		**915.40**	**−8.46**		**1142.90**	**14.29**		**1647.80**	**64.78**		**3.86**

Source: Standard & Poor's © The McGraw-Hill Companies, Ltd (2005) – All rights reserved – E&O E
Calculation basis: bid-bid (mid-mid for Investment Trusts), gross income reinvested (income reinvested net of basic rate tax for UK Insurance Funds) in UK Sterling.

Appendix 3

Issues and definitions

Ethical Investment Research Services (EIRIS)

Although a majority of people, when asked, express the view that they would prefer to invest their money in a manner that reflected moral as well as financial criteria, many would have difficulty defining what was their own moral view. Of course, they'll know right from wrong when they see it but may have more difficulty calling to mind, at the time they are discussing investment possibilities, all of the things that have concerned them in the past. It's just not something that people think about all of the time. However, a key plank in the case for ethical and socially responsible investment is that most investors can find a fund that closely reflects their own priorities: however, they will need first to crystallize and define those priorities in order to know what they are seeking to find reflected in the investment policy of a fund.

Ethical Investment Research Services (EIRIS) has made that step a great deal more organized by identifying the issues that most concern most people. This appendix from EIRIS helpfully explains why an issue is an issue, and then defines the specific concerns covered by each issue. Use this with Appendix 1, 'Funds' ethical policies and processes', which sets out each fund's investment approach, to find which funds' approach most closely reflects an investor's own views.

Alcohol

Why is this an issue?

Although alcohol can be consumed without harm, it is also a toxic and addictive substance which causes illness, accidents, violence and family suffering. While many ethical funds avoid drinks companies, traditionally individual investors have seemed less concerned about this issue and in EIRIS's experience many have been more likely to cite tobacco as a no-go area. However, there have been indications that this may now change following the wave of public concern and adverse publicity over the marketing techniques of certain alcohol manufacturers and retailers.

As evidence of the health risks associated with alcohol consumption becomes more widespread, manufacturers have sought replacement consumers and launched new products. The drinks industry has been criticized by campaigning groups such as Alcohol Concern for targeting young or under-age drinkers. Concerns have been expressed in particular over 'alcopops', sweet-tasting drinks which have the alcohol content of a strong lager. The government recently abandoned plans to impose statutory control on their sale, relying instead on industry self-regulation.

While the number of companies in the drinks manufacturing sector has shrunk, the companies themselves have grown enormously and are now among some of the biggest and most well known in the UK. Many are said to be attempting to change the public's image of pubs as dark and dingy places for men, and are now making pubs more child- and woman-friendly. This greater accessibility and social acceptability has also caused further alarm among some health and child protection groups.

Definitions

Alcohol production – the brewing of beers, distilling of spirits, production of ciders or wines, and the blending or bottling of alcoholic drinks.

Alcohol sale – retailing or wholesaling. We also include the auctioning, import, export, contract distribution or sale of alcohol through concessions where these are indicated in the source we use.

Turnover – annual turnover over £1 million. By annual turnover we mean the turnover of the entire company, including subsidiaries and associated companies.

Animal testing

Why is this an issue?

Many people who would not necessarily regard themselves as 'ethical' consumers draw the line at buying products such as make-up, shampoos and perfumes that have been tested on animals. The proliferation of such products that carry the 'not tested on animals' or 'against animal testing' tags is testimony to the level of consumer feeling on this issue.

The testing of cosmetic finished products and ingredients on animals is no longer allowed in the UK. But the testing of new cosmetic ingredients on animals will carry on abroad, as regulations may specify animal tests for safety purposes. Therefore cosmetics testing is still an issue. Of the 2.64 million animal tests in the UK in 1997, the majority were carried out for medical research and pharmaceutical purposes. Some concerned consumers and investors therefore look more widely at animal testing, believing it to be equally unacceptable in the production of other chemical products, such as food flavourings or household cleaners; others take a harder line, excluding pharmaceutical production involving animal testing as well.

A further issue is the definition of what constitutes 'not tested on animals'. One approach has been the five-year rolling rule whereby products and ingredients must not have been tested on animals within the last five years. Another approach is that a policy not to test on animals should be based on a fixed cut-off date, which entails a commitment not to test in the future. Groups campaigning against animal testing in the cosmetics industry now clearly favour the fixed cut-off date policy, which includes a requirement that ingredients suppliers must also adhere to the manufacturer's policy.

Definitions

Animal testing services – the conducting of animal testing on behalf of others (contract research organizations).

Cosmetics and toiletries – the definition of cosmetics as set out in Directive 93/35; that is any substance or preparation intended to be placed in contact with the various external parts of the human body or with teeth and the mucous membranes of the oral cavity with a view to cleaning, perfuming, changing appearance and/or correcting body odours and/or protecting them or keeping them in good condition. This includes: perfumes, make-up, haircare products, soaps and shower gels, deodorants, suntan creams, oral hygiene products and cleaning wipes. We also include delivery systems, such as controlled release mechanisms. The term *cosmetic(s)* used on its own covers cosmetics and toiletries.

Although testing of cosmetic finished products and ingredients on animals is no longer allowed in the UK, this testing for cosmetics purposes, especially of new ingredients, can be carried out in mainland Europe, the United States and other countries.

Cosmetic intermediates – ingredients which are supplied to the cosmetics industry and have been tested (a) for cosmetic purposes or (b) for other purposes but are mainly (50 per cent or more) used by the cosmetics industry.

Fixed cut-off date – any past date adopted by the company after which a policy not to test on animals will apply.

Ingredient suppliers – ingredient suppliers for finished products but not for intermediate products.

Medicines – the development of new drugs, delivery systems (eg controlled release mechanisms), self-medication products, vaccines, wound care products, vitamins and other dietary supplements. It also includes medical devices, such as dental and opthalmic products, surgical instruments, pacemakers, artificial joint replacements and other implantable devices, and infusion products. We include companies receiving payments on the achievement of development milestones or royalty payments from medicines tested on animals within the last five years.

Other products – agrochemicals, pesticide or veterinary products, food additives, industrial or household chemical products or intermediates. These are products identified in Home Office animal testing statistics. We also include tobacco products, because, although no tests on animals are allowed on these in the UK, tests could still be carried out in other countries.

Own-brand cosmetics or toiletries – products manufactured by a third party contract manufacturer which are sold under the company's own label.

Range of a brand which is manufactured according to a strict fixed cut-off date policy – at least three products from a manufacturer which has a fixed cut-off date for both itself and its ingredients suppliers, and which monitors its ingredients suppliers.

Sold – includes retailing, wholesaling and sale through concessions.

Tested – conducting or commissioning animal tests on either products or ingredients.

Corporate governance: Board practice

Why is this an issue?

Concerns about the governance of public companies increased after corporate scandals such as Polly Peck and Maxwell. The Cadbury Committee, which reported in December 1992, was set up by the City in response to these concerns. Cadbury's recommendations aimed to tighten corporate procedures by having a clearer separation of powers within boards of directors. For example, it encouraged separation of the roles of chief executive and chair and required the appointment of at least three (external) non-executive directors to help improve the level of independent auditing and internal control within companies.

The Cadbury recommendations on governance structures were followed up in 1995 by complementary recommendations relating to directors' remuneration made by the Greenbury Committee. The best-practice provisions on directors' remuneration endorsed by the Greenbury Committee were appended to the Stock Exchange listing rules in 1996. This responded to shareholder concerns about directors' pay issues, by for example increasing the amount of information companies are required to disclose about directors' pay and encouraging shorter notice periods for directors' service contracts.

In 1998, a further committee chaired by Sir Ronald Hampel drafted the Combined Code, which brings together the recommendations of both the Cadbury and Greenbury committees.

Only a limited number of the Combined Code's provisions were new, with the majority of its recommendations being derived directly from the findings of the Cadbury and Greenbury committees. The Hampel Committee envisaged that, whilst it would not be possible for all companies to comply with every section of the Combined Code's recommendations straight away, steps should be taken over time to encourage increased compliance.

Since 1999 the Stock Exchange has introduced a requirement for companies to report on how they comply with relevant recommendations contained within the Combined Code and in addition, should they breach any parts of the Combined Code, to explain their reasons for non-compliance.

Whilst improved procedures cannot provide a foolproof safeguard against deliberate fraud, many investors see their existence as evidence of sound management practice within a company and therefore look for adoption of the Combined Code by companies in which they wish to invest.

EIRIS reports which companies do not meet those requirements of the Cadbury Code now contained within the Combined Code. EIRIS does not presently consider those aspects of the Combined Code which relate to the recommendations of the Greenbury Committee, but has separately researched criteria in relation to the issue of directors' pay.

For companies that breach recommendations of the Combined Code that were derived from the Cadbury Code, EIRIS lists those sections of the Combined Code that they breach. Also, although it was not formally part of the Cadbury Code, the recommendation for separation of roles between chair and chief executive is monitored by EIRIS as a specialized criterion.

Definitions

Cadbury Code – the Code of Best Practice issued as the report of the Cadbury Committee on the Financial Aspects of Corporate Governance, on 1 December 1992.

Combined Code – the Principles of Good Governance and Code of Best Practice issued by the Committee on Corporate Governance chaired by Sir Ronald Hampel, which are appended to the Stock Exchange Listing Rules. We record breaches of those sections of the Combined Code that are derived from the Cadbury Code. EIRIS covers all UK companies for this criterion but does not cover new issues. If a company is taken over by another company we remove corporate governance details for the company that was taken over.

Chief executive – where no chief executive director is specified in the annual report, we include a sole executive managing director. The recommendation that companies should split the roles of chair and chief executive does not form part of either the Cadbury Code or Combined Code and so is not in itself a formal breach.

Corporate governance: Bribery and corruption

Why is this an issue?

Corruption has many adverse effects. By definition, as well as distorting fair competition, corrupt practices are damaging to all societies. If permitted to flourish, corruption can in the worst instances hinder the development of entire nations. The World Bank and Transparency International, the global anti-corruption NGO, have demonstrated that in some developing countries corruption has reduced growth by deterring foreign investment and channelling funds into 'white elephant' projects of primary benefit to corrupt decision makers.

Over the years, governments and international organizations have sought to eliminate corrupt practices from business activities. For example, members of the

Organisation for Economic Co-operation and Development (OECD) have endorsed conventions to implement laws outlawing the payment of bribes to public officials.

A company which does not actively make clear that it does not condone corrupt practices may be at risk of suffering reputational damage, should its employees or agents ever become implicated in bribery scandals.

Corporate governance: Codes of ethics

Why is this an issue?

For many institutional investors, the value a company attaches to stakeholder/social issues is increasingly seen as being as important to its long-term sustainability as its approach to environmental issues. The Turnbull guidelines endorsed by the London Stock Exchange expressly mention corporate reputation issues as factors which may need to be incorporated into a company group's risk assessment systems. Having a corporate code of ethics or conduct which encourages its employees to follow principles of good business behaviour is commonly regarded as a minimum requirement for ensuring effective reputation management. By having a public code, employees have a benchmark from which to continually improve behaviour, for the benefit of all stakeholders.

Definitions

Code of ethics – clear evidence of a policy which encourages employees to follow principles of good business behaviour. The policy may be contained in either a specific set of guidelines or within written commitments found in company literature which when taken as a whole can be deemed to shape the company's strategy and activities. This may include: an explicit or implicit statement published by the company in its annual reports, brochures, leaflets, website or other publicly available literature. Alternatively, corporate commitments may also be construed where it is clear from available evidence of company practices, procedures and performance that the company seeks to meet the required standards.

Communicates a code of ethics – the company has published and distributed its code/policy at least to its employees and ideally to other stakeholders as well.

Corporate governance: Directors' pay

Why is this an issue?

The massive media and public interest in this issue can be seen in the so-called 'fat-cat' scandals about large pay rises for the directors of formerly nationalized utilities. These rises attracted criticism both from unions and from shareholders. The

Greenbury Committee reported in July 1995 on improving procedures for directors' remuneration.

EIRIS has a number of criteria which look at different aspects of the issue. For instance, we highlight companies which have the largest gaps between the percentage pay change for directors and that for employees, or whose highest-paid director receives more than 25 times the average UK wage. On the positive side, EIRIS also highlights companies which include non-financial performance criteria as part of determining their directors' performance-related pay.

Definitions

Non-financial targets – include the attainment of customer service standards and the achievement of environmental or health and safety targets.

One of the largest gaps between the percentage pay change for directors and that for employees – that there is a gap of over +100 percentage points between the percentage pay change for average directors' pay and the percentage pay change for average employees' pay. This criterion identifies approximately 1.3 per cent of companies on the EIRIS index.

One of the largest increases in the directors' share of the wage bill – companies that have increased the directors' share of the wage bill by 50 per cent or more. This criterion identifies approximately 3.8 per cent of companies on the EIRIS index.

Pay – all remuneration and emoluments including, where known, pension contributions and bonus payments.

Pay for directors and for employees – the average director's pay and the average employee's pay according to *Corporate Register*. The average number of directors is calculated by *Corporate Register*. It is not always possible to account for the dates of appointment and resignation of all directors when calculating this number.

No allowance is made for variations in directors' pay caused by individual directors choosing to forgo part of their remuneration for a period.

UK average earnings – the estimate of average annual gross earnings for all manual and non-manual workers published by the New Earnings Survey of the Office for National Statistics. This was £20,472.40 for the year ending January 1999.

Wage bill – the sum of total directors' pay and total employees' pay for the most recent financial year reported in *Corporate Register*.

Percentage pay change – the percentage increase or decrease between the pay for the most recent financial year and the previous financial year, according to *Corporate Register*.

Corporate governance: Responsibility for stakeholders

Why is this an issue?

The Turnbull guidelines endorsed by the London Stock Exchange expressly mention social and environmental impacts and related corporate reputation issues as factors which may need to be incorporated into a company group's risk assessment systems. The developing importance of these topics makes them of increasing interest to many investors.

A widely acknowledged principle of good corporate governance is that there should be clear board-level accountability for important issues and subject areas. The discipline of having a named senior individual responsible for a topic is considered to improve accountability as it encourages greater transparency and reporting of issues within the company.

In view of the growing pressure on companies to improve their policies and performance on social issues and to engage more deeply with their stakeholders, more and more investors are demanding explicit board-level accountability for social-issue topics. Accordingly, when reviewing companies, EIRIS asks if they have a named board member or senior executive with responsibility for different social and stakeholder topics.

Definitions

Stakeholder issues – any of the following six areas:

- Equal opportunities and diversity.
- Health and safety.
- Job creation and job security.
- Training and employee development.
- Relationships with customers and suppliers.
- Community involvement.

Corporate governance: Women on the board

Why is this an issue?

The 'glass ceiling' beyond which many women are unable to progress in their careers is most evident in the boardroom. According to research by Opportunity 2000, a business-led campaign to improve prospects for women, there are 109 positions held by women on the boards of directors of the British companies listed in '*The Times* Top 200'. This represents only 5 per cent of the total number of 2,000 positions. Opportunity 2000 says that, although there is evidence that the number of women directors is growing, they remain under-represented. The group argues that '81% of women directors are the only woman on the board, and without a significantly higher number of women at the top decision-making levels, it will be hard to achieve the desired culture change towards equal opportunities'. Accordingly, ethical investors concerned about equal opportunities may wish to select companies that take steps to appoint more women directors.

Corporate governance: Disclosure

Why is this an issue?

As investors, the public and government increasingly recognize the need for quality information on corporate policy and practice. For investors to be able to pick and choose between companies it is essential they have sufficient information to make an informed decision. The Cadbury, Greenbury, Hampel and Turnbull reports have all called for greater disclosure and transparency regarding corporate governance. Michael Meacher, former Minister for the Environment, called on companies to publish environmental reports. Shareholder resolutions have been put to company annual general meetings asking them to explain certain practices. Organizations such as EIRIS seek to improve dialogue with companies in order to better inform investors about corporate activities and behaviour. An absence of disclosure and transparency makes this task more difficult.

Investors who are concerned about non-disclosure by companies may wish to use these criteria. This may be to influence their investment decisions but also, perhaps, in order to put pressure on non-disclosing companies to be more open.

Definitions

Responded – the companies that have written, telephoned or faxed an acknowledgement or comments on the contents of the EIRIS Company Report giving details about them, or that have answered a recent EIRIS questionnaire. We do not include companies that responded saying they refused.

Environment: Environmental policy, management, reporting and performance

Why is this an issue?

Public concerns about the degradation of the environment are becoming increasingly widespread. Protests, shareholder actions, boycotts and other campaigns have brought these concerns to the attention of business. Companies have responded to this in a variety of ways. They can produce a policy statement or commit themselves to a set of principles established by organizations such as the International Chamber of Commerce (ICC). They can implement an environmental management system, either using one developed by statutory bodies or developing their own. They can also communicate and report their environmental performance and impacts. The resulting picture is characterized by a plethora of initiatives and approaches. Developments have inevitably been uneven with companies progressing at different speeds. But today it is possible to find companies:

- Working with rather than against the likes of Greenpeace and the World Wide Fund for Nature.
- Engaging in stakeholder discussion panels with their 'critics'.
- Implementing an environmental management system across many of their operations.
- Publishing their environmental performance on the internet for anybody to scrutinize.
- Speaking the language of sustainable development and 'triple-bottom-line' reporting.

Definitions

High-, medium- and low-impact classifications – companies may be involved in one or more of the business sectors listed in Table A3.1. Where more than 15 per cent of a company's turnover derives from high-impact or medium-impact sectors, the company is classified as high or medium impact accordingly. If the company only has significant activities in low-impact sectors then it is classified as low impact.

Table A3.1 Business sector classifications

High impact	Medium impact	Low impact
Agriculture	DIY and building supplies	Information technology
Air transport	Electronic and electrical equipment	Media
Airports	Energy and fuel distribution	Leisure not elsewhere classified (gyms and gaming)
Building materials (includes quarrying)	Engineering and machinery	Consumer/mortgage finance
Chemicals and pharmaceuticals	Financials not elsewhere classified	Property investors
Construction	Hotels, catering and facilities management	Research and development
Fast-food chains	Manufacturers not elsewhere classified	Support services
Forestry and paper	Printing and newspaper publishing	Wholesale distribution
Major systems engineering	Property developers	
Mining and metals	Public transport	
Oil and gas	Retailers not elsewhere classified	
Pest control	Vehicle hire	
Power generation		
Road distribution and shipping		
Supermarkets		
Vehicle manufacture		
Waste		
Water		

Environment: Environmental policy

Why is this an issue?

Companies can produce a policy statement or commit themselves to a set of principles established by organizations such as the International Chamber of Commerce (ICC).

Definitions

Environmental commitment – the act of signing declarations, charters, etc, or membership of organizations, forums or industry sector initiatives, by which the company has expressed a public intention to adhere to a set of environmental principles or commitments.

Environmental policy – an explicit statement published by the company in its annual report, environmental report, brochures, leaflets, website or any other of its publicly available literature. Alternatively it may be an interpretation made by EIRIS of the contents of text found in these publications which implicitly describe the company's attitude and commitments and can be regarded as amounting to an environmental policy even if it is not explicitly designated as such. We do not include information provided in correspondence, or in internal or staff documents.

Environment: Environmental management

Why is this an issue?

Companies can implement an environmental management system to help monitor impacts and performance, either using one developed by international bodies or developing their own.

Definitions

Environmental management system – environmental management systems that have either been certified or devised by the company itself.

Environmental management systems that have been certified – those that have been certified to either EMAS or ISO14001 standard.

EMAS – the Eco-Management and Audit Scheme whereby particular company sites can obtain registration certificates, and the audit reports must be publicly available. It has only been applicable for manufacturing, mining, power stations and recycling/waste disposal operations, but revisions to its governing regulation are expected to lead to it encompassing all sectors of economic activity. As a European Union scheme, registration only occurs for sites within its borders plus Norway, although companies may have sites elsewhere with environmental management systems designed and operating on the same basis, which we would also include.

ISO14001 – the international environmental management standard established by the International Standards Organization that is open to any organization. This superseded BS7750 in the United Kingdom in October 1997 and similar national standards in other countries.

Environment: Environmental reporting

Why is this an issue?

Companies can address their critics and become more transparent by publishing information on their environmental commitments, impacts and performance. This may occur in a variety of formats.

Definitions

Environmental reporting – that contained within either a stand-alone environmental report, a dedicated section in a company's annual report and accounts or on its website.

Made a commitment to report publicly – companies who have made clear in their own policy that they intend to, or are signatories or supporters of, the ICC Business Charter for Sustainable Development, the United Nations Environment Programme's initiatives for insurance and financial institutions, or other similar initiatives that EIRIS may include under Environmental Policy that incorporate such a commitment. For companies who have just made such a commitment, a 'reporting year's' grace is provided.

Report publicly – either a stand-alone environmental report, a dedicated section in a company's annual report and accounts or on its website.

Stand-alone environmental report – reports of environmental performance published separately from the annual report and accounts. We also include those reports which have clear environmental content but may be called Health, Safety and Environment (HSE) Reports, Sustainability Reports, Stakeholder Reports, Stewardship Reports or similar. Commonly these are produced by the parent company, but we also include those reports if produced by a significant part of the company. By **significant part** we mean a division, subsidiary or operating unit with at least 10 per cent of the company's annual reported turnover.

Environment: Environmental performance

Why is this an issue?

Many companies have introduced environmental management systems (EMS) in order to control their environmental risks, reduce their impact on the environment and deliver continuous improvements in environmental performance, beyond legal compliance.

Socially responsible investors are increasingly seeking to invest in companies that are managing their environmental impacts. Good environmental management is often seen as proxy for good management generally, and can potentially deliver costs savings as well as environmental benefits.

Many companies are now reporting publicly on their environmental performance, although the format and content of these reports varies widely from one company to another. As more companies adopt certified EMS the spotlight is now turning to what companies have actually achieved in performance terms. A method to consistently analyse the often confusing array of data provided by companies is therefore needed.

Why is biodiversity important?

Biodiversity is vital for maintaining ecosystems on which all life depends. It is known that diverse ecosystems are better able to withstand environmental changes, such as climate change. Conserving biodiversity is therefore essential in ensuring the continued functioning of the ecosystems on which we all depend.

Biodiversity also has practical implications for business. Many businesses, for example forestry, fishing and agriculture, depend directly on biological resources. Others may depend on the quality of the local environment or require ecosystem 'services', for example the purification of sewage discharges by river systems. Some businesses operate near to habitats under statutory protection, and many own or occupy large landholdings which have potential for promoting biodiversity conservation. The restoration of disused sites can create valuable new habitats.

Definitions

Biodiversity – the total variety and variability of all life on earth, including microorganisms, plants and animals. Biodiversity includes both common and rare species, the ecosystems in which they occur, and genetic variation within species (Case studies in business and biodiversity, *Earthwatch*, March 2000).

Biodiversity policy – a general policy defining a company's approach to biodiversity and strategy for implementation which may cover all or part of a company's operations or sites. For example, a forestry company's policy may be to manage forests in a sustainable manner, which enhances biodiversity while maintaining economic yields.

Demonstrated improvement – the reduction in a company's environmental impact relative to production or sales volumes over a specified time period, indicated by data either published or provided to EIRIS in response to an information request.

Environmental performance – the overall impact of the company on the environment, as measured by appropriate key performance indicators (KPIs).

Primary impact – companies whose operations directly impact upon biodiversity. Activities in this category include: airports and other transport infrastructure providers, agriculture, food production, forestry, mining, quarrying, ports and shipping, food production, oil and gas exploration and production, water, construction, civil engineering and utilities (usually through large landholdings).

Secondary impact – companies whose operations have an immediate indirect impact on biodiversity through their processes, supply chain or products. Activities in this category include: transport companies, supermarkets and DIY retailers, chemical and pharmaceutical companies, building materials, steel and other metal processors and property developers.

Environment: Greenhouse gases

Why is this an issue?

Evidence of climate change is mounting: Antarctic ice sheets are melting, record temperatures have been observed in recent years, and many regions have witnessed severe storms, flooding and drought. The international science community has now accepted that one cause of climate change is likely to be the increase in greenhouse gas emissions, particularly carbon dioxide, that has occurred since the industrial revolution.

The IPCC, an international panel of scientists, predicts that, if carbon dioxide levels increase to much more than double their pre-industrial levels, then the earth's temperature could rise by up to 3.5°C by the end of the next century. Likely effects are predicted to include rising sea levels, resulting in the loss of low-lying lands, an increase in storms and droughts, and the melting of the frozen Arctic soil, causing landslides and destroying roads, railways and buildings. Climate change could also prove catastrophic for the world's biodiversity as forests that cannot adapt to the changed conditions will be lost.

The prospect of such drastic consequences convinced many governments to take action, and so the Climate Change Convention was agreed at the Rio Earth Summit in 1992. Under the Kyoto Protocol to the convention, industrialized nations have now agreed to reduce their emissions of greenhouse gases by 5 per cent on average over the next decade. Efforts are being made to improve energy efficiency and develop cost-efficient renewable energy sources such as wind and solar power, which produce no carbon dioxide. But far greater efforts will be required in future to reduce our dependency on fossil fuels if we are to achieve the 60 per cent reduction in carbon dioxide emissions that is thought necessary to avoid dangerous climate change.

Definitions

Energy-intensive industries – sectors whose share of energy consumption was at least twice their contribution to UK output, for manufacturing industries as a whole in 1989. (This is the latest year for which figures are available from the Department of Energy.) The sectors are bricks and ceramics; cement, lime and plaster; mineral extraction; glass and glassware; basic chemicals; paper and board; iron and steel; and ferrous foundries.

Energy-intensive industry subsectors – brick and tile manufacturers, ceramics manufacturers, ready-mixed concrete and aggregates, concrete producers, pre-cast concrete manufacturers, glass industry, mining and quarrying, industrial chemical manufacturers, forging industry, iron founders, steel producers, paper and board manufacturers.

Fossil fuels – coal, oil or gas, including liquefied petroleum gas (LPG).

Fossil fuel industries – the extraction, refining or distribution of fossil fuels.

Renewable energy – solar, wind, wave, biomass or geothermal power.

Environment: Mining and quarrying

Why is this an issue?

Ethical investors may have a variety of reasons to be concerned about mining and the extraction of commodities. Some may be concerned about pollution and the effect individual operations have on the landscape and local communities. The production processes associated with opencast or strip mining may be of particular concern to these investors. Others argue that the nature of extractive industries is inherently damaging to the environment not just because of the production process but also because the end products serve to increase greenhouse gas emissions, waste energy, and discourage recycling of resources. EIRIS identifies companies directly involved in mining and the extraction of raw materials.

Definitions

Aggregates – rocks that consist of a number of different minerals such as sand or gravel. We do not cover the extraction of oil and natural gas under this heading.

Extraction – can be from mines that are underground or above ground (opencast mining). Products such as sand, gravel and granite are extracted at quarries and open-air pits. Extraction can also be done by special dredging equipment, removing minerals from under a river, lake or the sea.

Mining – the extraction of ores, aggregates and other minerals.

Ores – minerals, such as copper or iron ores, from which elements such as metals can be derived.

Turnover – annual turnover over £1 million. By annual turnover we mean the turnover of the entire company, including subsidiaries and associated companies.

Environment: Nuclear power

Why is this an issue?

The threat of radioactive contamination from an incident at a nuclear power station like the Chernobyl disaster typifies what worries people most about nuclear power. But less serious incidents happen every year and these, together with legal radioactive discharges, are a cause for concern. According to campaigning organizations, such as Friends of the Earth, the nuclear power industry has so far failed to come up with a solution to the problem of intermediate and high-level radioactive waste. Efforts by Nirex to find a disposal site for the UK's radioactive waste suffered a serious setback in 1997, when they were refused planning permission to construct an underground test laboratory near Sellafield. Another concern is that nuclear reprocessing also produces plutonium, the raw material for nuclear weapons.

Definitions

Own or operate nuclear power stations – we exclude those which are permanently shut down. Ownership of these is covered under decommissioning, which falls within the policy question 'supply products or services for the nuclear parts of plants: major'.

Conventional area – areas that are common to all power stations, such as the turbine building and transformers, the diesel generator building, and the cooling tower and intake structures, including the building which houses the circulating water pumps.

Nuclear area – the reactor building, auxiliary building and control room, the fuel-handling building, and radioactive waste storage and reprocessing buildings. EIRIS has differentiated company groups supplying products or services for the nuclear parts of plants into 'major' and 'minor', taking into account such issues as specificity, scale and the supply chain. In some cases one aspect may override another; for example, if a software company's involvement consists of one project, it could be categorized as 'minor'.

Nuclear power industry associations – national and international trade associations which promote nuclear power. We include trade associations which make their membership lists publicly available, including the British Nuclear Industry Forum, the Spanish Nuclear Industry Forum, the Canadian Nuclear Association, the German Atomic Forum, the Uranium Institute, and Foratom.

Environment: Ozone-depleting chemicals

Why is this an issue?

Ozone in the upper atmosphere shields the earth's surface from damaging ultraviolet rays from the sun. Ozone-depleting chemicals such as CFCs react with and destroy ozone, leading to the thinning of the ozone layer and the so-called 'ozone hole' that appears over the Antarctic each year. Depletion of the ozone layer allows an increased amount of ultraviolet radiation to reach the earth's surface. This can lead to increases in skin cancer and cataracts and damage to micro-organisms that form the base of marine food chains. Record levels of ozone destruction in both the northern and southern hemispheres have been recorded in recent years: over the Arctic the ozone levels fall by an average of 25 per cent in early springtime, while in the Antarctic up to 70 per cent of ozone is destroyed. Although the concentration of chlorine and bromine in the upper atmosphere is thought to be at its peak, severe ozone depletion is expected to continue for another 10 to 20 years, and it will be at least 50 years before the ozone layer recovers.

The adoption of the Montreal Protocol in 1987 led to a schedule for phasing out all ozone depleters, beginning with the most damaging chemicals, such as CFCs, which were widely used in refrigeration, aerosols and foam production, and halons, which were used in fire extinguishers. Although the production and import of these chemicals is largely banned in developed nations, their use is still permitted while stocks last. Some production is allowed for essential purposes, and also for export to developing countries. In developing countries, production is permitted until 2010, although efforts are already being made in several countries to phase out the use of CFCs. Despite the progress made under the Montreal Protocol, there has been widespread concern over the illegal trade in CFCs, which are smuggled from countries such as China into Europe and the United States.

Timetables have also been agreed for the phase-out of less damaging ozone depleters, including HCFCs, the interim CFC substitutes, and methyl bromide, an agricultural pesticide. But it will be well into the next century before a complete phase-out of all ODCs is achieved under current regulations.

Definitions

Industrial or commercial refrigeration equipment – that used in oil, gas and petrochemical processing, chemicals and pharmaceuticals manufacture, refrigerated storage and transport, food and drink processing/manufacture, and by large retailers of food and drink such as supermarkets, and large hotel and pub chains. We do not include the use of refrigeration by small food and drink retailers such as off-licences, newsagents, petrol station shops, restaurants, cafés, fast-food outlets catering, and vending machines.

Manufacture or supply products containing ozone-depleting chemicals – the manufacture, distribution or installation by specialist contractors of refrigeration, air-conditioning and fire-extinguishing equipment containing ODCs, the manufacture or supply of rigid insulating foam containing HCFCs, and pesticides containing methyl bromide. We also include service and maintenance contractors.

Ozone-depletion potential (ODP) – indicates how destructive a particular chemical is. It is calculated from the quantity of chlorine or bromine atoms it contains and its lifetime in the upper atmosphere, compared with CFC-11, which is assigned an ODP of 1.0. CFCs have an ODP of around 1.0; methyl bromide has an ODP of 0.4; and most HCFCs have an ODP in the range 0.02 to 0.1. ODP is usually calculated over a time frame of 100 years, which can mask the short-term effects of, for example, methyl bromide.

High- or medium-rated ozone-depleting chemicals – CFCs, halons, methyl bromide and the solvents 1,1,1-trichloroethane and carbon tetrachloride. **Low-rated ozone-depleting chemicals** – HCFCs.

In developed countries high- and medium-rated ODCs have now been replaced by non-ozone-depleting alternatives in many applications for which they were formerly used, for example as aerosol propellants. They continue to be used as refrigerant gases, as propellants in asthma inhalers, in some fire-extinguishing equipment and, in some applications, as industrial solvents. Methyl bromide is an agricultural fumigant used to kill pests in soil and in stored foods. HCFCs are commonly used as refrigerants and in the manufacture of rigid insulating foam.

These criteria do not cover the ODC replacements such as HFCs (hydrofluorocarbons) and PFCs (perfluorocarbons), which are powerful greenhouse gases, but do not deplete the ozone layer.

Environment: Pesticides

Why is this an issue?

Growing sales of organically produced fruit and vegetables in part reflect the public's increasing concern about the way in which pesticides can affect the food chain. Consumer groups have been at the forefront of highlighting the build-up of pesticide residues in the food and water supply. They point to the resulting health hazards for humans and the ecosystem generally. Awareness of the increasing immunity of certain pests and the depletion of soil fertility caused by monoculture and overuse of fertilizers has contributed to doubts about the long-term sustainability of prevalent intensive farming practices.

Amongst the health hazards arising out of excessive pesticide use are the build-up of chemical residues through the food chain, damage to birds and insects, injuries and deaths among farm workers, and damage to animal and human immune systems. Some pesticide ingredients, for example methyl bromide, are also ozone-depleting chemicals.

Because of these concerns, there is growing regulation of pesticide manufacture and use. EIRIS's criteria focus on identifying companies involved in the distribution of pesticides (such as paraquat) which have either been banned or restricted in more than five countries, or which have been restricted in the UK for posing threats to the aquatic environment.

Investors concerned about these issues may choose to avoid particular types of pesticide which have caused the most concern, or seek to avoid the industry entirely.

Definitions

The Department for the Environment, Food and Rural Affairs (DEFRA) and the Health and Safety Executive (HSE) define a pesticide as 'any substance, preparation or organism prepared or used, among other uses, to protect plants or wood or other plant products from harmful organisms. A pesticide product can also serve to regulate the growth of plants, to give protection against harmful creatures, or to render such creatures harmless. Pesticides therefore have a very broad definition which embraces herbicide, fungicides, insecticides, rodenticides, soil-sterilants, wood preservatives and surface biocides among others.'

Licence to market – companies that have received official approval from DEFRA or the HSE to advertise, sell, supply, store, wholesale or retail pesticides in the UK. Some of these companies also formulate or manufacture the pesticide products concerned.

Red List – a list of substances that DEFRA believes present the greatest potential hazard to the aquatic environment, due to their toxicity, persistence in the environment and ability to accumulate in the food chain. The substances currently on the list are:

- Aldrin
- Azinphos-methyl
- Atrazine
- Cadmium and its compounds
- DDT
- Dichlorvos
- 1,2-Dichloroethane
- Dieldrin
- Endosulfan
- Endrin
- Fenitrothion
- Gamma lindane (gamma hexachlorocyclohexane)
- Hexachlorobenzene
- Hexachlorobutadiene
- Malathion
- Mercury and its compounds
- Pentachlorophenol
- Polychlorinated biphenyls
- Simazine
- Tributyltin compounds
- Trichlorobenzene
- Trifluralin
- Triphenyltin

Environment: Pollution convictions

Why is this an issue?

The effects of many industrial pollutants on human health and the environment are well established. But in recent years attention has been focused on the possible links between poor air quality and asthma and other respiratory complaints, with atmospheric emissions from road traffic and industrial sources thought to contribute to thousands of deaths every year. Concern is also growing over the effects of complex organic chemicals such as pesticides, industrial chemicals and by-products such as dioxins, which are extremely persistent in the environment and can accumulate in the food chain and in the fat tissue of humans and animals. The long-term effects of many synthetic chemicals on ecosystems and human health are unclear, but of increasing concern is the ability of some organic pollutants to act as hormone disrupters.

The system of Integrated Pollution Control (IPC) was introduced under the Environmental Protection Act 1990 (EPA 90), and was designed to prevent or minimize pollution from the most seriously polluting industrial processes. IPC covers major solid, liquid and gaseous emissions from such processes to air, land and water. Under IPC companies are required to use the Best Available Techniques Not Entailing Excessive Cost (BATNEEC) to minimize or prevent the release of substances into the environment.

Companies operating processes regulated by IPC are issued with an authorization setting conditions that must be met in order to minimize such releases. Contravention of these conditions may lead to a legal notice being served. A small number of prosecutions are carried out each year by the Environment Agency or SEPA following a serious pollution incident or as a result of continued non-compliance with conditions set out in a legal notice.

Definitions

The **Environment Agency** regulates the most seriously polluting industrial processes in England and Wales under the Environmental Protection Act 1990, which was previously the responsibility of Her Majesty's Inspectorate of Pollution (HMIP).

The **Scottish Environment Protection Agency (SEPA)** regulates the most seriously polluting industrial processes in Scotland, under the Environmental Protection Act 1990.

EPA 90 is the Environmental Protection Act 1990.

RSA 93 is the Radioactive Substances Act 1993, which controls the release of radioactive discharges or waste.

Environment: PVC and phthalates

Why is this an issue?

Critics of PVC cite increasing evidence that synthetic chemicals such as phthalates and dioxins can act as hormone disrupters. Phthalates are added to PVC to soften it and make it more flexible. Dioxins are given off both in the manufacture of PVC and its ultimate disposal through incineration. Hormone disruption can lead to reduced sperm counts and testicular cancer, suppression of the immune system, and intelligence and behaviour dysfunctions. These hormone disrupters persist in body fat and can accumulate in the food chain. In some cases it is thought that 1 part in 10,000 billion can do damage. The scientific evidence is not fully conclusive. However, some may ask if society should wait for definitive proof of harmful effects before action is taken.

In Western Europe, some governments have introduced policies and legislation curbing PVC, one of the main contributors to the hormone disruption problem. The British government announced in September 1997 that the polluting of the North Sea with harmful chemicals should cease by 2020 in line with the aims of the Oslo–Paris Convention (OSPAR). This is likely to curb the use of phthalates. The European Commission deferred a European-wide ban in 1998 on the use of phthalates in toys for children under three, but eight countries have subsequently banned or restricted their use. Some toy manufacturers are now re-evaluating the use of these chemicals.

Definitions

Leader in the PVC industry – members of the European Council of Vinyl Manufacturers (ECVM), which is the trade body for the PVC industry. The **European Council of Vinyl Manufacturers (ECVM)**, according to its 1996 Review, 'represents the specific interests of the European PVC industry' and its members account 'for virtually all Western European production'.

Manufacture of PVC – includes the production of vinyl chloride monomer (VCM), the raw material of PVC, and compounds of PVC.

Manufacture of PVC-based products – semi-finished products such as blocks, castings, coated materials, films, sheets and tubings and finished products including building and construction materials such as pipes, windows and doors, packaging, and wiring and cabling. We do not cover PVC-based products used in toys, furniture, medical products, transport equipment, clothing and footwear, which are relatively minor users of PVC.

Phthalates – a group of chemicals that are added to PVC to plasticize or soften it. There is concern that they are hormone disrupting. They include diethylhexylphthalate (DEHP), diiosonoylphthalate (DINP), butylbenzylphthalate (BBP) and dibutylphthalate (DBP). By **hormone disrupting** we mean the alleged adverse effects upon human reproductive organs including reduced sperm counts and testicular cancer, suppression of the immune system, intelligence and behaviour dysfunctions. They are also alleged to adversely affect wildlife.

Environment: Tropical hardwood

Why is this an issue?

Tropical forests are home to over half of all species on earth. The loss and degradation of these forests therefore has dramatic consequences for the world's biodiversity. Around 15 million hectares of tropical forest are still lost each year, which is thought to cause 75 species to become extinct every day. Forests have other vital roles: they help to regulate the climate and protect soils and river systems, in addition to providing a livelihood for many indigenous communities. Burning forests to clear land releases huge amounts of carbon dioxide – a potent greenhouse gas – into the atmosphere. Deforestation can also exacerbate the effects of climate change. This was seen in Central America in 1998 when the area was hit by Hurricane Mitch; land that had been previously cleared of trees became destabilized, resulting in mudslides that buried whole villages.

Deforestation has several causes, including the clearance of land for agriculture, plantations and development, commercial logging and the collection of fuel wood. Even where land is not completely cleared, the selective logging of commercially valuable species degrades the overall quality of the forest, threatening the survival of many mammals and birds. Some of the tree species themselves are endangered by over-exploitation. Logging can have a further, indirect, effect: by driving roads through previously untouched forests, logging companies open up the way to even greater destruction as they provide access for migrant farmers.

Two-thirds of the world's remaining forests are commercially exploited for the production of timber and pulp. Responsible management is therefore essential to prevent the continuing degradation and loss of the world's forests. Widespread public concern has led to calls for the 'sustainable' management of forests, which would ensure the long-term production of timber, a valuable renewable resource, as well as protecting the ecological systems and livelihoods of communities that depend on the forests.

A labelling system has been developed for products derived from well-managed forests, which gives the consumer a guarantee of sustainability. The scheme is run by the Forest Stewardship Council (FSC), an independent, non-profit-making organization. The FSC scheme applies to all types of forest, including temperate and boreal forests such as those in North America, Russia and Scandinavia, where commercial logging threatens some old-growth forests. Plantations are also covered by the scheme, since these often have damaging effects on the environment and rarely provide good habitats for wildlife.

Definitions

Construction includes property development and refurbishment by major property developers, and fitting out of shops, whether carried out by the company directly or by independent contractors on the company's behalf. We also include construction or fitting out of ships and boats. We do not include companies that construct only their own buildings such as stores, offices or hotels.

FSC-certified products are manufactured under a chain-of-custody certificate awarded by an organization accredited by the Forest Stewardship Council (FSC). This provides a guarantee that the source of the raw material can be traced back to a certified well-managed forest.

The **Forest Stewardship Council (FSC)** is an independent, non-profit, non-governmental body that supports environmentally appropriate, socially beneficial and economically viable management of the world's forests.

Joinery – doors, window frames, staircase parts, fitted kitchens, conservatories, flooring, partitions and coffins.

Members of the **WWF forest products buyers groups**, such as the UK 1995+ Group, are committed to purchasing increasing amounts of forest products from independently certified, well-managed sources. This includes products from all types of forest, including tropical, temperate and boreal forests and plantations. Some groups are being established at present, and records will be added to the database when membership details become available. The buyers groups may include companies or parts of companies that do not purchase or use any tropical hardwood.

Mining – mineral extraction. We also include oil or gas exploration.

Other purposes – road construction or other infrastructure development.

Tropical hardwood – species listed by Friends of the Earth in *The Good Wood Guide* (1990) in Table 1: An A–Z of Tropical Hardwoods.

Uncertified – products sourced from forests that have not been certified as being well managed by an organization accredited to the Forest Stewardship Council (FSC). The FSC is an independent, non-profit, non-governmental body that supports environmentally appropriate, socially beneficial and economically viable management of the world's forests.

Environment: Water pollution

Why is this an issue?

Water is the most important natural resource and its pollution has both environmental and economic impacts. The consequences of water pollution depend both on the type and level of pollution and the use to which the receiving water is put. Sewage discharges have polluted bathing waters and threatened the health of bathers. Water supplies may be contaminated by pollution if the receiving water is used as a source of drinking water. Toxic discharges may kill fish and other aquatic wildlife, and may ultimately affect the marine environment. International attention is currently focused on the potential long-term effects on human health and wildlife of many complex chemicals that cannot be broken down naturally and persist in the environment.

In the UK, rivers are classed according to their ability to support different types of fisheries, although the EU is proposing a future system that will take account of a wider range of ecological factors. There have been great improvements in general water quality in recent years, although these have been offset by climatic factors such as reduced rainfall and warmer temperatures. Improving water quality confers several benefits, including increased recreation and amenity value, the support of higher-quality fisheries and other aquatic life, and providing additional sources of drinking water.

Most of the UK's poorer-quality rivers are in industrial areas. The regulatory agencies set limits for industrial discharges in accordance with water quality objectives determined either nationally or in compliance with EU standards. Although it is an offence to exceed the limits set for a particular discharge, a large number are breached every year. Accidental spills also occur, which may require costly clean-up procedures. Although the most serious incidents result in a prosecution (if there is sufficient evidence), relatively little regulatory action is taken when site operators are found to be in breach of their discharge consents. Even when prosecutions are successful, it has often been suggested that the level of fines imposed by the courts is unlikely to present a real deterrent to polluters.

Definitions

Discharge consent – a discharge consent must be obtained from the Environment Agency or SEPA by any individual or organization wishing to discharge effluent into rivers, estuaries or underground or coastal waters. If the consent is granted it sets permitted limits for different parameters for discharges at a particular location. It also specifies **sampling points** at which monitoring will take place.

Different types of consent are granted for different types of effluent. We have only examined **trade effluent** consents, which are also referred to as industrial effluent consents. The other main type of consent is the sewage consent, and these are held primarily by the water companies. Compliance with sewage consents is included in the criteria covering **water suppliers**. We do not examine agricultural discharge consents.

Breached a discharge consent means that samples taken by the Environment Agency or SEPA showed results for one or more parameters that were outside of the permitted range.

Parameters of a consent are limits set for aspects of the discharge that affect water quality, such as **biochemical oxygen demand** (BOD) and suspended solids. BOD measures the amount of oxygen required to break down the organic matter present. **Suspended solids** measures the total free (usually visible) solids in the water. Limits for other substances, such as metals, may be imposed to maintain water quality and comply with European legislation.

The **Environment Agency** is a government agency which has various responsibilities, including those of safeguarding and improving the natural water environment in England and Wales. The **Scottish Environment Protection Agency (SEPA)** fulfils a similar function to the Environment Agency, but prosecutions in Scotland are carried out by the Procurator Fiscal on the advice of SEPA.

A Formal Caution is issued by the Environment Agency or SEPA when an operator admits to an offence but no prosecution follows. The Formal Caution is signed by the operator, returned to the Environment Agency and is added to the public register.

The **Red List** is a list of substances that the Department of the Environment believes present the greatest potential hazard to the aquatic environment, due to their toxicity, persistence in the environment and their ability to accumulate in the food chain. The current list:

- Aldrin
- Azinphos-methyl
- Atrazine
- Cadmium and its compounds
- DDT
- Dichlorvos
- 1,2-dichloroethane
- Dieldrin
- Endosulfan
- Endrin

- Fenitrothion
- Gamma lindane (gamma hexachlorocyclohexane)
- Hexachlorobenzene
- Hexachlorobutadiene
- Malathion
- Mercury and its compounds
- Pentachlorophenol
- Polychlorinated biphenyls
- Simazine
- Tributyltin compounds
- Trichlorobenzene
- Trifluralin
- Triphenyltin

Financial institutions

Why is this an issue?

Recent announcements of major mergers in the financial world may be regarded by some investors as an indication of the growing power and influence of these institutions. Enormous flows of capital are channelled through financial companies. Pension funds, often controlled or managed by insurance companies and other financial companies, own a large proportion of the shares in quoted companies as well as private companies. Others provide financial backing for governments and their institutions, exports of goods and services around the world, and a host of other services.

Some investors may be particularly concerned about the investments financial institutions hold, or about the loans they make and the services they provide. For example, an investor wishing to avoid companies involved in alcohol or animal testing may also wish to avoid financial institutions which provide financial services to those companies or which invest in them.

EIRIS is not able to monitor fully the loans and investments of financial institutions. Banks with subsidiary or associated company investments in some of the areas EIRIS researches may be identified under those headings. For example, a bank may have an investment in a company involved in arms or alcohol production. Where EIRIS is aware of this type of involvement by financial institutions we record it. However, if investors want to be certain to avoid financial companies that may have investments in areas they disapprove of, choosing some of the criteria above may help them.

Definitions

Classification is based upon the following definitions used by the FTSE Actuaries Industry Classification System:

Asset managers – asset managers.

Consumer finance – credit card companies, providers of financial services (re personal loans).

Mortgage finance – institutional producers of mortgages and mortgages not engaging in other types of retail or commercial banking.

Other financial – financial holding companies and companies engaged in financial activities not specified elsewhere.

Banks – banks providing a broad range of financial services, with significant retail banking and money transmission.

Investment banks – banks providing a range of specialist financial services, primarily to corporate client stockbrokers.

Insurance brokers – insurance and life assurance.

Insurance – non-life – companies engaging in fire, accident, marine and other classes of insurance business.

Insurance (Lloyd's Funds) – principally investment companies and trusts involved in insurance underwriting.

Reinsurance – reinsurance companies.

Other insurance – insurance companies with life assurance, non-life insurance and reinsurance interests, no one of which predominates.

Life assurance – companies engaging principally in the life assurance business, and/or disability business.

Fur

Why is this an issue?

Anti-fur campaigners believe that the use of fur for clothing is cruel and unnecessary, whether the fur comes from trapping wild animals or from fur farms. Real fur is viewed as a luxury item for which there can be little ethical justification.

Definitions

Fur products – items of clothing or accessories, principally coats and capes, made from animal fur. We do not include fur trims on garments made principally of other material. By **animal fur** we mean the skins of fur-bearing animals bred or hunted for their coats. We do not include leather or sheepskin.

Gambling

Why is this an issue?

As with alcohol and tobacco, gambling has long been a cause for concern amongst the ethical funds. With the advent of the National Lottery, and the deregulation of the UK gambling industry which took place in 1996, there have been claims that addiction to gambling is on the increase in Britain. A government-sponsored report which came out in 1996 estimated that there were 1.5 million problem gamblers in Britain.

The National Lottery has made gambling more socially acceptable, more accessible and more attractive to young people and women. Since its launch in 1994, the lottery has been subject to frequent criticism from gambling-concern groups, church bodies and the medical profession for encouraging compulsive behaviour, greed, poverty and illness. There are fears that low-income families are diverting much-needed cash away from basic necessities into gambling, and that the lottery is effectively a tax on the poor. The average weekly spend on the lottery is around £4.00, with more than 7 in 10 households playing regularly.

A broad range of businesses have blamed the lottery for reduced profitability over the past two years, in particular smaller retail outlets without lottery terminals. There has also been a drop in donations by individuals to charities. Whilst some charities have benefited from lottery grants, the National Council for Voluntary Organisations has estimated a net fall in overall charitable giving.

Most gambling is restricted to those aged over 18, but the age limit for playing the National Lottery was reduced to 16. Grave concern has been expressed by children's organizations and OFLOT itself over the issue of under-age gambling. Research commissioned by OFLOT and published in February 1998 suggests that 5 per cent of young people may have a problem with gambling, with fruit machines and scratch-cards being of particular concern. Deregulation plus the influence of the National Lottery has been partly blamed for the boom in other types of gambling, such as casinos and bingo. A study of reformed gamblers found that they are lured back into their addiction by the Lottery, and calls to Gamblers Anonymous have risen by 17 per cent since the Lottery started.

The internet and television have made it possible to place bets and gamble online, attracting a new breed of gambler who would not normally visit traditional gambling venues such as betting shops or casinos. Online gambling is still relatively new, but, as with the National Lottery, its introduction may make gambling more accessible and convenient, potentially leading to an increase in the number of problem gamblers.

Definitions

Gambling – the operation of betting shops, horse and greyhound racing tracks, licensed bingo halls, casinos, gaming clubs, provision of online betting services. We have treated the National Lottery separately. We include passenger ships that have casinos on board, football pools, and the manufacture or supply of gaming or amusement-with-prize machines. We also include companies with sports clubs (such as football and rugby clubs) operating cash lotteries where the proceeds go directly to the company. We do not include the ownership or operation of pubs, arcades or other facilities that house such machines, the manufacture of parts of such machines, spot-the-ball or other prize competitions that are run mainly in shops or in newspapers or the retail of National Lottery tickets.

Turnover – annual turnover. By annual turnover we mean the turnover of the entire company, including subsidiaries and associated companies.

Turnover up to 3 per cent – annual turnover over £1 million. By annual turnover we mean the turnover of the entire company, including subsidiaries and associated companies.

Turnover of 3 per cent and above – the turnover in the accounts of the parent company and normally excluding associated companies.

Genetic engineering

Why is this an issue?

Genetic engineering is generally perceived to be a radically new way of manipulating nature. The ability to transfer genes across species barriers, so that genes found in bacteria can be incorporated into the genetic make-up of a plant, or human genes can be transferred into a sheep, is viewed with distrust by many outside the biotechnology industry. Different applications of genetic engineering raise different concerns:

- **Genetic engineering in agriculture.** This is the application which has given rise to most protest and direct action. The cultivation of genetically modified (GM) crops and their use in everyday foods have led to concerns about the following: environmental pollution and the threat to local biodiversity, food safety, consumer rights and choices, farmers' rights and the threat to their traditional method of planting crops from saved seeds, food security for the developing world, and the increasing dominance of multinational corporations.

- **The genetic engineering of animals.** This raises issues specifically about animal welfare and the use which humans make of animals. Animals are being genetically engineered to produce human medicines, and to produce animals for research laboratories.
- **The genetic engineering of micro-organisms.** This is used in the production of insulin and other industrial products. This process has raised concerns about accidental releases and survival rates in the environment of genetically modified organisms (GMOs), and the implications this could have for public health.
- **Genetic engineering for healthcare purposes.** The potential development of gene-based drugs, for example, is generally seen as more acceptable than GM applications in agriculture. However, the emphasis on genetics has been criticized as misdirecting resources away from environmental causes of ill health. The hunt for gene traits, such as the 'gay gene' or the 'motherhood gene', has been labelled as oversimplistic genetic determinism. The potential for gene therapy to alter germline cells (which make sperms and eggs) in human beings, and the increased use of genetic testing are seen as possibly leading to 'designer babies' and the creation of a genetic underclass.
- **Patenting.** Biotechnology companies are seeking to patent not only GM animals and plants, but also newly discovered genes. Broadening the patent system to include living things is seen by some as a commodification of life itself. It is also argued that information on human genes should be in the public domain to encourage medical research. The rush by private companies to patent natural resources in the South (where most of the genetic resources of the world are to be found) has been labelled **biopiracy**. It has been seen as a new colonization process, with as yet no laws to halt the 'gold rush'.

Definitions

Animals – all living vertebrate animals (except man); this includes fish and birds.

Catering and hospitality sector – includes restaurants, fast-food outlets, hotels, public houses, contract food services and cruise lines.

Cloning – the artificial production of genetically identical copies of an animal.

Contained setting – the contained use of GMOs under circumstances in which the organisms are prevented from escaping, for example in fermentation tanks, laboratories or factories. In practice this covers principally the genetic engineering of micro-organisms such as bacteria and yeast. However, it could cover genetic engineering of plants or insects too. We do not distinguish at the criteria level between those companies carrying out research and those which are using the technology on a large industrial scale. However, the scale of companies' activities is made clear in the EIRIS Company Reports.

Food products – along with foods such as biscuits, bread, confectionery and so on, we also include soft drinks and animal feed.

For any purpose including medical – the use of genetic engineering in a contained setting for research, development or production relating to industrial and medical products. By **for any purpose excluding medical** we exclude genetic engineering for research, development or production of human medicines.

Genetic engineering – the use of recombinant DNA technology, which is the technology of transferring genes between organisms that would not naturally interbreed. **DNA** is the hereditary substance, which contains a complete set of information determining the structure and function of a living organism. A **gene** is a stretch of DNA which carries the information required for constructing proteins, such as enzymes and hormones, which control the development and functioning of all organisms. Genetic engineering is the central technology within **modern biotechnology**, which includes cloning and xenotransplantation, and the patenting of genes.

GM soya and maize ingredients which are not required by law to be labelled – those ingredients which are derived from GM soya or maize, but which may not contain detectable traces of the foreign DNA or protein, or which may not be subject to the EU's Council Regulation no. 1139/98.

Ingredients derived from soya or maize – **all ingredients which are made from soya or maize, including** soya beans, soya flour, soya protein, tofu, soya milk, textured soya, lecithin made from soya, refined vegetable oil made from soya, starch from soya, soya sauce, hydrolyzed soya protein, maize grains, maize flour, maize protein, refined corn oil, starch from maize, maltodextrins, dextrose, and glucose syrups. The European Union legislation on labelling GMOs in food (Council Regulation no. 1139/98) is limited to those ingredients which contain detectable amounts (over a certain threshold level) of the foreign DNA or protein. In addition it exempts ingredients like lecithin from this regulation because they are covered under other legislation. EIRIS does not limit its definition of genetically modified soya and maize ingredients in this way because consumer and environmental groups consider that attention should be focused simply on whether the ingredient is **derived** from GM soya or maize.

EIRIS has focused on soya and maize because in the United Kingdom at present these are the only two genetically modified food crops which are being marketed (apart from Zeneca's GM tomato paste, which is only sold under the Sainsbury and Safeway own-brand labels). Other GM crops may be marketed in the European Union in the near future, including sugar beet, potatoes and rape. EIRIS will regularly review the situation with respect to the introduction of new GM food crops. Ingredients derived from soya are used in over 60 per cent of processed foods, including biscuits, bread, chocolates, ice cream and ready-prepared meals. Maize derivatives are also widely used in processed foods and soft drinks, for example as sweeteners.

Intended for deliberate release into the environment – the release or marketing of genetically modified organisms (GMOs). In practice at present this relates primarily to GM plants.

Manufacture – includes own-brand sale, processing and development of new food products. By **own-brand** we mean products manufactured by a third-party contract manufacturer which are sold under the company's own label.

Organisms – living things, including animals, plants, insects, and micro-organisms, such as bacteria, viruses and yeast and fungi.

Patent genes – the application to patent sequences of DNA. The sources we are using at present include company information and publications from the Genetics Forum. The EIRIS data for this criterion is not yet comprehensive for all companies, and therefore we are looking into the possibility of using additional sources of information.

Reformulated – ingredients derived from soya and maize are taken out of a food product, and replaced by ingredients from other sources which are not genetically modified.

Refused to reply to EIRIS – the company has either told EIRIS that they will not provide the information requested in the EIRIS questionnaire, or that the company has not responded after a reasonable time period during which EIRIS has been in communication with the company urging them to respond.

Relevant food lines – those products which contain ingredients derived from soya or maize. A **food line** is one particular product, for example one particular type of margarine. The percentage figures work in this way: for example, a company has a moderate GMO avoidance and labelling policy if it has 100 food lines which contain soya or maize, and for 10 of those it sources non-GM soya and maize, or has reformulated 10, or has labelled at least 2 GM soya or maize ingredients across all the relevant food lines.

Poor GMO avoidance and labelling policy – the company: does not source non-genetically modified (non-GM) soya and maize ingredients for at least 10 per cent of its relevant food lines; or has not reformulated at least 10 per cent of its relevant food lines to exclude GM soya and maize ingredients; or does not label at least 2 GM soya or maize ingredients which are not required by law to be labelled.

Moderate GMO avoidance and labelling policy – the company: is sourcing non-GM soya or maize ingredients for 10–50 per cent of its relevant food lines; or has reformulated 10–50 per cent of its relevant food lines to exclude GM soya and maize ingredients; or has labelled at least 2 GM soya or maize ingredients which are not required by law to be labelled.

Good GMO avoidance and labelling policy – the company: is sourcing non-GM soya and maize ingredients for over 50 per cent but under 100 per cent of its relevant food lines; or has reformulated over 50 per cent but under 100 per cent of its relevant food lines to exclude GM soya and maize ingredients; or has labelled all GM soya or maize ingredients which are not required by law to be labelled across all the relevant food lines.

Exceptional GMO avoidance policy – the company: is sourcing all non-GM soya and maize ingredients for all relevant food lines, and does not source any other ingredients from GM crops.

Human rights

Why is this an issue?

The issue of human rights has become increasingly central to the corporate social responsibility agenda over the last few years. This is partly driven by the debate about whether globalization is detrimental or beneficial for developing companies. It is also partly driven by concern about whether corporate behaviour is reinforcing or undermining human rights. A number of campaigns focusing on corporate behaviour, initially in South Africa and more recently in Burma and elsewhere, has placed the spotlight on particular countries where human rights are seen as most at risk (whilst not detracting from the fact that violations of human rights occur in all countries). While governments have primary responsibility to promote and protect human rights, corporations and other organs of society also have responsibilities. Companies have direct responsibility for their own operations, for example that their labour rights policies apply throughout their global operations. Recently, however, companies are starting to be assessed on their wider social impact on local communities, under the banner of fundamental human rights as recognized in the Universal Declaration of Human Rights.

Investors have traditionally boycotted certain countries, but increasingly it is being argued that countries need investment to improve basic social and economic rights. For example, Mary Robinson, the former UN High Commissioner on Human Rights, has highlighted extreme poverty as a major human rights violation. Against this background it is what the company does in a country that is of interest. Is it an influence for good, or does the business either benefit from or somehow support a climate of repression? The arguments are not always clear cut, and the debate about how to assess a company's overall performance on human rights is still at a relatively early stage.

Companies in the oil and gas and mining sector typically have direct links with central governments, often working in joint ventures with them and investing large sums over a long period in the countries concerned. The nature of their industries means that the effect on local communities can be pronounced with displacement of local people, potential pollution threatening livelihoods and security forces guarding pipelines and installations.

Oil and gas and mining companies typically procure licences to carry out exploration work, and buy into joint ventures where equity stakes can be lower than 20 per cent. The issue of security at oil and gas and mining operations has been highlighted by human rights abuses in Colombia, Nigeria, India and elsewhere. In response to this the UK and US governments met with several companies and human rights NGOs in 2000 to develop the Voluntary Principles on Security and Human Rights. These cover corporate policies and practice on private and public security forces, and draw on UN principles on the use of force and law enforcement. In order to be graded higher than basic on policy, companies in this sector need to have policy guidelines on security.

With regard to supply chain standards we cover sectors of high concern, which include: retailers (including general, food, drugs, apparel, household goods, etc), apparel manufacture (clothing, textile, footwear), toy manufacture, sports goods manufacture, food producers and processors, and tobacco.

These sectors have been identified because they have the greatest concentration of activities involving global supply chains, which have been the subject of significant public concern in relation to working conditions. (In future, other sectors and activities may be added.)

For example, clothes and sports goods manufacturers have been targeted by campaigns seeking to improve working conditions, because companies in these sectors have both highly visible operations and also typically a high degree of influence over their supplier companies, which are often wholly dependent on them for orders.

Similarly, retailers and food producers and processors often source products from all around the world, and have a high degree of leverage over their suppliers due to their purchasing power.

EIRIS includes all companies identified in these sectors as having operations in a sector of high concern *unless* it is made clear that the majority of the company's operations do not in practice involve global supply chains (eg a company making a limited range of food products sourced from only one country).

Definitions

Burma – sanctions against the military dictatorship in Burma relate to its dire human rights record, in particular the system of forced labour used for large infrastructure projects, the large number of political prisoners and the suppression of the democratic opposition party, the National League for Democracy (NLD). The NLD's leader, Aung San Suu Kyi, has been in dialogue with the generals in summer 2002, which seems to be leading to greater freedom of movement for herself and other party members. However, it is as yet unclear what the political future holds under the dictatorship.

Category A countries – this list is drawn up annually by EIRIS using a variety of sources, including the Freedom House *Annual Survey*, Human Rights Watch annual reports and Amnesty International annual reports. The methodology is the following:

EIRIS uses the latest Freedom House list of 'not free' countries, and cross-references this with the latest annual reports from Human Rights Watch and Amnesty International. EIRIS looks beyond the Freedom House 'not free' list for other countries of most concern for human rights. An example is Colombia, where armed conflict and killing of trade unionists has led ethical investors and NGOs to question company policies on human rights.

Another filter is used – that of number of EIRIS companies operating in the country of concern (threshold is 25+) to screen out countries where foreign direct investment is not sufficiently high to affect numbers of companies identified. An example is Burundi, for which EIRIS data shows just six companies operating – all of which are identified by operations in several other countries of most concern.

This 'number of companies' filter is not used in cases involving the most authoritarian regimes or where conflict has led to a breakdown of society, for example North Korea, Somalia and Sudan.

Category B countries – those that Freedom House classifies as 'partly free' (3.0 or worse) *and* which *The Observer's* Human Rights Index 1999 marks as having a relative intensity of human rights violations of greater than 10. (This category includes the Category A countries by default.)

Current oppressive regimes list
See Table A3.2.

Freedom House – a non-profit organization founded 60 years ago in the USA as a 'vigorous proponent of democratic values'. It produces a 'Freedom in the World' survey each year, which assigns each country and territory the status of free, partly free or not free, based on combined average ratings for political rights and civil liberties (1–7, with 1 being most free). These are assessed against such rights as the existence of free and fair elections, free trade unions and protection from political terror, exile or torture.

International Labour Organization's Core Standards – these are the eight core conventions which the ILO has designated as 'fundamental to the achievement of basic human rights' and 'decent work'. They relate to: child labour, forced labour, freedom of association and collective bargaining and equal opportunities.

Large presence – EIRIS has categorized the company as having significant operations in A list countries. This means the company is identified by at least one of the following indicators in relation to its operations in oppressive regime countries: 1,000-plus employees; or £100 million-plus turnover or assets.

For the question about oil and gas and mining companies' exploration and production activities in developing countries, rather than the smaller subset of A list countries, 'large presence' means the company is identified by one of the indicators above for its non-OECD country operations.

The Observer's **Human Rights Index 1999 –** ranks countries according to incidence of abuse by head of population under 10 general headings, such as extra-judicial executions, torture, and detention without charge or trial. The scale is 24–0, with the highest scores being the worst abusers.

Oil and mining – as explained above, the EIRIS criteria on human rights are applied to companies with operations in countries considered as oppressive regimes. Operations are defined as 20 per cent-plus equity stake in a company incorporated in these countries, except for oil and gas and mining exploration and production where operations refer to all exploration and production activities.

Table A3.2   EIRIS oppressive regimes list 2003

Category A	Category B
Afghanistan	Category A countries, plus:
Algeria	Burundi
Angola	Cambodia
Bahrain	Chad
Brunei	Cuba
Burma	Equatorial Guinea
Cameroon	Eritrea
China	Ethiopia
Colombia	Guinea-Bissau
Democratic Republic of Congo	Haiti
Egypt	India** (Kashmir)
Iran	Indonesia
Iraq	Israel** (Israeli Administered
Kazakhstan	Territories, and Palestinian
Kenya	Authority Administered
Libya	Territories)
North Korea	Lesotho
Oman	Liberia
Pakistan	Mexico
Rwanda	Morocco* (Western Sahara)
Saudi Arabia	Nepal
Somalia	Nigeria
Sudan	People's Republic of Congo
Syria	Peru
Tunisia	Senegal
United Arab Emirates	Serbia and Montenegro
Vietnam	Sierra Leone
Yemen	Sri Lanka
Zimbabwe	Tanzania
	Togo
	Turkey
	Uganda
	Uzbekistan
	Venezuela

* The country itself is ranked as an A or B list country, in addition to its disputed territory.
** The country's ranking is solely due to that country's disputed territory.

Related and disputed territories – the Freedom House lists include related and disputed territories, which are attributed to the country with which they are linked: these are marked on the list (see Table A3.2) with asterisks.

Strategic business – the concept of strategic businesses is employed by EIRIS to cover companies engaged in activities considered likely to have particular economic or political significance that gives them a particular responsibility for upholding human rights.

Sectors of the FTSE Global Classification System provided an initial starting point for the definition of strategic businesses, in combination with the work of the Amnesty International UK Business Group's list of strategic sectors. A degree of flexibility is applied to the FTSE classification where appropriate. For example, note is taken of the company's business description in its annual report and any comments the company has made to EIRIS with regard to the nature of its business activities. There are some sectors for which companies are reviewed on a case-by-case basis to see if their business includes a significant degree of activity relating to strategic sectors.

The following shows the business sectors which are considered generically strategic (FTSE sector codes provided in brackets):

- Mining (04)
- Oil and gas (07)
- Chemicals (11)
- Construction and building materials (13)
- Steel and other metals (18)
- Aerospace and defence (21) (other than minor components)
- Electronic and electrical (25) (unless consumer goods)
- Engineering and machinery (26) (unless exclusively food, medical or safety equipment)
- Telecommunication services (67)
- Electricity (72)
- Banks (81) (other than exclusively retail banking)
- Information technology hardware (93)
- Software and computer services (97)

Other sectors which can be included:

- Diversified industrials (24)
- Support services (58) (security guards)
- Speciality and other finance (87)

Intensive farming and meat sale

Why is this an issue?

The UK has witnessed growing public interest in vegetarianism in recent years. Surveys suggest that 'true' vegetarians – that is people who don't eat meat of any kind – now account for 4.5 per cent of the UK population, while a further 6.7 per cent draw the line at red meat. This represents a doubling of the equivalent figures from 10 years ago. No doubt many of those who have given up meat for ethical reasons would also like to avoid investing in companies involved in meat production and sale.

But misgivings over the treatment of animals used in food production – for example, the conditions in which they are kept, how they are transported and the methods of slaughter – are by no means the exclusive province of vegetarians. There is also concern about the quality of food produced, particularly about food contamination (in the wake of BSE), antibiotic residues and the use of growth hormones and pesticides. As a result of all this, an increasing number of people are turning their backs on intensive farming.

Definitions

Fish farms – the rearing of fish in tanks or cages. We include the farming of smolts and fingerlings. We do not include the farming of fish for the restocking of rivers or recreational fisheries. We do not include shellfish.

Intensive methods – in relation to pig farming we mean farming systems that use dry sow stalls, tether stalls, farrowing crates, piglet cages, flat deck houses or fully enclosed fattening units.

Poultry farming – the farming of turkeys, broiler chickens and egg-laying hens, unless free-range. Under poultry farming we also include poultry breeding.

Turnover – the turnover reported in the most recent accounts of the parent company. This normally includes subsidiaries and excludes associated companies. By annual turnover we mean the turnover of the entire company, including associated companies.

Sale or processing of meat – the manufacture or butchering or sale of meat or poultry products such as sausages, soups, ready meals and pet foods containing meat. We include supermarkets that sell or process meat. Under **sale or processing of slaughterhouse by-products** we include rendering, processing or sale of leather, animal fats, collagen and gelatine.

Military production and sale

Why is this an issue?

Many people share the fundamental conviction that, because the taking of human life is wrong, warfare is wrong too. Some take this to mean that the use of military force is unacceptable, either for defensive or, more commonly, for offensive purposes. Others disapprove of what they regard as the harmful diversion of government funds from social spending to unproductive and destructive military programmes, both in the developed and the developing worlds.

The proliferation of weapons in poor countries and areas of political instability or war is another concern. In recent years there has been considerable public outcry over landmines and over arms exports to oppressive regimes. The Labour government's espousal of an ethical foreign policy has also raised public awareness of the issues. Sales of warplanes and tanks to countries such as Indonesia have resulted in protests and shareholder resolutions at company annual general meetings. Investment in arms-exporting companies by some charities has also been in the news, which has increased investors' attention on their holdings in such companies. It is hardly surprising, therefore, that avoiding businesses with military links is a top priority for many ethical investors. For some it is the scale of contracts a company has with the Ministry of Defence that may be of concern, especially for those worried about the diversion of government funds from social expenditure.

Definitions

Base – any installation at which weapons systems are deployed, maintained, refitted, stored or developed.

Campaign Against Arms Trade (CAAT) is a pressure group working to end the international arms trade and Britain's role as one of the world's leading arms exporters.

Civilian products or services – non-combat clothing and accessories, accommodation, office and leisure facilities, furnishings and accessories, and civilian passenger vehicles.

End product or service – one that is in a finished state and can be used in its current form either on its own or as part of, or in conjunction with, another product or service. By **essential** we mean indispensable to, or a precondition for, the functioning of a weapon system or military operation. The absence of such a strategic product would preclude this functioning. By **military operation** we mean the use of armed force or preparation or support for it.

General products or services – all products and services which are not civilian (as defined above). Those that are not strategic (see below) include unfinished products or raw materials such as steel, chemicals and wood. Also included in this category are finished products ranging from nuts and bolts through to heating and ventilation equipment.

International military sales activities – the sale of goods, services or intellectual property (including technology) from one country to another; or the supply of goods, services or intellectual property to a state which is not the state of the parent company, or the exhibition or advertisement of these goods or services in internationally available military-related publications, or at international defence exhibitions.

Major exports – the scale of exports achieved by those companies classified as major arms traders of military goods or services by CAAT.

Nuclear bases – military bases where nuclear weapons systems are deployed, maintained, refitted, stored or developed. We do not include services when we are sure that they are not directly related to the deployment of nuclear weapons systems.

Nuclear weapons system – weapons system where the weapon involved is a nuclear weapon or the weapons system is nuclear capable. We include uranium as a strategic product for nuclear weapons when the uranium is sold to a country known to possess nuclear weapons.

Overseas military purchasers – those buying products or services from the exhibitions or catalogues or journals referred to above.

Production of weapons systems includes the refitting of such systems.

Products or services – anything from nuclear weapons to office furniture. We do *not* include alcohol, food, drink, medical equipment or tobacco that are sold to the military.

Sold to the military – the direct sale of products or services to the military, the act of exhibiting at defence sales fairs, being quality assessed to supply goods or services by the defence ministry of the UK or other countries, or promoting goods or services in defence directories.

Strategic parts – end products or services that are essential to modern weapon systems or military operations. Examples of strategic parts for weapons systems include combat and communications equipment, training equipment, and arming devices for missile warheads. Examples of strategic services include computing, communications services and flight simulation training. An example of a strategic part for a nuclear weapons system would include power plants for Trident submarines. An example of a strategic service would include refits on nuclear weapon platforms such as B-2 nuclear bombers.

Strategic products or services – end products or services that are essential to modern weapons systems or military operations. Examples of strategic goods include combat and communications equipment, training equipment, armour and machine tools. Examples of strategic services include computing, communications services and civil engineering.

Strategic services – those that are essential to running of a military or nuclear base. An example of a strategic service for military or nuclear bases would include major civil engineering projects at bases such as the Devonport Royal Navy Dockyards or Aldermaston Atomic Weapons Establishment.

Weapons – products sold for military users that are designed to kill, maim or destroy. This can include ships, tanks, armoured vehicles, aircraft, guns, grenades, bombs, mines, munitions, ammunition, submarine torpedoes, bombs and missiles.

Weapons system – weapons and platforms for weapons.

Political donations

Why is this an issue?

Many large companies have over the years given considerable amounts to political parties. This prompts different types of criticism. Many shareholders disagree with the policies of the political parties to which money is donated. Others may feel that companies should not make political donations unless it can be demonstrated that this is in the interests of the company and is expressly agreed to by a majority of shareholders. More fundamentally, some may regard the giving of money by companies as a corrupting influence on the political process. They may be concerned that a party's close connections with a company may lead it to act in the interests of the company rather than the country and its citizens.

UK companies are required to disclose in their annual reports all donations worth over £250 a year to political parties and affiliated organizations. EIRIS records all these donations and their recipients.

Definitions

Political donations are defined in the Companies Act as being those which go, directly or indirectly, to support a political party of the United Kingdom or any part of it. This includes donations or subscriptions to those who engage in activities which are likely to affect public support for a political party. This question only applies to companies that have made any political donations at all in the last five years.

Pornography and adult entertainment services

Why is this an issue?

Objections to pornography have traditionally centred on its tendency to 'deprave and corrupt'. Current opponents of pornography argue that it is degrading to both men and women, transmitting the message that women are sex objects available solely for male gratification without any form of emotional attachment. Recent research has provided evidence suggesting that it is likely that pornography can be one of the factors that contribute to sexual violence and sex discrimination. Sex offenders for example can make use of pornography to persuade children that the abuse is acceptable behaviour.

EIRIS uses the definition of pornography put forward by Dr Catherine Itzin in a publication edited by her, *Pornography: Women, violence and civil liberation* (1992, OUP): the graphic, sexually explicit subordination of women, which includes sexual objectification or sexual violence.

There has been rising public concern recently about internet pornography, especially child pornography, which is illegal, and also worries about children using the internet and accessing offensive material.

Definitions

Adult entertainment services – programmes or channels described as adult entertainment by the television producers or by the company in its annual report, sales or other literature. We include in this category: the Adult Channel, Playboy TV and TVX Fantasy Channel, game shows or sporting competitions featuring topless female or nude participants, table-dancing or lap-dancing, which involves women stripping and dancing for customers.

Cut 18 certificate films or videos – the British Board of Film Classification (BBFC) requiring cuts to be made before giving the film or video an 18 certificate. Scenes are usually cut because the BBFC considers that they are either excessively violent or that they contain sexual violence or material that is not suitable for general distribution on the grounds of decency. We include cut 18 certificate advertisements and trailers for films and videos.

Pornographic – material that falls within Catherine Itzin's proposed legal definition of pornography, ie the graphic, sexually explicit subordination of women through pictures and/or words, which includes sexual objectification or sexual violence.

Provide – the production or distribution via satellite or cable services, and the staging of live shows.

Positive products and services

Why is this an issue?

Knowing whether the product or service provided by a company contributes positively to society is something that has been of interest to many ethical investors for a number of years. Of course, there may be different views about what products or services should be regarded as positive; and perhaps one can supply a basically 'good' product or service in a way that does not benefit the world. But at the same time companies do put considerable effort into selling and developing their products and services. If these products and services are something you regard as being, broadly speaking, a good thing, then you may feel that the growth and prosperity of the company concerned has a positive impact as its products and services are used more widely and as it meets important needs amongst its customers.

EIRIS has identified six groups of activity which can be seen as providing basic necessities, environmental products and other services which help in solving problems and making the world a safer place.

The six groupings are:

- Environmental technology, including products such as machinery for recycling, wind power generators, and pollution abatement technology.
- Waste disposal companies.
- Public transport and bicycles, including provision of bus services and maintenance of railway tracks.
- Safety and protection, for example alarm systems for elderly people living alone, fire alarms, life jackets and protective clothing.
- Health care, including medicines, hearing aids and spectacles.
- Housing, food and clothing.

For each of these groups of activity, EIRIS measures whether a company's level of involvement amounts to over 10 per cent of reported annual turnover.

Definitions

Environmental technology – technologies associated with pollution and natural resources.

Food, clothing or housing – the manufacture or sale of products or supply of services. We exclude luxury ranges.

Health care – the provision of pharmaceuticals (including research and development of new drugs), medical technology, nursing homes, healthcare centres, hospitals, medical information, dental equipment, hearing aids and ophthalmic products including lenses. We include ownership and operation of healthcare facilities, the provision of medical personnel and the management of healthcare facilities.

Natural resources – both non-renewable and renewable. We include non-renewable resources such as coal, gas, oil and minerals, and also renewable sources such as trees or water. By **conserve** we mean reduce the rate of depletion of the resources or replace the usage by an alternative renewable source. We include such technologies as recycling (eg of glass, paper, board, polythene, oil, plastic, aluminium, and ferrous metals); energy efficiency products (eg compact fluorescent lightbulbs, combined heat and power systems, insulation materials), alternative energy sources (eg solar power, wave power, wind power, geothermal and biomass energy) and water-saving technologies.

Pollution – emissions into the air, discharges into water, and contamination of land. By **control** we mean the measuring, monitoring, reducing and elimination of pollution. We include such technologies as flue gas desulphurization systems for coal power stations, waste gas cleaning systems to remove dioxins, alternative fuels for cars and buses, and drinking water treatment plants.

Public transport – the operation of bus, coach or train services, or the manufacture of buses, coaches, railway rolling stock, components or systems, or bicycles. Under **bus, coach or train services** we include trams, underground trains, light railways and rail freight services. **Operation of train services** – both the operation of trains and the operation and maintenance of the rail network. Under **manufacture of buses, coaches, railway rolling stock, components and systems, or bicycles** we include chassis body builders and bespoke engines for buses, coaches, trains, trams, underground trains, light railways, goods wagons, railway track, signalling and other equipment.

Safety equipment – goods or services whose purpose is to save or protect human life: fire and smoke alarms; locks; security alarm systems for residential dwellings; fall arrest equipment; emergency escape equipment; survival equipment; safety surfaces; safety glass; road safety equipment; protective clothing; explosion protection equipment; surge protection devices; emergency lighting; services and equipment for monitoring food and consumer goods; services or information relating to health and safety law.

Turnover – the turnover in the accounts of the parent company and normally excluding associated companies.

Waste disposal – the collection, treatment or disposal of any kind of waste including sewage, domestic waste and industrial waste. We also include the manufacture of waste disposal or treatment machinery such as sewage flushers, composting equipment and waste shredders.

Size

Why is this an issue?

This section is primarily for information purposes. However, the market value of a company group can also give an indication of the degree to which it dominates its Stock Exchange sector. The fact that a company accounts for a large share of its sector's market value may, in part, reflect its share of the market in which it operates. However, one should be cautious about making a direct correlation. Some companies may account for a large part of their sector and account for a large share of their area of business. But if the sector is one with few quoted companies in it (the rest being foreign owned or private) then it may not have a large share of its market regardless of its share of Stock Exchange sector. In addition, share price can be affected by other factors such as future prospects and profitability which have nothing to do with the size of the company.

Those who are concerned about companies possibly having a disproportionate share of their sector may wish to use these criteria.

Definitions

Market value – the value of all the company's issued share capital.

Stock Exchange subsector – the sector in which that company is classified in the *Stock Exchange Daily Official List*.

Stakeholder policy, systems, engagement and reporting

Why is this an issue?

Business activities have a variety of impacts on different sections of society. These can include positive factors such as providing meaningful employment and good working conditions, support for charities or significantly improving the quality of the goods and services available to customers. Conversely, company activities may involve negative impacts, such as the exploitation of unsafe or poorly paid working conditions.

Without a suitable management system in place, a company may fail to meet key policy commitments towards stakeholders. Investors concerned about stakeholder issues need to check therefore if companies have an effective structure of practices, procedures and processes for identifying, managing and continually improving significant impacts on their stakeholders.

A range of different topics are considered in order to provide an assessment of a company's overall systems for managing stakeholder issues. Relevant indicators that can be used to measure the quality of a company group's systems include the extent of board-level accountability and governance for issues, the use of relevant quality assurance standards and the reporting of appropriate data points.

A range of different topics are considered in order to provide an assessment of a company's overall policy on stakeholder issues. Topics covered are:

- bribery and corruption;
- equal opportunities policy;
- job creation and security;
- training and development;
- corporate governance allocation of board-level accountability for stakeholders.

In practice, there are wide variations in reporting standards on social issues between companies operating both within and between different sectors and countries. The long-standing and increasing public interest in these topics means that more companies are beginning to publish social data, and the extent and quality of social reports is gradually improving.

Although organizations such as the Global Reporting Initiative have published guidance documents in an attempt to standardize the format of reports, the lack of standardized reporting requirements can make it difficult for investors to objectively compare different companies. This task is made harder by the fact that most companies publish little or no meaningful performance data that can be used to make fair comparisons.

Moreover, the practice of 'greenwashing', that is to say companies attempting to mollify ethical and environmental concerns by publishing glossy reports that purport to address these issues without actually implementing appropriate policy changes or providing meaningful performance data, remains a common criticism of corporate reporting.

It is important for investors to be able to distinguish therefore between indicators in reports that are meaningful and helpful in comparing companies and the types of data that are less helpful and/or primarily published for promotional purposes. For example, a report stating the total amount a company gives to charity is not as helpful as a report breaking down the amounts given and detailing the actual projects to which the company contributes. Likewise, a report which has been independently verified by a third party is superior evidence of a company's commitment to social reporting than an unverified report.

Employee issues: Equal opportunities

Why is this an issue?

The treatment of workers and the improvement of employment conditions form a major part of people's perceptions of a company's attitude to its stakeholders and its policies on social issues. An increasingly important element to be considered when assessing labour conditions is a company's attitude towards equal opportunities and diversity.

Despite the many strides made globally in combating discrimination during the last century, much remains to be done to achieve true equality in the workplace. In the United Kingdom, despite the many changes in social attitudes in the last three decades and equal pay legislation and EU directives to ensure added legal protection, women overall still receive only around four-fifths of men's hourly pay. Similarly, despite positive developments since the introduction of the 1976 Race Relations Act in the UK, many people from ethnic minorities are, consciously or otherwise, prevented from progressing within, or in some cases even entering, parts of the workforce.

Changes in social attitudes have increased recognition of the harm done by discrimination and led to growing awareness of other forms of discrimination in addition to sex and race. Employers now more widely recognize all types of discrimination as being bad for business because it limits the skills pool from which they can draw talent and creates a closed mindset towards developing new markets and opportunities. More and more companies now see improving diversity as not just a way to avoid criticism or lawsuits, but as a means towards building reputation and gaining competitive advantage. For example, by not discriminating on the grounds of age, a company can take advantage of highly experienced staff who are often overlooked in the marketplace. Companies can achieve similar results by being proactive in combating discrimination on the grounds of religion or sexual orientation and, moreover, use this to their advantage in helping to market their services more widely.

Equal opportunity is increasingly an issue of global concern. However, progress towards equality is often at different stages of development in different countries. In some countries legislation leads public opinion, whilst in others public opinion creates pressure for legislative reform. There are also some conceptual differences in how the challenge is understood.

The case for gender equality is now widely accepted, as are calls for all forms of discrimination against women, direct and indirect, to be removed. In practice, however, there is a vast difference between the workplace situation in Scandinavia and that in Japan. Social practices, legislation and public opinion all differ greatly. There are also indications globally that the glass ceiling operates differently according to the size of the company concerned.

Equal opportunities in relation to ethnic or other minorities are seen differently around the world. In Australia, for example, the notion is applied to non-English speakers, and issues associated with the indigenous, aboriginal population are seen separately. In much of North America the focus is on diversity policies and the need to create a diverse workforce. As company activities become more global, there is an increasing demand on companies to be seen to be proactive in relation to this issue.

Without effective systems in place to monitor and improve a company's practices on this issue, it can often be difficult for the company to effect real change for the better. The existence of adequate monitoring systems is also important to investors seeking quantitative evidence of the company's performance on this issue.

National regulatory requirements influence the type of disclosure made by companies, so for example within Northern Ireland and the United States equal opportunities legislation requires significant disclosure of the religious and racial compositions of their workforce respectively, whilst in other countries the collection of such statistics based on ethnicity is illegal.

In relation to the reporting of the latter type of figure, EIRIS makes allowance in its scoring system for companies which confirm that they are mainly operating in a country where this is not permitted.

Definitions

Policy – a specific set of guidelines, or collection of written commitments found in company literature which when taken as a whole can be deemed to shape the company's strategy and activities.

Equal opportunity development initiatives – membership of or support for programmes and organizations which give a positive indication that a company is taking proactive steps to increase the scope and effectiveness of its equal opportunities policy. Such organizations may be involved, for example, in providing mentoring or networking opportunities to disadvantaged groups. Examples of relevant organizations in the UK are:

- Opportunity 2000;
- Employer's Forum on Child Care;
- Employer's Forums on Age and Disability;
- Business in the Community – Race for Opportunity.

Employee issues: Health and safety

Why is this an issue?

In most modern industrial societies, there is a general consensus that employees have the right to work in a safe environment and that employers should not put employees' health and safety at risk.

In the UK, the Health and Safety at Work Act 1974 (reinforced by European Union initiatives) provides the framework for the supervision and enforcement of health and safety requirements by the Health and Safety Commission and the Health and Safety Executive (HSE). The HSE has helped to keep the number of workplace fatalities in the UK to under 300 a year. However, there remains understandable public concern about this issue, highlighted by a trend towards ever-stiffer fines for high-profile breaches.

Investors can show their disapproval of companies that break the rules by avoiding investment in those that have been successfully prosecuted by the Health and Safety Executive. One potential drawback with this approach is that prosecutions necessarily reflect past events; they give no clues as to whether companies have made efforts to improve their health and safety standards since prosecution.

Definitions

Health and Safety Executive (HSE) – a statutory body which enforces the Health and Safety at Work Act 1974 and related legislation.

Prosecuted by the Health and Safety Executive – prosecuted by one of the HSE inspectorates in England and Wales or by the Procurator Fiscal on the advice of the HSE in Scotland.

The main Health and Safety Executive inspectorates are the Factory and Agricultural inspectorates. They operate jointly from 20 area offices in Great Britain. These area offices carry out approximately 80 per cent of health and safety prosecutions. The other HSE inspectorates responsible for enforcing health and safety legislation are the Explosives Inspectorate, the Mines Inspectorate, the Nuclear Installations Inspectorate, the Offshore Safety Division, the Pipelines Inspectorate, and the Railway Inspectorate. In total these other HSE inspectorates account for less than 5 per cent of health and safety court prosecutions.

We do not include prosecutions by local authorities. These account for the remaining 15–20 per cent of prosecutions, which are mainly carried out by environmental health departments. Local authorities are responsible for enforcing health and safety legislation in shops, hotels, offices, warehouses and catering premises. Health and safety convictions in these areas are not included in our database.

Employee issues: Job creation and security

Why is this an issue?

The value a company attaches to social issues is increasingly seen as being as important to its long-term sustainability as its approach to environmental issues. It is important therefore for a company to ensure that it is not seen as taking advantage of workers by laying off workers without adequate consultation and considering all proper alternatives, or by not providing proper job security.

Although in some countries there is significant legislation obliging companies to consult their workforces ahead of restructuring operations, this is nonetheless seen as inadequate by some investors concerned about workers' rights. Such investors may therefore wish to seek out companies which have a proactive attitude to avoiding job losses, or at least providing support to workers who are made redundant, and/or are major creators of new jobs.

By encouraging job security and taking efforts during restructuring to help employees who have to be laid off to find new employment, or capital with which to start new businesses, companies can make a significant contribution to their stakeholders even during difficult periods.

Definitions

By **organic job creation**, we mean any net increase, excluding jobs gained as a result of mergers and takeovers.

Employee issues: Trade unions and employee participation

Why is this an issue?

Trade unions and collective bargaining can provide a valuable safeguard for workers from exploitation and victimization. This is particularly so in less wealthy countries and in less profitable industries, which usually have poorer employment conditions. It is not of course always necessary for trade unions to be recognized by a company in order for it to provide good or above-average working conditions. Indeed, many non-unionized companies have been regarded as highly progressive employers.

Nonetheless, even in wealthy countries and very profitable industries, a correlation can be found between increased unionization and overall improvements in the wages and working conditions of the workforce as a whole. More tellingly, decreases in unionization have often preceded redundancies and reductions in overall working conditions.

Investors concerned about employees' ability to bargain may therefore seek out those companies which recognize trade unions for collective bargaining on behalf of most of their workers. In the absence of trade unions, works councils provide a formal mechanism for consultation between employers and their staff. This criterion may therefore also be useful to investors concerned about workers' rights.

Employee ownership

In the UK and the USA, the concept of increased employee participation through ownership of company shares has taken off in the past 10 years. Employee ownership has support from all major political parties, and is favoured by workers' and employers' organizations alike, because of the increased stake it gives employees in the profitability of the companies they work for.

The compilers of the UK Employee Ownership Index, which tracks the shares of companies with exceptionally high levels of employee ownership (over 10 per cent), claim that such companies are also more profitable overall, because of the incentives and increased control provided by the employees' higher stakes.

Definitions

All employees – means that the shares must be owned and/or share options must be granted, under schemes open to every person employed by the company. Schemes which are only open to, or only used by, directors and senior executives are excluded from these criteria. Examples of schemes to encourage ownership of the company's shares amongst its employees are Employee Share Ownership Plans (ESOPs), Sharesave schemes and Employee Benefit Trusts.

Home country – the country containing the company's headquarters. If a company's home country contains less than 100 employees and it has more than 100 employees in other countries, or if more comprehensive information is provided for these latter countries, we will substitute the country where it has the most employees for which information is available, in place of the country containing the company's headquarters.

Share value – the issued ordinary share capital.

Trade unions – bona fide independent trade unions, as for example defined in the UK under the 1988 Employment Act.

Employee issues: Training

Why is this an issue?

In an increasingly competitive economy, training has taken on added importance. By providing improved and continuous training to all its workers, a company may gain a competitive advantage by attracting and retaining the best employees. The Department of Employment's Investors in People scheme is a government initiative which aims to encourage and accredit best practice in training and personal development throughout British industry. EIRIS identifies companies which have parts accredited under this scheme and the number of employees covered by these schemes.

Definitions

Company met – one or more parts (a subsidiary, associated company, division or unit) of the company that has been recognized as an Investor in People.

Investors in People scheme – the Department of Employment's Investors in People initiative, which aims to encourage best practice in training and development throughout British industry. To be officially recognized as an Investor in People an organization must be able to demonstrate that its own arrangements meet the requirements of the Investors in People National Standard. There are four of these National Standards, which are assessed by Training and Enterprise Councils in England and Wales and Local Enterprise Councils in Scotland.

Requirements – the four National Standards of the Investors in People initiative.

Customers and suppliers: Advertising complaints

Why is this an issue?

The power and influence of advertising has been seen as a potentially damaging force within society for several decades. The public can complain to regulatory bodies in the UK about advertisements which they consider misleading, dishonest, irresponsible or likely to cause offence. The Advertising Standards Authority (ASA) regulates the press, outdoor posters, direct mail, sales promotions, cinema advertisements, and advertisements in electronic media such as computer games and the internet. The Independent Television Commission (ITC) regulates advertising on commercial television. EIRIS records public complaints against companies we cover which are upheld by the ASA or ITC.

Definitions

Advertising alcohol – advertisements that may encourage excessive or under-age drinking, or suggest that alcoholic drinks can enhance capabilities.

Advertising to children – advertisements that may result in physical, mental or moral harm to children, or exploit their credulity, lack of experience or sense of loyalty.

Advertising cigarettes – advertisements that breach the Cigarette Code.

Advertising complaints – complaints from individual members of the public or from organizations representing the public's interests, such as consumer councils, or trading standards departments lodging complaints on behalf of consumers.

Advertising Standards Authority (ASA) – a body funded by the advertising industry, which receives complaints about advertisements from the public. The ASA decides whether the advertisements in question meet the advertising industry's Codes of Practice. It publishes its decisions in the monthly ASA *Case Report*.

The Codes used by the ASA include a number of particular sections relating to the following headings:

- Alcoholic drinks
- Cigarettes
- Children and young people
- Decency
- Environmental claims
- Financial services and products
- Health and medicines
- Social responsibility

EIRIS also uses these same headings, where appropriate to incorporate the ITC complaints.

Decency of advertisements – advertisements that contain any matter that is likely to cause grave or widespread offence. This category includes advertisements that are offensive on the grounds of race, religion, sex, sexual orientation or disability.

Environmental claims – advertisements containing misleading or unsubstantiated claims that the product or service is beneficial to the environment.

Financial services and products – advertisements for financial services and products, investment opportunities, credit facilities and financial information. Advertisers have to ensure that members of the public fully grasp the nature of any commitment into which they may enter if they respond to such advertisements.

Health claims or medicines – advertisements containing health and scientific claims made about beauty and health-related products. It also includes complaints upheld which relate to slimming.

Independent Television Commission (ITC) – a statutory body created by the Broadcasting Act 1990 to license and regulate commercial television in the UK. The ITC sets standards for television through its Code of Advertising Standards and Practice. The ITC enforces compliance through a combination of pre-vetting requirements and direct intervention. The ITC considers all complaints which it receives about advertising, and publishes its decisions in the monthly *Television Advertising Complaints Report*.

Same part – any subsidiary, associated or parent company.

Social responsibility – a wide range of general offences. It includes advertisements that play on fear or excite distress without good reason. It also includes advertisements that condone or encourage violence or anti-social behaviour, or show or advocate dangerous behaviour or unsafe practices. In addition this section covers advertisements that fail to protect an individual's right to privacy, or that result in unsolicited home visits.

Customers and suppliers: Customer/supplier relations

Why is this an issue?

Given the increasing importance attached to corporate reputation issues, it is vital that companies do all they can to actively engage with their stakeholders to improve the quality of their products and services. Such engagement can include the regular carrying out of customer surveys, to help develop better goods and services.

Without effective systems in place to monitor and improve a company's practices on this issue, it can often be difficult for the company to effect real change for the better.

The existence of adequate monitoring systems, therefore, is also important to investors seeking quantitative evidence of the company's performance on this issue.

Community involvement

Why is this an issue?

The giving of money by companies to worthy causes would at first glance seem to be self-evidently 'a good thing'. Certainly, there are strong arguments in favour of identifying and encouraging companies that make a positive effort to contribute to the communities they work in and to society at large, whether via donations or other means. However, not all investors will necessarily share the same priorities as companies in choosing which causes to support.

Definitions

Little or no evidence of, some, clear and a very clear commitment to community or charity work – relates to a company's activities in relation to the following:

- Operates employee secondment schemes
- Makes gifts in kind to the community
- Operates a payroll giving scheme
- Donates more than £50,000 annually to charity
- Publishes a community report or equivalent, giving details of projects supported (ie a breakdown of donations and/or explanations for supporting specific schemes)
- Publishes figures showing improvements over time in the company's community involvement schemes
- Makes significant healthcare and educational provision to local communities

Third World

Why is this an issue?

Many investors are concerned about the impact of companies' activities in the Third World. They believe that such investment too often fails to bring any overall benefit to the countries concerned.

In particular there is concern at the speed and manner in which natural commodities such as oil and timber are extracted from Third World countries by Western corporations, often at prices favourable to the wealthier nations and seemingly with little regard for the fact that they are using up finite resources. Dependence by a Third World country on a narrow export base of commodities can also exacerbate its poverty when prices fall. Similarly, Western corporations are criticized for encouraging Third World producers to grow crops for cash, rather than food. The benefits of such exports are often unfairly spread, with the consequence that poor people have less easy access to basic foods.

Accordingly, EIRIS identifies ownership of companies directly involved in commodity extraction or production. But not all involvement in the Third World is necessarily exploitative: a growing number of organizations are involved in 'fair trade', which ensures that Third World workers receive a decent living from the goods they produce. Also, large Western companies can arguably be instrumental in improving workplace conditions in the Third World.

The Third World debt crisis was first highlighted in the 1980s by leading international development agencies such as Christian Aid. Its origins can be traced to inappropriate lending by many banks during the 1970s. Money was frequently lent to unviable prestige projects or was wasted by corruption, leaving many countries with no means of repaying the original debt. This left many countries with a growing burden caused by continuing interest payments, and has led to the situation where some countries have paid in interest several times the sum originally borrowed.

The adverse effects of the debt crisis on the poor are well documented, as the poor are most affected by the financial policies imposed on countries in order to ensure debt payments continue to be made.

The inappropriate promotion of breast-milk substitutes in the Third World is regarded as a major cause for concern by the World Health Organization and UNICEF. As well as imposing a financial burden on poor people, substitutes are known to be generally less effective than breast milk in helping infants build up necessary immunities. They can also be dangerous where people do not have access to clean water to formulate the milk.

In 1981 WHO developed a strict code of marketing practice to outlaw the inappropriate marketing of breast-milk substitutes. EIRIS looks for reports of companies breaching this code.

Pharmaceutical companies' involvement with developing countries has been controversial. The World Health Organization, Health Action International and other consumer groups have criticized the sector for pursuing profit at the expense of appropriate healthcare policies. For example, some companies have been accused of undermining programmes for developing countries to produce their own basic generic drugs or have been criticized for irresponsible advertising. It is said that this type of misleading and aggressive marketing can cause customers to buy unnecessary or harmful products such as ineffective or overpriced drugs.

EIRIS monitors pharmaceutical companies for breaches of the industry's own code of good marketing practice.

In some countries the spread of tobacco, with its many negative health consequences, has begun to be checked by improved health education, public restrictions on sale and advertising and the impact of litigation. Globally though, particularly in the Third World, sales of tobacco are continuing to grow. Much of this growth in Third World countries is aided by marketing methods aimed at the young, which are outlawed elsewhere. Investors concerned about tobacco will therefore want to know if a company markets tobacco in the Third World.

Definitions

Broken means that the responsibilities outlined by the IFPMA code have not been fulfilled, according to MaLAM or HAI.

Code of Pharmaceutical Marketing Practices – the code of conduct issued by the International Federation of Pharmaceutical Manufacturers Associations (IFPMA) governing the marketing of pharmaceuticals. The IFPMA promotes and supports continuous development throughout the pharmaceutical industry of ethical principles and practices, which have been voluntarily agreed.

Commodity – we use the *Collins Dictionary* definition of 'commodity' as 'an exchangeable unit of economic wealth especially a primary product or raw material'.

Debt – the absolute sum of money which is due to be paid by a Third World country to the creditor bank. Debt against which an accounting provision has been made by the bank is included.

Extract – mining and quarrying, oil and gas exploration and production, and extraction of tropical timber.

Grow – the owning, operating or managing of plantations. By plantations we mean the large-scale growing of cash crops primarily for export.

HAI (Health Action International) is an informal network of some 100 consumer, health, development action and other public interest groups involved in health and pharmaceutical issues around the world.

International Code of Marketing Breast-Milk Substitutes – the code of that name issued by the World Health Organization and United Nations Children's Fund and adopted by the World Health Assembly in 1981. This code outlines the marketing responsibilities of baby-food manufacturing companies.

MaLAM (the Medical Lobby on Appropriate Marketing) was set up to encourage pharmaceutical companies to provide adequate information about the effectiveness and adverse effects of drugs to enable informed, appropriate prescribing.

Pharmaceuticals – medical drugs.

Poorest countries – a rank of less than 0.5 on the United Nations Development Programme's (UNDP) Human Development Index. The **Human Development Index (HDI)** is a composite measure of human development. It combines measures of life expectancy, educational attainment and income (gross domestic product per capita). Educational attainment includes adult literacy and average years of schooling. Gross domestic product is the total value of all goods and services produced domestically by a nation during a year. A rank of less than 0.5 is judged to be low by the UNDP (see Table A3.3).

Third World – the countries of Africa, Asia (excluding Israel and Japan) and Latin America (including the Caribbean).

Tobacco – cigarettes and other tobacco products. We do not include tobacco-related activities such as cigarette components or tobacco machinery.

Tobacco

Why is this an issue?

Over recent years, the tide of public opinion in Britain has turned against smokers. Tobacco is the largest cause of preventable death in the UK, claiming over 100,000 lives every year. It is responsible for at least 90 per cent of deaths from lung cancer, chronic bronchitis and emphysema, and it is a factor in over 20 per cent of all deaths from heart disease. A decline in adult smoking and fears about the effects of 'passive' smoking in particular have encouraged smoking to be banned in many public areas such as restaurants, offices and public transport. Some smokers, however, see such moves as an attack on their civil liberties. That fact notwithstanding, many investors have serious concerns about investing in tobacco because of the health implications.

The tobacco market is still a significant size and is open enough for further product proliferation. Although cigarette prices have risen following government attempts to reduce smoking by increasing duty on tobacco products, new brands have continued to appear on the market, and cheaper 'own-brand' cigarette sales are on the increase.

Table A3.3 Countries with low HDI ranking

Countries with HDI between 0.5 and 0.25	Countries with HDI of less than 0.25
Angola	Afghanistan
Bangladesh	Burkina Faso
Benin	Burundi
Bhutan	Ethiopia
Cambodia	Mali
Cameroon	Niger
Central African Republic	Rwanda
Chad	Sierra Leone
Comoros	Somalia
Côte d'Ivoire	
Djibouti	
Equatorial Guinea	
Gambia	
Ghana	
Guinea	
Guinea-Bissau	
Haiti	
India	
Kenya	
Laos	
Lesotho	
Liberia	
Madagascar	
Malawi	
Mauritania	
Mozambique	
Myanmar	
Nepal	
Nigeria	
Pakistan	
Senegal	
Sudan	
Tanzania	
Togo	
Uganda	
Yemen	
Zaire	
Zambia	

The issue of smoking has been the subject of increased media coverage recently as a result of two major developments. The first has been the litigation in the USA, where tobacco companies and anti-tobacco lawyers have wrestled over compensation claims brought by smokers and health authorities. The second has been the proposed European Union ban on all forms of tobacco advertising including newspapers, magazines, billboards and sponsorship, a move which has been applauded by the British Medical Association and the Imperial Cancer Research Fund among others.

While anti-tobacco campaigners may have been winning the litigation war, it is claimed that global tobacco companies are funding their US liabilities from profits generated by marketing in the Third World. Third World tobacco marketing is another area of research covered by EIRIS. Investors concerned about this issue should refer to the 'Third World' section.

Definitions

Contract distribution – contracts with a producer of tobacco products to transport these goods.

Production – the ownership of tobacco plantations and the manufacture of cigarettes and other tobacco products.

Sale – the retailing or wholesaling of cigarettes or other tobacco products. We also include the import, export, contract distribution or wholesaling of tobacco products where these are indicated in the sources we use. We include the sale of tobacco through concessions. We cannot tell for every company whether they are taking rent or a percentage of turnover from concessions, so we treat concessions as if the company was selling the product directly.

Turnover – annual turnover. By annual turnover we mean the turnover of the entire company, including subsidiaries and associated companies.

© Copyright EIRIS.

Appendix 4

How investors can sort out their own concerns

John Hancock

ORGANIZED BELIEFS

Of course, generalities are useful but only so far. If investors would prefer their investments to be in tune with their own beliefs about what is right and what is wrong, to support that which they support and avoid that which they eschew, then they will need, at some stage, to organize those beliefs. This may sound a little callous for an investment philosophy that is about broader values than profit alone, although it must be emphasized that there is nothing wrong with profit as long as it is decently obtained and results from a true added value rather than being the other side of somebody else's loss or the sequestering of future value. However, it is in the hope of profit that most people conduct their working and investing lives although not all would measure that profit in just monetary terms. Nevertheless, given the wide choice of funds available and the wide range of priorities that they have incorporated to their standards and protocols, if investors have not analysed and organized their own beliefs, however are they going to know which fund managers will invest in the way that will support those beliefs?

WHAT DO PEOPLE THINK?

Sorting out personal concerns is not a difficult job. Many people will start by writing down those issues that can make them think when, for instance, they come up as an item in the news. Are they moved by events involving and affecting people or do they find their own feelings run strongest when places and artefacts are threatened? When they hear of a mine closing, do they inwardly rejoice that there will be one less slagheap scarring the countryside and wonder how the land will be restored? Or do they despair for the families whose livelihood has been cut away and wonder whether there will be any new development on the site to restore the dignity of work and maintain the spirit of a community? If their first concern is for the land, then the environment may be their prime motivation while those who think first of the people may have an ethical emphasis in their concerns. Neither is better than the other and each could argue the case for their own view being the one that would secure the long-term good of the community. Of course, it is perfectly possible to hold a combination of those feelings and wish for a sensible outcome that will balance the desire to restore the land with a pragmatic acceptance that there will need to be new development but in a manner that is sympathetic to the area.

Are there particular issues about which, for one reason or another, investors feel passionately? Have they lost a loved one in an industrial accident and now wish to ensure that employers do not play fast and loose with health and safety? Has their community been cut in half by road building and subsequently seemed to lose its cohesion and that spirit that marks out a community from a collection of buildings and people? Have they experienced at close hand the devastation that alcohol and gambling can wreak, or lost a dear relative to cancer or another condition following a lifetime of cigarette smoking or working in a toxic environment? Do they find themselves moved by the plight of people in faraway places being killed and injured by munitions that have been manufactured in this country?

It may take an afternoon or even more to sort out their own priorities. Like most concerned people, they may be surprised at how many matters there are over which they would like to effect some influence for change. But, with the best will in the world, any single investor will not be able to address them all and so ought to ascribe a score (say, out of 10) to each concern in order to impose an order and a set of priorities.

One technique is initially to use the method applied by market researchers of ascribing to each possibility a weighted view. It works like this. Take each issue covered in Appendix 3, plus any other that may be particular to an individual investor's own concerns, and write it down as a statement starting either with the phrase 'I support...' or with 'I am against...' Hence, the investor might say, 'I support fair trade' or 'I am against animal testing for non-medical purposes.' Alongside each statement write a number as follows:

1   I strongly agree with the statement.
2   I agree with the statement.
3   I neither agree nor disagree with the statement.
4   I disagree with the statement.
5   I strongly disagree with the statement.

Now group the statements according to their scores and it will be possible to identify the investor's main and secondary concerns – 'strongly agree' and 'agree' – from the issues over which he or she has little or no concern – the rest. You could, of course, further refine the list by applying a similar exercise to each group until all concerns are listed in a sequence but, quite honestly, life is too short.

Then, it might be a useful exercise to create the investment terms of an investor's ideal fund in much the same way that fans create ideal combinations and teams in fantasy sport competitions. While it is unlikely that there will be a fund run along exactly the lines which any particular investor would follow, you will at least now have a starting point from which to work.

A CHOICE OF FUNDS

Having profiled an ideal fund and having chosen an investment vehicle (unit trust, ISA, etc) suitable to an investor's circumstances and requirements, you will now wish to identify a group of funds that are managed to similar priorities. You may go to Appendix 1 to discover the investment priorities and methods of each of the funds that responded to Ethical Investment Research Services (EIRIS)'s survey in 2004. Then go through the same exercise for each fund under consideration to see which ones most closely match the ideal for a particular investor. There will, of course, be other factors that will need to be considered including past performance (not a guarantee of future performance but certainly an indicator), fund size, savings and investment vehicles available. Appendix 2 has been provided by the rating experts Standard & Poor's and list all UK-based ethical and SRI funds with their performances over a number of periods up to 1 October 2004.

If you would feel more comfortable using a more prescribed selection system, then invest in a copy of the EIRIS publication *The Guide to Ethical Funds* (a book in itself), which includes a comprehensive, step-by-step fund selector.

KNOWLEDGE IS STRENGTH

In practice, the selection of a suitable ethical or environmental investment is much the same as selecting any suitable investment. The one exception is that, because the criteria by which concerned investors judge performance include some subjective elements, a little more time must be invested in understanding the feelings and beliefs from which those elements arise and prioritizing those elements. The advantage of this is that, just as socially accountable fund managers know more about their investments as a result of their higher levels of research, so the individual investor will better understand his or her own feelings with the benefit of having had to evaluate them in this way (and the advisor will better understand his or her client).

Index

NB: page numbers in *italic* indicate figures or tables